Enterprise Information Security and Privacy

For quite a long time, computer security was a rather narrow field of study that was populated mainly by theoretical computer scientists, electrical engineers, and applied mathematicians. With the proliferation of open systems in general, and of the Internet and the World Wide Web (WWW) in particular, this situation has changed fundamentally. Today, computer and network practitioners are equally interested in computer security, since they require technologies and solutions that can be used to secure applications related to electronic commerce. Against this background, the field of computer security has become very broad and includes many topics of interest. The aim of this series is to publish state-of-the-art, high standard technical books on topics related to computer security. Further information about the series can be found on the WWW at the following URL:

http://www.esecurity.ch/serieseditor.html

Also, if you'd like to contribute to the series by writing a book about a topic related to computer security, feel free to contact either the Commissioning Editor or the Series Editor at Artech House.

For a listing of recent titles in the
Artech House Information Security and Privacy Series,
turn to the back of this book.

Enterprise Information Security and Privacy

C. Warren Axelrod
Jennifer L. Bayuk
Daniel Schutzer

Editors

ARTECH
HOUSE

BOSTON | LONDON
artechhouse.com

Library of Congress Cataloging-in-Publication Data
A catalog record for this book is available from the U.S. Library of Congress.

British Library Cataloguing in Publication Data
A catalogue record for this book is available from the British Library.

Cover design by Igor Valdman

ISBN 13: 978-1-59693-190-9

© 2009 ARTECH HOUSE, INC.
685 Canton Street
Norwood, MA 02062

10 9 8 7 6 5 4 3 2 1

Contents

Foreword

If there is one lesson you can learn from this book, it is that information security is an art, not a science, and the mastery of information security requires a multidisciplinary knowledge of a huge amount of information, experience, and skill. You will see much of the necessary information here in this book as the authors take you through the subject in a security systems development life cycle using scenarios of real life situations to emphasize each topic. The authors provide the experience and skill from many years of real life experience combined with their academic approach to provide a rich learning experience that they expertly present in this book. You have chosen the book well.

Since you are reading this book, you are likely in or working toward a career in information security or at least have some serious information security interest. You must anticipate that just about everybody hates the constraints that your work of increasing security will put upon them, both the good guys and the bad guys–except for malicious hackers who love the security you install as a challenge to be beaten. I concentrate on fighting the bad guys in security because when security is developed against bad guys it also applies to accidents and errors, but when developed against accidental problems, it tends to be ineffective against enemies acting with intent.

I have spent 35 years of my life working in a field that most people hate but still found it exciting and rewarding working with computers and pitting my wits against malicious people. Security controls and practices include logging on, using passwords, encrypting vital information, locking doors and drawers, motivating stakeholders to support security, and installing pipes to spray water down on your fragile computers in case of fire. These are means of protection that have no benefit except rarely when adversities occur. Good security is when nothing bad happens, and when nothing bad happens, who needs security. So why do we engage in security? Nowadays we do it because the law says that we must do it, e.g., we are required to use seat belts and air bags–especially if we deal with the personal information of others, electronic money, intellectual property, and keeping ahead of the competition.

There is great satisfaction knowing that your employer's information, communications, systems, and people are secure, and getting paid a good salary, being the center of attention in emergencies, and knowing that you are matching your wits against the bad guys all make up for the downsides of your work. It is no job for perfectionists, because you will almost never be fully successful, and there will always be vulnerabilities that you aren't aware of or that you haven't fixed yet. The enemy has a great advantage over us. He has to find only one vulnerability and one target to attack in a known place, electronically or physically, while we must defend from potentially millions of enemies' attacks against all of our assets and vulnerabilities that are no longer in one computer room but are spread all over the world by wire and now by air. It's like playing a game in which you don't know your opponents and where they are, what they are doing, why they are doing it, and are changing the rules as they play. You must be highly ethical, defensive, secretive, and cautious about bragging about the great security that you are employing that might tip off the enemy. Enjoy the few successes that you experience for you will not even know about some of them.

There is a story that describes the kind of war you are entering into. A small country inducted a young man into their ill-equipped army. They had no guns; so they issued a broom to the new recruit for training purposes. In basic training, the young man asked, "What do I do with this broom?"

They took him out to the rifle range and told him to pretend it is a gun, aim it at the target, and say, "bang, bang, bang." He did that. Then they took him out to bayonet practice, and he said, "What do I do with this broom?"

They said, "Pretend it is a gun with a bayonet on it and say, 'stab, stab, stab.'"

He did that also. Then the war started, they still didn't have guns; so the young man found himself out on the front line with enemy soldiers running toward him across a field, and all he had was his trusty broom. So he could only do what he was trained to do, aimed the broom at the enemy soldiers, and said, "bang, bang, bang." Some of the enemy soldiers fell down, but many kept coming. Some got so close that he had to shout, "stab, stab, stab," and more enemy soldiers fell down. However, there was one stubborn enemy soldier (there is always one in these stories) running toward him. He said, "bang, bang, bang," but to no effect. The enemy continued to get closer. He got so close that the recruit had to say, "stab, stab, stab," but it still had no effect. In fact, the enemy soldier ran right over the recruit, left him lying in the dirt, and broke his broom in half. However, as the enemy soldier ran by, the recruit heard the enemy muttering under his breath, "tank, tank, tank."

I tell this story at the end of my many lectures on computer crime and security to impress on my audience that if you are going to win against crime, you must know the rules, and it is the criminal who is making up his secret rules as he goes along. This makes winning very difficult.

When I was lecturing in Rio de Janeiro, a young lady performed simultaneous translation into Portuguese for my audience of several hundred people, all with earphones clapped over their ears. In such situations, I have no idea what my audience is hearing, and after telling my joke nobody laughed. They just sat there with puzzled looks on their faces. After the lecture, I asked the translator what had happened. She had translated "tank, tank, tank" into "water tank, water tank, water tank." I and the recruit were both deceived that time.

Three weeks later, I was lecturing to an audience of French bankers at the George V Hotel in Paris. I had a bilingual friend listen to the translation of my talk. The same thing happened as in Rio. Nobody laughed. Afterwards, I asked my friend what had happened. He said, "You will never believe this, but the translator translated 'tank, tank, tank' into 'merci, merci, merci.'" Even in telling the joke I didn't know the rules to the game.

Remember that when working in security, you are in a virtual army defending your employer and stakeholders from their enemies, and from your point of view they will probably think and act irrationally, but from their perspective they are perfectly rational with serious personal problems to solve and gains to be made by violating your security. You are no longer a techie with the challenging job of installing technological controls in systems and networks. Most of your work should be assisting potential victims to protect themselves from information adversities and dealing with your smart but often irrational enemies even though you rarely see or even get close to them. I spent a major part of my security career hunting down computer criminals and interviewing them and their victims trying to obtain knowledge from them to do a better job of defending from their attacks. You, likewise, should also use every opportunity to seek them out and get to know them. This experience gives you great cachet as a real and unique expert even with only minimal exposure to a few enemies.

Comprehensiveness is an important part of the game you play for real stakes because the enemy will likely seek the easiest way to attack the vulnerabilities and assets that you haven't fully protected yet. For example, one of the most common threats is endangerment of assets, which means putting information assets in harm's way, yet I rarely find it on threat lists. Endangerment is also one of the most common mistakes that security professionals make. You must be thorough, meticulous, document everything (in case your competence is questioned and to meet the requirements of the Sarbanes–Oxley Law), and keep the documents safely locked away. Be careful and document so that when an adversity hits and you lose the game, you will have proof of having been diligent in spite of the loss. Otherwise, your career could be damaged, or at least your effectiveness will be diminished. For example, if the loss is due to management failing to give you an adequate budget and support for the security that you know that you need, you must have documented that before the incident occurs. Don't brag about how great your security is, because it can always be beaten. Keep, expand, and use everyday check lists of everything–threats, vulnerabilities, assets, key potential victims and suspects of wrongdoing, security supporters and those that don't bother with security, attacks, enemies, criminal justice resources, auditors, regulators, and legal council. To assist your stakeholders, who are the real defenders of their information and systems, in managing their security, you must identify what they must protect and measure the real extent of their security. And make sure that those to whom you report and higher management understand the nature of your job and its limitations.

You will have a huge collection of sensitive passwords to do your job. Use the best possible passwords to set a good example, write them down, and keep the list safely in your wallet next to your credit card. Know as much about the systems and networks in your organization as possible and have access to the expert people that know the rest. Make good friends of the local and national criminal justice people, your organization's lawyers, insurance risk managers, human resources people, talent, facilities managers and auditors. Audit is one of the most powerful controls that your organization has. Remember that people hate security and must be properly motivated with penalties and rewards to make it work. Seek ways to make security invisible or transparent to stakeholders, yet effective. Don't recommend or install controls or practices that they won't support, because they will beat you every time by making it look like the controls are effective but are not–a situation worse than no security at all.

One of the most exciting parts of the job is the insight you gain about the inner workings and secrets of your organization and its culture that you must thoroughly understand. As an information security consultant, I was privileged to learn about the culture and secrets of more than 250 of the largest international corporations throughout the world. I had the opportunity to interview and advise the most powerful business giants if even for only a few minutes of their valuable time. You should always be ready to use the five minutes that you get with them once every year or so as your silver bullet to use with top management for the greatest benefit of their security. Carefully learn the limits of their security appetites. Know the nature of the business whether it is a government department or a hotly competitive business. I once found myself in a meeting with the board of directors intensely and seriously discussing and suppressing my snickering about the protection of their greatest trade secret, the manufacturing process of their new disposable diapers.

Finally, we come to the last important bit of advice. Be trustworthy and develop mutual trust among your peers. Your most important objectives are not risk reduction and increased security; they are diligence to avoid negligence, exceeding compliance with all of the laws and standards and auditors, and enablement when security becomes a competitive or a budget issue. To achieve these objectives, you must develop a trusting exchange of the most sensitive security intelligence among your peers in your and other security people's organizations so that you know where your organization stands in protection relative to them. You need to know what the generally accepted current security solutions are and especially those used in your competitors' businesses or other related organizations. Therefore, you need to exchange this highly sensitive information among your peers. If the information exchanged is exposed, it could ruin your and others' careers as well as be a disaster for your or their organizations. Your personal and ethical performance must be spotless, and you must protect your reputation at all costs. Pay particular attention to ethics. You must be discrete and careful by testing and growing the ongoing peer trust to facilitate the sharing of sensitive security information.

Donn Parker
Senior Information Security
Consultant, Retired

Preface

Our Age of Anxiety is, in great part, the result of trying to do today's job with yesterday's tools and yesterday's concepts.

We shape our tools and afterwards our tools shape us.

Most of our assumptions have outlived their usefulness.

—Marshall McLuhan

What makes otherwise sensible but overloaded men and women take the time and put in the effort to create a book such as this—a book that questions the very foundation and practice of a profession that has provided our livelihoods. Perhaps one reason is that we have something in common. We are all passionate about improving the state of security and privacy in an ever more threatened and vulnerable world.

Our authors were carefully chosen from a relatively small cadre of talented, engaged professionals, who are not only directly involved in "real world" activities, but contribute extensively to the evolution of the information security field via participation in numerous professional and industry committees, associations, conferences, and other initiatives. Additionally, many of us are frequently write and lecture on best practice on a purely voluntary basis, seeking to raise the proficiency of the information security profession.

In a recent interview published in the January/February 2008 edition of the *IEEE Security & Privacy* journal, Bob Blakely, a principal analyst with the Burton Group, is quoted as saying, "Despite the fact that both attacks and losses have approximately doubled every year since 1992, we continue to rely on old models that are demonstrably ill-suited to the current reality" [1].

And there's the rub. For the most part, we security professionals continue to use ill-suited traditional approaches to deal with new threats and vulnerabilities. The accelerating rate of incident growth and resulting losses, despite increased attention and expenditures on security, points to the lack of effective methods for taming the threat and vulnerability tigers that are accompanying the rapid proliferation of new information technologies. It has become clear that many of us in the security profession are trying to solve today's and tomorrow's problems with yesterday's solutions, which is turning out to be a no-win situation as witnessed by the continuing increases in frequency and size of security and privacy breaches.

Of course, there has been some progress and innovation in the security and privacy space, thanks to a veritable hoard of companies developing and purveying products and services. Also, many academic and research institutions are engaged in leading edge, though not always practical, research and development. Despite all that effort, we still find ourselves lagging far behind the "bad guys." Could it be that we are slow to adapt to new challenges or to adopt new, more effective technologies? Or, is it that pure and applied research and product development are just not keeping up, or not addressing real pragmatic concerns of real world practioners? It is interesting to see how our authors interpret and respond to the situation.

This book takes a fresh, and (we hope) refreshing, approach. The author guidelines were to examine and question current and traditional approaches, to determine their weaknesses and strengths, and to suggest paths forward that will overcome their deficiencies. Because of their strong practical backgrounds, the authors' recommendations are realistic, visionary, and doable within the context of the rapidly changing technical and social worlds in which we live.

Trying to gauge the futures of security and privacy is a daunting task, but it is one that the contributors to this book live with every day of their lives and are therefore eminently capable of addressing. Some of our authors are contrarian, others more conservative, but all are thoughtful and practical and sufficiently concerned that they made this effort to bring their messages to the reader. You will find yourself agreeing with some positions and disagreeing with others. That is to be expected and to be encouraged. In fact, in a novel format suggested by one of the editors, we have introduced comments by the editors throughout the text in order to stimulate thought and discussion. You cannot and should not suppress free and open thinkers or restrict their thinking to what you believe in. That is the price of encouraging creative thinking and innovation. We hope that you will agree that it is a small price for the benefits derived from the out-of-the-box thinking from these caring and resourceful professionals.

We, as security and privacy professionals and practitioners, are at a crossroads and must decide which path to take. We can continue with business as usual and see the number and size of breaches and losses continue to mount, or we can examine each new situation with the pragmatic approach needed to get ahead of the monster. But, before we run off with our rallying cries and impassioned pleas, we need to really understand what approaches have a chance at actually working. This book's purpose is to provide you with a basis for countermanding those who still support tired and ineffective methods. We are not seeking change for change's sake, but are looking for change that will be productive and effective and will keep us ahead of the security-breach tsunami that is threatening to swamp us all.

A brief note about the structure of the book. The book consists of three major sections. At the beginning of each section we have a few pages of introduction. Your editors wrote the introductions to each part. Then sprinkled throughout the chapters, we have editorial comments and discussions, much like blogs with their point and counterpoint repartee.

In Part I, we will trace back the history of security, privacy and information technology to see what got us into this mess in the first place. Chapters on the evolution of security and privacy from a variety of technological and organizational views will give you the perspective and energy needed to tackle even greater future demands.

In Part II, we tackle the thorny topic of risk. Donn Parker's contrarian views on this subject set the stage. Should the doctrine of risk-based security and privacy assessments be thrown out the window, or are we losing something by doing so? We shall see whether or not our authors can make the case for such controversial areas as security metrics, risk analysis, and return on security investment.

Then, in Part III, we invite those who have extensive knowledge and expertise in specific public and private sectors to tell us what security and privacy issues dominate their industry or sector.

Reference

[1]   Saydjari, O. Sami, "Virtual Roundtable: Information Assurance Technology Forecast 2008," *IEEE Security & Privacy Journal,* Vol. 6, No. 1, January/February 2008, pp. 16-23.

Acknowledgments

Author acknowledgements follow some chapters of this book. In this space, our editors acknowledge the influences and support that allowed them to complete this volume.

Warren Axelrod wishes to thank Wayne Yuhasz, executive acquisitions editor for Artech House Publishers, for proposing the book. The concept for this book, namely, to have it written by practitioners for practitioners, came out of our discussions. Wayne also suggested that I recruit two outstanding coeditors, which I did in the persons of Jennifer Bayuk and Daniel Schutzer. Jennifer and Dan have been extremely supportive throughout the process and we each picked up the slack when others were diverted by other projects or job situations. It was this aspect of editors and authors having "day jobs" that created the real challenge in developing the book. And so I thank all the authors who generously gave of their time and effort to write their outstanding contributions despite their other commitments. Finally, I thank my wife Judy for putting up with the intrusions on our personal lives as a result of this and other projects.

Jennifer Bayuk acknowledges the influential thinkers which she was lucky enough to have as mentors and coaches in various InfoSec roles over the years. In chronological order, these are: Ed Amoroso, her professor at Stevens Institute of Technology and colleague at AT&T Bell Laboratories; Mike Donahue, a past international president of the Information Systems Audit and Control Association and her coach at Price Waterhouse; Rich Corneilson, the director of internal audit at AT&T Capital Corporation wherein she managed IT Audit, and Pat Ripley, the highest ranking information security officer at Bear Stearns before the title chief information security officer became commonplace. In addition, Jennifer acknowledges her husband Michael, whose constant support makes such extracurricular tasks as authoring textbooks possible.

Dan Schutzer acknowledges all the smart people he has been lucky enough to have met in his long career, and the wisdom they have provided through the years. This includes many of his colleagues at Citi including Steve Katz, David Solo, Mark Clancy, and Bob Wilkinson. He also acknowledges his wife Myra for her understanding and support in his undertaking this project.

Part I: Trends

Each chapter in this section consists of four parts:

- Background,
- Observations,
- Recommendations,
- Future trends.

The background provides either a history or a survey of the issue identified in the title of the chapter. Observations show how the author is approaching the issue and includes his or her thoughts on how today's state of affairs evolved. Recommendations give practical advice on how to think about the issue in order to best serve the objectives of security and privacy with respect to information. Future trends outline the next steps that will likely be taken by the industry as a whole.

The subject matter covered in Part I allows a glance at the field of security at a whole. The five chapters on different aspects of security and privacy provide a base level of understanding of the evolution of the field to date. Though not a comprehensive portrait of the profession,[1] the staged introduction of each issue provides the reader with a well-rounded impression of the state of affairs faced by the infomation security practitioner.

---

1. For a history of the profession, see Jennifer Bayuk, *Stepping Through the InfoSec Program*, Information Systems Audit and Control Association (ISACA), 2007, Chapter 1.

As in any profession, it cannot be expected to make progress without the recognition that it is hard to understand how to move forward without studying the past. As the great poet and philosopher, George Santayana, said, "Those who cannot remember the past are condemned to repeat it."

Nevertheless, the chapters in this section are not purely history lessons. They combine history lessons with matter-of-fact observations on today's state of affairs. They build on the observations to provide useful insight for information security practitioners facing dilemmas of the future.

1

Privacy Roles and Responsibilities

Sam DeKay and Ken Belva

As a relative newcomer to the information security profession and particularly to the privacy field, I was under the impression that modern-day privacy legislation and regulations originated with the 1995 EU (European Union) Directive 95/46/EC on the protection of personal data. I had been told that the Europeans are particularly sensitive to the privacy rights of individuals following the abuses of personal information by the Nazis before and during World War II and hence they had very demanding privacy rights legislation. However, while the requirements mandated in the EU Directive might be considered more stringent than those in the United States, other aspects, such as the need to inform individuals that their information has been compromised and could be used for illegal purposes, are apparently not as broad as in the United States. Consequently we have little idea as to the extent of data breaches in Europe. Be that as it may, compliance with the European Union's Directive on data protection means that many other countries must meet higher standards than in their own country, making for issues with the free flow of personal data around the world.

I was also aware of a number of data protection and privacy laws and directives from other countries, such as New Zealand, Japan, and the United Kingdom. However, I did not know about the long history and the origins of privacy concepts and laws as described in this chapter by Sam DeKay and Ken Belva going back more than 100 years. I was particularly interested in learning about the evolving theatre of privacy in the United States in the 1960s and 1970s with the landmark 1974 Privacy Act.

The authors have provided us with a context that I have not seen elsewhere. This review of the history helps us better understand the context in which more modern laws and regulations have been written. Tom Smedinghoff, who is a leading expert in security and privacy law, provides a particularly comprehensive legal perspective in Chapter 8.

The authors also address two issues, namely data classification and the relationship between security and privacy, which are at the forefront of concerns of practitioners.

The topic of data classification is handled in more detail in Chapter 4. As the reader will see, the jury is still out on our ability to actually achieve meaningful data classification in the private sector, since the cost of doing a complete job and maintaining the data inventory is overwhelming to say the least.

It is very useful to plow through the distinctions between privacy and security as delineated by the authors. I see that loose definitions and much confusion are common here, so it is refreshing to see this attempt at clarification.

Sam and Ken have tackled a difficult set of topics in an easily understood chapter and so have provided a service to many of us who have struggled to put together a realistic model of privacy and security. The authors do not resolve all the issues, but give the reader a basis for understanding them and going forward with a realistic template.

—C.W.A.

1.1 Background

The right to privacy was first defined by Brandeis and Warren in their 1890 *Harvard Law Journal* article, "The Right to Privacy." It is well noted that this article was written in response to Warren's aristocratic lifestyle appearing in the gossip pages of the daily Boston newspapers. While the intrusions into Warren's life certainly seemed unethical, until Warren's and Brandeis' landmark paper it was unclear how to legally demonstrate why this was the case. Brandeis and Warren were the first to ground an individual's right to privacy in common law rights, as well as the psychological health of the individual. Namely, without such rights psychological harm would come to those who are not able to handle certain aspects of their life in private, outside of public scrutiny.[1]

Glancy notes that "Warren's and Brandeis' original concept of the right to privacy thus embodied a psychological insight, at that time relatively unexplored, that an individual's personality, especially his or her self-image, can be affected, and sometimes distorted or injured, when information about that individual's private life is made available to other people."[2] Glancy further writes,

---

1. Glancy, D. J., "The Invention of the Right to Privacy," *Arizona Law Review,* Vol. 21, No. 1, 1979, p. 2.
2. Ibid.

"In the simplest of terms, for Warren and Brandeis the right to privacy was the right of each individual to protect his or her psychological integrity by exercising control over information which both reflected and affected that individual's personality."[3] Warren and Brandeis realized that an individual's control over his or her personal information was being altered by new technology.

Technology influences the right to privacy by extending one's ability to freeze moments in time and replay them. When Brandeis and Warren wrote the "The Right to Privacy," landmark inventions such as the telegraph, inexpensive photographic equipment, as well as the ability to record sound were becoming commonplace. Technology enables our ability to trace history through the creation and collection of well-documented, nearly indisputable records of past events. Upon examination we see a strong, yet often overlooked aspect of technology and privacy. By recording history, one's privacy may potentially be violated at any point in the present or future should these records be disclosed in a manner not intended by those who became part of the record. Moreover, recording and electronification allow pieces of information to be automatically linked. Information, which in isolation may not be considered private, in combination is often so considered (e.g., name and account number).

As technology becomes more powerful, the functionality of our system increases in its ability to intrude into the operations of people's lives. One needs to look no further than the telephoto photography of the paparazzi as ample evidence. Other cases are worth mentioning due to scale: government capture of all cellular transmissions worldwide, satellite photography used to spy across national borders, various taps into communications equipment (e.g., fiber optics, internet packet duplication). In short, our ability to record private events continually increases, which culminates in a collective history through documenting that which normally would otherwise be erased in the sands of time.

The concerns of Brandeis and Warren have been exacerbated as we become more technologically sophisticated. We not only have the capability to record events, but we have the historically unprecedented ability to correlate such records by synthesizing and aggregating data. Historically speaking, the privacy debate in the United States was driven by the fear of government collecting and abusing data stored in its information systems. In the early 1960s, the U.S. government proposed a National Data Center and considered creating a unified database to synthesize all data collected about individuals. According to its proponents, the purpose of the National Data Center was to increase efficiency and decrease costs, not create dossiers on individuals.[4] Its opponents, such as Representative Cornelius Gallagher, argued that the possible abuse of

---

3. Ibid.
4. "Data Vampire," http://www.time.com/time/magazine/article/0,9171,836161,00.html?promoid=googlep, Nov. 2007.

such a system outweighed its efficiency. Charles A. Reich, a professor of constitutional law, argued that such a government system would "establish a doctrine of no second chance, no forgiveness, one life, one chance only."[5] The National Data Center program was ultimately dropped due to lack of public support.

The early 1960s witnessed a period of great public distrust, in both the United States and Europe, concerning the concentration of personal data being stored in governmental and corporate databases. Vance Packard's best-selling *The Naked Society*, published in 1964, was perhaps the most influential alarm sounded against the dangers to privacy represented by the massive accumulation of personal information in electronic databases. Packard's warnings were echoed by Myron Brinton's *The Privacy Invaders* (1974). Three years later, Alan Westin's *Privacy and Freedom* reminded readers that technology remained a grave threat to the privacy of individuals.

These books presented a seemingly persuasive case that electronic data processing, despite the many efficiencies that it promised and often delivered, was also responsible for the gradual diminishing of citizens' privacy. Packard, Brinton, and Westin portrayed a future in which the technological resources of "big government" and "big business" could invasively spy upon and pry into the intimate details of individuals' lives.

Pronouncements from Washington seemed to fulfill these dire predictions. In the early 1960s, the Bureau of the Budget proposed establishing a National Data Center that would collect within a single database information previously residing in the records of four separate federal agencies. Eventually, according to the proposal, data from many additional agencies would be added to the single database. *Saturday Review* published an article praising this effort, emphasizing the productivity gained from eliminating redundant record keeping. However, the article failed to convince readers that the government proposal was a benign step toward progress. In fact, the article had an exactly opposite effect. Rather than persuading Americans that the new database represented an effective means of delivering services and performing governmental functions, the *Saturday Review* piece raised fears that the most personal information concerning individuals' lives would be available to Washington bureaucrats.[6]

As a result of growing public distrust with the notion of centralized electronic data collection, several congressional subcommittees convened hearings to discuss the proposed database and its implications for privacy. In 1963, Representative Cornelius Gallagher, a member of a House subcommittee, vehemently attacked those who would transform citizens into "computerized men," beings that were "stripped of identity and privacy."[7] Gallagher predicted that,

---

5. Ibid.
6. "Chapter 2, Database Nation," http://safari.oreilly.com/0596001053/dbnationtp-CHP-2, Nov. 2007.

should the national database be established, even the privacy of the home may not be inviolate. In order to ensure privacy, claimed Gallagher, Americans will have to ensure that "the essential ingredients of life will be carried on in sound-proof, peep-proof, prefabricated rooms where, hopefully, no one will be able to spy, but where life won't be worth living."[8] However, although the subcommittees interviewed hundreds of witnesses and issued thousands of pages of transcripts, nearly a decade passed before legislation finally emerged.

In 1973, the Department of Health, Education, and Welfare (HEW) issued a report condemning the trend toward making social security numbers a universal identifier. The report noted a growing public "distrust" with computerized recordkeeping systems and recommended a code of Fair Information Practices:

1. There must be no personal-data record-keeping systems whose very existence is secret.
2. There must be a way for an individual to find out what information about him is in a record and how it is stored.
3. There must be a way for an individual to prevent information about him obtained for one purpose from being used or made available for other purposes without his consent.
4. There must be a way for an individual to correct or amend a record of identifiable information about him.
5. Any organization creating, maintaining, using, or disseminating records of identifiable personal data must assure the reliability of data for their intended use and must take reasonable precautions to prevent misuse of the data.[9]

The HEW report made no explicit mention of information or data security, although the insistence upon "reliability of data for their intended use" may be interpreted as a security function. In general, however, the code of Fair Information Practices emphasized that privacy and electronic recordkeeping could coexist if individuals are allowed to ensure the accuracy of their own personal data, to know what information is recorded, and to be aware of how the information is being used.

On December 31, 1974, President Ford signed the Privacy Act. This legislation, which representation a culmination of the work of earlier congressional

---

7. Regan, P. M., Legislating Privacy: Technology, Social Values, and Public Policy, Chapel Hill: The University of North Carolina Press, p. 95.
8. "Data Vampire."
9. "The Code of Fair Information Practices," http://epic.org/privacy/consumer/code_fair_info.html, Nov. 2007.

subcommittees and of the HEW report, imposed strict controls on databanks in federal agencies and also established a Privacy Protection Study Commission. The Privacy Act, unlike the code of Fair Information Practices, included an explicit role for information security. Subsection 10 of Section E, "Agency Requirements," stated that federal agencies must "Establish appropriate administrative, technical, and physical safeguards to ensure security and confidentiality of records to protect against any anticipated threats or hazards."[10]

Donn B. Parker, writing two years after the passage of the Privacy Act, noted that the legislation was flawed. The statute included no mention of monitoring violations or determining the compliance of database custodians. In addition, the Act included no provisions requiring that, in the event of a data breach, individuals must be informed that their personal information may have been compromised or disclosed in an unauthorized manner.[11] Nearly a quarter of a century would elapse before Parker's suggestions were incorporated into federal legislation. However, the Privacy Act successfully established a role for information security as a significant "safeguard" intended to protect the confidentiality of personal data. For the first time, a relationship between privacy and information security had been forged. Subsequent decades would witness a similar pattern: The relationship between privacy and security control is substantially grounded upon legislative fiat and regulatory requirement. Law—not business ethics, economics, or technological advancement—has served as the primary bond between concern for individual privacy and information security.

1.2   Observations

In the late 1990s, as computer systems became more accessible to corporate entities and the general user, the worry about data abuse moved from the government to corporations. While some corporate entities began mining their collected data, other businesses collected, synthesized, and aggregated data from public and private sources to sell as products. To ease this concern, governments worldwide passed a number of laws across different industries to prevent abuse, misuse, and negligence of the data collected and used.[12]

Once we know what we want to protect and who has it, the question is "how." Information security as a discipline uses the concepts of confidentiality,

---

10. Parker, D. B., *Crime by Computer,* New York: Charles Scribner's Sons, 1976, p. 237-238.

11. Oravec, J. A., "The Transformation of Privacy and Anonymity: Beyond the Right to Be Let Alone," *Sociological Imagination,* 2003, p. 6, http://www.stv.umb.edu/n05oravec, Nov. 2007.

12. New Zealand Privacy Act (1993); Hong Kong Personal Data Ordinance (1995); U.S. Health Insurance Portability and Accountability Act (1996); European Union Data Protection Directive (1998); US Gramm-Leach-Bliley Act (1999).

integrity, and availability (CIA) as frameworks for thinking about how data should be protected. For any given piece of data we must ask: Is it protected from being disclosed to those who should not access it? Is it protected from being created, changed or deleted by those who do not have permission to do so? And, is it available to those who need it? Information security uses mechanisms such as encryption, access control lists, authentication, intrusion detection, recovery procedures, and penetration testing to create and enforce the CIA triad. These protective mechanisms are implemented at different levels and components in the architecture of the systems environment.

Brandeis and Warren helped us to understand that we have a right to privacy and how this right is grounded in law and psychology. The mechanics of implementation is separate from one's privacy policy, leaving space for two distinct fields. The role of information security is to implement the mechanisms that establish and enforce privacy rights. Privacy theoretically drives security, but, as we shall see later in this chapter, cannot do so totally for pragmatic reasons when actually implemented.

More than three decades ago, Parker wrote that "almost everything that could be said about the right of privacy and the roles that computers play had been said by about 1968."[13] Obviously, Parker's statement is not literally true: Statutes and regulations governing the privacy of electronic records in health, financial services, and other industries did not emerge in the United States until the late 1990s. In fact, state and federal governments continue to wrestle with methods to combat identity fraud and other threats to individual privacy posed by the Internet, mobile computing devices, and an unceasing supply of emerging technologies. However, a less literal interpretation of Parker's observation reveals that, from an historical perspective, the complex relationship between privacy and information technology was well established by 1968. Information security, however, did not occupy a role in this relationship until 1974.

The Privacy Act of 1974 mandated that the resources of information security professionals must be deployed to ensure the privacy of information concerning individuals when that information is maintained by federal agencies in the United States. However, beginning in the late 1990s, the relationship between information security and privacy has broadened to include data stored or transmitted by private businesses. In addition, federal and state governments commenced to implement an assortment of legislative initiatives intended to prevent unauthorized access to or modification of personally identifiable information.

The Gramm-Leach-Bliley Act, enacted in November 1999, required financial services institutions to establish security controls to ensure that the "nonpublic personal information" of consumers is not disclosed to

---

13. Parker, p. 249.

unauthorized third parties. The Act, and its accompanying regulatory guidance, did not provide an unambiguous listing of data elements that comprise "nonpublic personal information." Rather, these data were described as any information:[14]

- Provided by a consumer to a financial institution; or

- Resulting from a transaction with the consumer or any service performed for the consumer; or

- Otherwise obtained by the financial institution.

The objective of this component of the legislation was to prevent an unauthorized individual from obtaining a consumer's personal information and then using this information to conduct financial transactions (identity theft). Gramm-Leach-Bliley requires financial institutions to establish written information security programs that describe technical and administrative controls established to safeguard the privacy of consumer nonpublic personal information.

The Health Insurance Portability and Accountability Act (HIPAA), which was fully implemented in July 2006, mandated that health insurance companies, clearinghouses, and individual medical providers must safeguard health information if that information can be associated, or identified with, a specific individual. The central intent of this legislation, as with Gramm-Leach-Bliley, is to protect information against unauthorized disclosure. HIPAA, however, was not primarily enacted as a safeguard against identity theft; rather, this Act sought to prevent the possible misuse of confidential medical information by unauthorized third parties.

HIPAA includes both a Privacy Rule and a Security Rule. The Privacy Rule specifies the kinds of data that must be protected and the conditions under which confidentiality is required. The Security Rule, which complements the Privacy Rule, applies to information that is electronically stored or transmitted. HIPAA's Security Rule requires that information security controls, such as access control mechanisms and encryption technology, must be applied to individually identifiable health information.

Several data elements—including patient name, telephone number, fax number, social security number, medical record number, and email address—are considered identifiers of medical information. Thus, medical data associated with these identifiers are considered highly sensitive and must receive appropriate security control.

---

14. "Gramm-Leach-Bliley Act," 15 USC Subchapter I §6809, http://ftc.gov/privacy/glbact/glbsub1.htm, Nov. 2007.

In July 2003, the California legislature enacted a statute requiring any company that conducts business with a state resident to inform the resident if his or her personal data has been, or may have been, purposefully or accidentally disclosed to an unauthorized third party. The California statute, SB 1386, provides a very clear definition of the types of data that, if disclosed, must trigger the customer notification requirement:

"Personal information" is an individual's name in combination with one or more of the following data elements when either the name or the data element is not encrypted or otherwise rendered unreadable or unusable:[15]

- Social security number;
- Driver's license or state identification card number; or
- Account number or credit or debit card number in combination with any required security code, access code or password that would permit access to an individual's financial account.

The purpose of this legislation is to provide customers with timely notification that sensitive personal information may have been compromised and that appropriate action should be taken (e.g., notifying credit card companies) to prevent identity theft. As of April 2007, 33 states and one municipality (New York City) had enacted "data breach notification" laws; most are similar to the California legislation, but many states have implemented unique provisions that are not duplicated elsewhere.

Information security is explicitly involved with the enforcement of these laws because of the requirement that customers must be notified only if protected information is disclosed in an unencrypted form. Thus, information security professionals are obligated to encrypt sensitive information to ensure that a potential or actual data breach will not damage a company's reputation or result in costly litigation.

The continuing proliferation of privacy-related legislation has established an awkward terrain within which information security professionals must navigate. Gramm-Leach-Bliley, HIPAA, and the state "data breach notification laws" mandate that an assortment of data elements must be protected against unauthorized disclosure. The enabling legislation occasionally provides very specific examples of protected data; state laws, for example, usually categorize a customer name and associated driver's license or state identification card number as "personal information." However, Gramm-Leach-Bliley and HIPAA prefer more ambiguous definitions of personally identifiable information.

---

15. "Bill Number: SB 1386 Chaptered," http://info.sen.ca.gov/pub/01-02/bill/sen/sb_1351-1400/sb_1386_bill_20020926_chaptered_html, Nov. 2007.

1.3   Recommendations

History reveals that privacy is the "why" and information security is the "how." By this statement it is meant that privacy is derived from an underlying philosophical and legal concept; information security is the method or set of methods implemented to achieve privacy. Privacy reflects the values of the given culture and power structure of the organization creating the policy. By contrast, information security is a pragmatic function that effects compliance with the policy that describes one's right (or lack thereof) to privacy.

For information security professionals, the most prudent method to ensure compliance with legislative mandates is to ensure that all data associated with individual customers or employees are provided the highest level of security control. In order to provide this control, the first and most critical task of risk management must occur: data classification, which is discussed in detail in Chapter 4.

Privacy-related information—data elements that, either singly or in combination with other data, pertain to an individual—must be classified in the most secure category. Organizations often designate this category as "top secret," "personally identifiable information," "restricted," "confidential," "sensitive," or by a similarly descriptive label. Many compliance officers prefer that classifications should be self-explanatory; thus, the terms "nonpublic personal information" or "personally identifiable information" may be preferable as the type of classification that describes privacy-related data. The specific name selected is less important than the establishment of a category that explicitly includes data that are associated with individual persons. In addition, a written policy, explaining the various kinds of data included within the classification and accompanied by easily comprehended examples, must be developed and published for internal organizational use. Information security will contribute to the formulation of this policy, although the actual document may be authored by the legal department, compliance, or a similar control function. The policy should be accessible to all employees.

The task of identifying privacy-related data—which also includes documenting the electronic locations of these data and the methods by which data are communicated within the organization and to external entities—is best performed by business stakeholders and the technologists who support systems and applications used by the stakeholders. However, information security, in its role as enforcer of mandated privacy regulations, is not merely a passive observer of the identification and classification processes. In fact, information security personnel must ensure that classification occurs in a manner that will permit technical security controls (e.g., encryption, secure architecture design, access control mechanisms) to perform their intended functions properly.

For example, customer names and associated account numbers may be stored in specific databases. Access management and encryption may be appropriate tools to secure the confidentiality of these personally identifiable data. However, the same information, when verbally communicated during a telephone conversation, is not amenable to technical information security controls. Sensitive information transmitted by telephone is more efficiently safeguarded by the establishment of customer relationship procedures established by specific business units.

Unfortunately, the task of data classification—especially in large organizations with hundreds of applications and databases—is rarely a systematic, thorough process. For example, a few years ago, a large American corporation deployed teams of technicians, business analysts, and information security personnel to classify all data elements resident within the thousands of applications used by business units and their supporting services. Several years were devoted to this effort. When the task was nearing completion, the organization merged with another large company. At this point, the classification project was discontinued.

In order to address the privacy-related mandates, however, it is not necessary to perform an enterprise-wide data classification effort. Rather, it is required only to identify those data elements that pertain to individual customers or employees. Although the scope of this work should not be minimized, it is far less formidable than a full classification of all available data.

The identification of personally identifiable data serves as the point of departure for subsequent risk assessment. More specifically, information security professionals must examine each application and database within which private information resides; in addition, the technical environment of these applications and databases must be scrutinized. This examination will consider three primary risk-related factors.

First, what are the possible vulnerabilities to which the data associated with each application or database is exposed? For example, is the application accessible via the Internet? Can data entry and modification or approval be performed by the same individual? Does the application fail to generate hardcopy reports that detail changes to data?

Second, are there potential threats that could exploit the identified vulnerabilities? For instance, could Internet-borne malware compromise the confidentiality or integrity of data residing in an application? Is it possible that inadequate access controls could contribute to the occurrence of fraud perpetrated by employees? Could the lack of hardcopy reports mask unauthorized transactions?

Third, what is the likelihood of these threats exploiting the vulnerabilities and, therefore, inappropriately disclosing privacy-related information? The response to this question must necessarily involve a subjective judgment, because it requires a prediction of possible future action. However, when making this prediction, information security professionals must consider that the mere *possibility* of a successful exploitation is not equivalent to a *likelihood* that compromise will occur. In his book, *Animal Farm,* George Orwell coined the rather cynical motto: "All animals are equal, but some animals are more equal than others." The information security risk assessment process is guided by a similar, although less sardonic, truth: "All possible exploits are dangerous, but some exploits are more possible (and dangerous) than others." Determining the degree of possibility and danger is the task of risk assessment.

However, identifying vulnerabilities and threats and ascertaining the likelihood of threats exploiting vulnerabilities is not the first responsibility of privacy-related risk management. Rather, these activities are dependent upon a critical preliminary: the identification and classification of data that require protection.

1.3.1   Roles and Responsibilities of Information Security

Privacy (or lack thereof) is a policy matter; the implementation of information security controls is a pragmatic one. Within the corporate environment the chief privacy officer and chief information security officer are assigned the tasks of fulfilling duties related to privacy and information security, respectively. However, the daily functions of these officers negate the notion that privacy dictates to security its pragmatic function.

We can evaluate the relationship between information security and privacy on two levels: top-down and bottom-up. From the top-down approach we understand why privacy and information security controls are implemented. The bottom-up approach, however, provides understanding of how these privacy and information security controls are implemented. Privacy and information security contain distinct, as well as overlapping, functions.

The major benefit of the top-down perspective is a holistic approach to integrating privacy requirements into the corporate culture. Other benefits include, but are not limited to, regulatory and legal compliance, instilling cultural values regarding privacy and a uniform pragmatic application of principles to corporate data. On inspection we find that certain functions overlap between the chief privacy officer and the chief information security officer. Overlapping privacy functions include: asset management, communications and operations management, access control, incident management, and business continuity management.[16] However, as mentioned earlier, there are specific non-overlapping functions which apply to the chief information security officer but

---

16. Axelrod, C. W., "Achieving Privacy Through Security Measures," *Information Systems Control Journal,* http://www.isaca.org, Vol. 2, 2007.

not to the chief privacy officer. These include security policy, organization of information security, human resource security, physical and environmental security, and system acquisition and maintenance.[17]

The bottom-up approach analyzes data in two ways. First we can understand privacy and security relating to data at rest and data in transit. For example, we may encrypt data on backup tapes when the data is at rest and we encrypt data in transit via SSL when it travels across the Internet. Second, we can apply privacy and security to specific data elements and not others. Personal, nonpublic data such as social security numbers and bank account numbers must be protected, whereas publicly available data is optional.

We can thus apply our top-down and bottom-up framework to the chief privacy officer and the chief information security officer roles and have a clear understanding why privacy will work in tandem with, but cannot drive, the information security program.

The chief privacy officer is responsible for creating a framework that includes legal, compliance, and cultural issues confronting the organization. On a conceptual level, the chief privacy officer interprets legal requirements and legal exposure. In the age of globalization, a cultural understanding of privacy expectations, and requirements is paramount. On a pragmatic level, the chief privacy officer's responsibilities may include the sending of privacy notices which are not of concern to the chief information security officer in the scope of functional responsibility.

The chief information security officer function is a role that includes pragmatic compliance with the corporate policy but is not limited to that role only. Managing information security has its own best practices that dictate how certain operations should be performed. In short, the discipline of information security manages risk over technology assets and dictates its own set of requirements, some of which are not within the purview of the chief privacy officer. As an example, the chief information security officer has a responsibility to ensure that the infrastructure is appropriately patched; this is not a role assumed by the chief privacy officer.

Increasingly, the chief privacy officer and chief information security officer will intimately need to know each other's perspective. Both functions are integrated in the sense that one cannot be a chief privacy officer without thinking about the operational risk of executing the technical provisions described in the privacy policy. And, one cannot be a chief information security officer without thinking about compliance and legal issues. Thus, the "why" and the "how" are intertwined in a ballet where the impact of one function necessarily influences the other. A failure of policy will result in an incomplete, and failed, execution; a failure of execution will be a failed policy.

---

17. Ibid.

1.3.2   The Impact of Outsourcing: Privacy, Security, and Enforcing Controls

Enforcing controls over data outside one's main environment is basically taken on faith. Corporate interests and various laws mandate that we include contractual provisions that require third parties to treat data in the same way we would treat data. We review various reports—SAS 70 type II, vulnerability assessments, auditor statements—that give us a comfort level that service providers are protecting data properly.

Data flow between companies may be thought of as similar to an Olympic track relay race. One company hands the baton of data to the next company waiting in line to process it. Each runner in the relay race follows accepted rules, or else the entire team is disqualified. Each runner is dependent on the skills of the other runners. Sometimes a runner steps out of bounds, sometimes a runner drops the baton. As a company, we hope to choose the best running mates. We practice with our teammates. We do our due diligence by requesting reports or perhaps even directly auditing the systems of service providers. Ultimately, and as much as we practice, we hope that when we pass the baton to our other running mates they will not drop the baton when they handle it and that they stay in bounds and within the rules so as not to disqualify themselves and the entire team. Unfortunately, our current technology does not allow us to tie the baton to our running mate when we pass it to them. Generally speaking, "Where the data flows, so must the proper controls...."[18]

1.3.3   Privacy and New Roles for Information Security

Laws intended to prevent the unauthorized disclosure of private information, coupled with the ceaseless development of new technologies, have both expanded and altered the traditional roles of information security. For example, the statutory focus on privacy concerns has blurred the distinction between physical and logical security.

In recent years, well publicized news stories concerning the loss or theft of magnetic tapes, laptops, and other media containing personally identifiable information have become commonplace. The situation has become sufficiently dire that a website, privacyrights.org, has been established to chronicle all reported unauthorized disclosures of sensitive personal information since 2005. According to the Privacy Clearing House, 217 million records have been inappropriately made public since the commencement of recordkeeping.[19]

---

18. Belva, K., "A nice little saying: Wherever the data flows, so must the proper controls," http://www.bloginfosec.com/2007/11/16/a-nice-little-saying-wherever-the-data-flows-so-must-the-proper-controls/, Nov. 2007.

19. "A Chronology of Data Breaches," http://www.privacyrights.org/ar/ChronDataBreaches.htm, Feb. 2008.

As a result, information security professionals are required to assist with the securing of physical media. This responsibility involves several issues:

- Establishing and assisting with the implementation of standards concerning the secure destruction and erasure of hard drives, magnetic tapes, optical disks, and other media containing personally identifiable information;

- Formulating standards and guidelines that focus upon the secure transport and storage of physical media;

- Developing policies intended to control the threat of unauthorized data disclosure posed by portable media, such as USB devices, cell phones, and music players;

- Devising controls intended to prevent the loss or disclosure of personal data due to the theft of laptops.

These issues are not the sole responsibility of information security. Physical security personnel, records and media management specialists, and legal professionals also contribute to the mitigation of security risks posed by the many vulnerabilities associated with portable, highly mobile devices and other physical media. However, information security must collaborate with these individuals to document and implement policies that incorporate realistic controls intended to reduce the likelihood of unauthorized disclosure due to loss or theft.

For example, many corporations recognize that the portability of laptops represents a security exposure. They are frequently lost, stolen, or left unattended in public locations. As a result, information security professionals have adopted policies that require power-on passwords to access data and applications resident on laptops. In addition, the full encryption of laptop hard drives is an increasingly accepted practice. Control of USB devices may be implemented by requiring the use of strong encryption. Also, numerous organizations have established technical controls that eliminate the possibility of downloading information from workstations or laptops to USB devices.

However, the role of information security as enforcer of privacy is not limited merely to the implementation of access controls and encryption. A clearly defined and documented reporting mechanism, activated when a potential or actual theft or loss of data has occurred, must be established and made available to all employees of the organization. Information security professionals are required to monitor these reports, to determine if personally identifiable information has been compromised, and to conduct relevant forensic analyses. Large organizations, recognizing the importance of this investigative function, have dedicated expanding numbers of information security personnel to the monitoring of incident reports and conducting forensic investigations. This trend has been prompted, to a considerable extent, by privacy concerns.

The numerous state data breach notification laws, initiated originally by California in 2003, provide a vivid example of the manner by which government-mandated privacy controls have altered the roles assumed by information security professionals. Compliance with these laws requires that organizations must develop programs for identifying the likelihood of a privacy-related data breach and for notifying individual customers if their personal information may have been compromised. Implementing such programs involves the acquisition of skills that have not traditionally been associated with the professional practice of information security: the ability to identify any legal definition for data content involved with a specific incident, awareness of legal or public relations measures that may reduce the severity of the breach, and facility with the communication of technical matters to legal, business, and public relations professionals. These skills, involving knowledge of data classification systems, privacy-focused risk assessments, and regulatory requirements, are increasingly critical to information security professionals attempting to cope with new roles necessitated by privacy concerns.

1.4 Future Trends

Writing in 1976, Donn Parker claimed that two major factors traditionally motivate the "imposition" of information security controls: (1) fear of losses, based on widely publicized experience of victims of computer abuse, and (2) establishment of laws and regulations.[20] As discussed earlier in this chapter, both of these elements were decisive to the forging of a relationship between privacy and information security. However, these were not the only influential factors. In addition to a broad sense of public distrust with technology, and also several statutory and regulatory initiatives enacted in response to this distrust, it was necessary to achieve consensus concerning concepts of "private" versus "public" information. In the United States, this consensus emerged primarily due to fear of identity theft, and also anxiety concerning the unauthorized disclosure of medical information. Further, the relationship between privacy and information security has been strengthened by the emergence of specific technologies (such as the Internet) that are generally perceived as posing threats to accepted concepts of privacy.

However, Parker's essential theme—that public fear, followed by legislation intended to mitigate fear, are the preconditions to involvement by information security controls—is as valid in the first decade of the twenty-first century

---

20. Parker, pp. 275, 276.

as in the 1970s. Information security remains an essentially reactive tool, responding to broader social and political forces, rather than a proactive agent that actually shapes social values.

To a considerable extent, information security professionals address issues related to privacy in very traditional ways by implementing those components of the security toolkit that are typically used to protect data confidentiality. These tools would include identity and intrusion management, access control technologies, and incident response mechanisms. However, the task of securing privacy-related data has also greatly expanded the traditional roles of information security.

For example, auditors and security-focused organizations have been advising information security professionals for many decades that the development and implementation of written policies and standards is a critical element of an effective security program. However, the task of providing adequate controls for privacy-related data transforms policy development into a mandatory obligation. Not only must data classification policies be established to identify protected data, the emergence of privacy concerns has blurred boundaries between physical and logical security; information security specialists can no longer assume that logical security is their only responsibility. In order to comply with regulations concerning privacy, security professionals must develop an awareness of issues related to disposal of hard drives, restrictions upon downloads to USB devices and other portable media, and problems associated with the loss and theft of devices containing personally identifiable data. Similarly, policies regarding data erasure, media destruction, secure transport and storage of information, and controls governing the use of portable, easily lost, media must be enforced at service provider and vendor locations.

Finally, the need to comply with regulations concerning privacy have thrust the information security function into the midst of an intricate web of issues pertaining to corporate governance. During the final two decades of the twentieth century, information security professionals were aware that the adequacy of their controls and programs is under continual scrutiny by the internal audit function. In turn, many internal auditors viewed their primary task as the assessment of information security. However, the introduction of privacy regulations has greatly altered this relationship. Due primarily to the increasing focus upon privacy, information security must now develop collaborative relationships with innumerable corporate functions—internal audit, compliance, legal, privacy officers, media and records management, physical security, and business units. Roles and responsibilities between these numerous, diverse functions are frequently overlapping and occasionally confused. In order to establish a consistent privacy program, issues of governance—especially pertaining to the authority assigned to each of these functions—must be addressed. In the absence of a well-defined governance structure, the implementation of privacy controls may degenerate into a hodgepodge of conflicting goals and responsibilities.

As mentioned previously, Donn Parker maintained that "Almost everything that could be said about the right of privacy and the roles that computers play had been said by about 1968."[21] Only now are we really listening to what was actually said.

---

21. Parker, pp. 239.

2

Data Protection

Joel Weise, Glenn Brunette, and Michelle Dennedy

> If you are an experienced infomation security and IT professional, you may find this chapter simple and obvious. You may find "the importance of standardization" a recurring theme not only in information security literature, but in IT literature. You might doubt whether endorsement of the holistic view of the management situation rates observation under the heading "future trends." If you have experienced economies of scale in IT management without numerous security exceptions, you will not find much new or innovative material in this chapter. However, it is still worth reading because the overarching theme still falls on deaf ears. Namely, it is impossible to maintain asset integrity or privacy without consistency in security implementation. The authors remind us that security is a management discipline that facilitates control over information. Moreover, like any other management discipline, it requires a strategic rather than a tactical approach. Given the ever-increasing number of new, nontechnical disciples to the information security community, this volume would be incomplete without these reminders.
>
> —J.L.B.

2.1 Background

As more and more devices are connected through the network, and as information is now more easily available through open and ubiquitous access methods, a shift is happening in the way people are using technology. Transitioning from just a supporting role, technology is today being used to connect people with each other to participate in and to share workflows, to compete for jobs, to purchase goods and services, and to learn and create. These activities will rarely, if ever, be entirely contained within traditional jurisdictional boundaries or even within traditional closed information technology (IT) networks, thus creating a challenge for legislators, enforcement agencies, users of systems, as well as security and privacy professionals.

This new era, dubbed the "Participation Age" by Sun Microsystems, is defined by an age where participants are not just acquiring information but are also contributing to that information, refining it, and sharing it. The Participation Age affects not only how people access and use information but also how IT systems and services must be designed to deliver and protect information. Today, IT services must support widespread access while also protecting the security and privacy of intellectual property (IP), personally identifiable information (PII), and other protected data categories.

For the purposes of this chapter, a brief discussion regarding a few basic definitions may help determine the scope of protection implied by data protection for various date elements.

Personally Identifiable Information   PII is a generic term used to describe the broad category of data that either directly identifies an individual or indirectly can be associated to an individual. For example, name, contact information, government-issued ID, social security number, bank account numbers, personal health information, and others. There are hundreds of laws or regulations around the world which seek to protect PII or some subset of it.

Confidential Information   This is any type of information that can be considered to be confidential given the timing and context of a particular data asset. The key differentiator here is that this type of data asset is bound by an agreement or understanding regarding the selective access and disclosure rights of data. For example, confidential information can be defined by parties on a contractual basis and can include such items as business documents, plans, account numbers, contracts, invoices, purchase orders, system data, or trade secrets.

Intellectual Property   This is a term that refers to the bundle of rights associated with documented creative expression such as inventions, literary and artistic works, and symbols, names, images, and designs used in commerce.

Data Asset   We collectively define these various categories as data assets for the purpose of discussing the interplay between security and data privacy in particular, and for all data categories in the general sense. A specific data element may fall into one or all of these data asset categories given the specific facts. The categorization of that asset can and often will determine the security strategy deployed.

As we look toward the future, modern IT services and the organizations that use them must, in turn, develop methods to measure and correct the ability of IT systems to support fair and appropriate use of data assets. In other words, services should be designed to promote systemic integrity and accountability by leveraging secure architecture techniques built upon open standards that can be validated by third parties. But is this enough? How does security compliment and relate to privacy in today's world? Can privacy exist in the absence of security? Does security even matter if we are not protecting something as valuable as the data that describes, explains, promotes, and indicates individual people? What of the interplay between the rights and responsibilities of the creators of IP and users in a distributed and often anonymous environment? These questions and the evolution of answers start to shape the technology, financial, process, and ethical decisions in the modern enterprise.

The relationship between security and data assets can be summed up with the oversimplified statement: You can have security and have no asset protection or privacy, but it is impossible to maintain asset integrity or privacy without security. When discussing the relative functions and features of data asset management and security in the enterprise context, it is useful to start with a discussion of business issues that define the basic goals of the organization:

- First, an organization must have a clear understanding of the scope of its IT services and workforce. Will the organization be present virtually or physically in one or many different geographies, for example? Will the organization employ its own workforce or rely on work performed by third parties, including open communities who may have no fiduciary relationship with the organization.

- Further, decisions must be made about the fundamental functions of information systems and who will have responsibility for building, accessing and maintaining these systems. Accordingly, even the users of various information services themselves should be considered when determining who should have access to what, when, why, and for how long.

Once these and other basic business decisions are formed, the IT, data asset governance and management and security professionals can enter into the equation, cooperating, hand-in-hand, to execute on these basic requirements. The IT function is primarily concerned with the successful delivery of IT services that meet the business and technical requirements that have been defined, including those related to security and privacy. A data asset management function is primarily concerned with value of information balanced against risk related to its loss, inappropriate use as well as its sharing or regulation. A privacy professional, IP creator or owner or other data asset guardian provides value to the organization when appropriate information reliably gets to the right people at the right time. Silence is not necessarily golden for the data asset professional, as the goal of preserving information in a timely and respectful fashion typically includes active sharing of data to drive business value.

The security professional delivers value to the organization by preserving the confidentiality, integrity and availability of information while guarding against inappropriate access by unauthorized parties. A security professional is most successful when information and infrastructure on which it resides is protected from compromise. Issues such as who requires access to what services and data and at what level of sensitivity must be well understood. The data asset management function determines how best to share, or otherwise use, those data to greatest effect while the security function must determine which techniques will be effective to keep the cost of incursion higher than the value of the data combined with the cost of protecting the infrastructure.

2.2 Observations

It is useful to look to the example of privacy and personally identifiable information, its interplay with security, and the notion of risk as a specific instance of data asset management. Although the practices of privacy and security often require near simultaneous work-streams, they are, in fact, distinct specialties requiring a distinct perspective. To further explore this relationship, it is important to understand security as a risk management tool. In this sense, security control mechanisms are used to reduce the attack surface of systems, networks, applications, processes, and physical elements such that one can be assured that one's privacy is not at risk beyond a level considered reasonable. In other words, PII may be considered secure when the risk of compromise is controlled to an identified and acceptable level, and the potential for limiting harm and decreasing proliferation of disclosure is maximized given the current state of technical tools, processes, and the people who are able to protect this particular data asset.

But what is an identified and acceptable level? Clearly, risk is not a universal constant, and neither is the value of information to organizations. This is where criticality and impact come into play. How critical is the information to be protected? What is the impact to the organization and other key stakeholders should the information be disclosed, altered, or outright destroyed? What level of privacy protection has the organization promised to its users either explicitly or through its brand? These are the critical questions to be asked, and unfortunately, these questions can only be answered by the organization itself. Once the organization has developed a standard model for criticality and impact, similar to what is described in the National Security Agency's Information Security Assessment Methodology,[1] the organization will be better prepared to classify its information, services, and infrastructure. The criticality and impact of risks will then depend on the purpose and context of the information, the method of its collection, processing, storage, and destruction, as well as the specifics as to who will have access to, or control, or possession of that information (influenced by regulatory, geographic, and cultural factors).

It should be clear that risk related to IT services and information cannot be reduced to zero, nor would anyone probably want to pay to do so, and the result is that there will also be residual risk to privacy and security interests. The good news is that security controls, when implemented correctly and within the context of a well-designed security architecture, can provide reasonable protection at a reasonable cost.

It is important to consider the key threats to security and data assets and how those threats adapt as organizational goals change. Previously we have talked about risks to information and systems such as disclosure, alteration, and destruction. Each of these pose real, tangible threats to individuals, organizations, and governments. As more systems become interconnected, and as more information is shared across greater numbers of services, there is an increased likelihood that a breach will occur.

- For individuals, many privacy-related breaches involve information being disclosed that leads to various forms of identity theft. The impact of identify theft must not be underestimated and, depending on the severity, can have a significant and long-lasting impact on the individual and his or her family.

- For organizations, privacy and other data asset issues can be just as tricky. Again, depending on the criticality of the breach, organizations may be required to pay hefty fines. A public breach involving their customers' information could lead not only to loss of business but potentially further litigation should the organization's data asset and information handling practices found lacking.

- For governments, data asset management and policy creation continues to pose significant challenges. On one hand, there are efficiencies that can be gained when multiple agencies share information about citizens. On the other hand, there is the perpetual and well-justified concern about how that information will be collected, stored, and used.

---

1. NSA IAM, http://www.nsa.gov/ia/industry/education/iam.cfm?MenuID=10.2.4.2

Sometimes the owner of the private information is his or her own worst enemy. People often compromise the security of their own PII for the sake of usability or other real or perceived benefits. For example, people will easily give up personal data just to get a $5 discount on a book from an online bookseller. What the individual may not realize is that the small pieces of data that are given up freely are aggregated together to build what can best be described as a dossier on them—including their personal and family information, their buying and shopping habits, what they eat, drink, read, and watch. People are familiar with the type of information collected in their credit reports, but this is just the tip of the iceberg. It is well known that some insurance companies use credit scores to set prices on their policies. What if an insurance company were to determine that you purchase tobacco products or eat too often at fast food restaurants?

There are other facets to data asset management that arise in a technologically wired world. Networks allow for the vast dissemination of data, and database systems allow for massive data stores and the opportunity for data mining. Concerns, for example, are often raised related to government surveillance, such as, what if the FBI tracks all of the books you read about anarchy for your doctoral dissertation and so determines you should be put on a watch list? What if your identity is stolen and the perpetrator is found to have committed crimes in your name that have put you on the TSA No Fly List? Will you ever know you are on these lists? How quickly? Once you discover the problem, how easily can you fix the errors? Will the errors be fixed in every place where that information is stored and similar decisions about you are made?

What can individuals do about this? One option to reduce the reliance on others is to avoid disclosing your information. This is certainly possible in a closed ecosystem such as your typical corporation that maintains HR information or within a hospital that maintains patient information; but these are rather simplistic examples. Very rarely do one's data exist within the confines of a single enterprise. Individuals will likely work for many corporations and those corporations will likely outsource elements of their operations which all increase the likelihood that an individual's information will be shared. Similarly, health care information will be shared with doctors, insurance companies, labs, and other health care entities thereby increasing its exposure. Unfortunately, we are left with the realization and expectation that our data will in fact be shared, and possibly without our consent.

For others, such isolation is simply not an option in this heavily interconnected world where everything from purchasing homes and cars, to flying on airplanes, to vacationing abroad involves handing over pieces of PII. Further, universally lacking significant rules and regulations for the sharing of PII, many organizations adopt a sharing approach in the name of interoperability, efficiency, or usability. So how do we balance the usability of services with the risks to peoples' data? Consider that once PII is given up to anyone, the owner will immediately and forever lose control over it. There are no guarantees that the information entrusted to that third party will be properly gathered, stored, used, and destroyed.

2.3 Recommendations

So where does this leave us? Unfortunately, there is no simple or easy answer for this challenge. Security and data asset threats can only be minimized and contained. The goal of this section is to discuss recommendations that can be adopted by organizations to better reduce their risk, protect PII in their charge, and enable controls for enhanced security. For individuals also concerned about data assets, we can only recommend that you share your sensitive information with only those organizations and entities that follow guidelines such as those listed below. Keep in mind that these recommendations:

- Will likely be customized to suit the needs of specific organizations;
- Must be implemented as part of an comprehensive security strategy (not as a series of independent constructs).

Before discussing the primary recommendations, it is useful to describe the characteristics of a successful organization, and by successful we mean an organization that is able to address threats to privacy sufficiently well that users, consumers, peers, and other entities are willing to entrust that organization with private and confidential information. An example of a definition for a high-performing organization can be found in the work of the Information Technology Process Institute, which states:[2]

> Based on our analysis, we have created the following working definition of high-performing IT organizations: They are effective and efficient and they succeed in applying resources to accomplish their stated business objectives with little or no wasted effort. These organizations have evolved a system of process improvement as a natural consequence of their business demands. They regularly implement formal, repeatable, and secure operational processes.

Given this definition, it can be stated that a successful organization (i.e., one that optimally reduces threats) ensures they maintain cost-effective and appropriate levels of the following characteristics:

2. Behr, K., et al, *Visible Ops Handbook,* Information Technology Process Institute, p. 73.

- *Availability*—data and processing resources are there when needed;
- *Reliability/integrity*—data resources are always consistent, correct and accurate enabling one the confidence to offer services that the competition cannot;
- *Agility/adaptability*—changes can be implemented faster than the competition along with responding to a changing business and technical climate faster than your competition;
- *Operational efficiency*—you can run your business faster and cheaper than your competition;
- *Security assurance*—confidentiality, integrity, and privacy are supported such that data resources are not disclosed or modified without authorization and accountability.

All of these characteristics are complementary to the use of security and when applied in a coherent, integrated, holistic, and optimized manner they will reduce the threats to privacy. These characteristics are embodied within the following recommendations that will be discussed in more detail below:

- Formalize a trust model;
- Utilize an integrated and holistic approach to security and governance;
- Implement a risk-based systemic security architecture;
- Support an adaptive security strategy;
- Build systems, applications, networks, protocols, and so forth using accepted standards.

2.3.1 Formalize a Trust Model

We have stated that privacy cannot exist in the absence of security. We now further extend this concept by stating that privacy cannot exist without trust. There are multiple types of trust, each of which serves a different purpose and target audience. Depending upon the needs of a particular constituent, a different trust model may be in order.

Organizations must design, develop, and run services and infrastructure that matches peoples' expectations of privacy and trust in terms of identity, authentication, and other security qualities, including those described above. Yet the inherent insecurity of many modern business systems is, in fact, the failure of the underlying security architecture upon which those systems are built. In particular, deficient trust models often fail to address every layer: business, technology, people, and process, and the consequence might be an implementation with weaker security than the designer intended. The trust model relies on complete requirements that include business, technical, legal, regulatory, and fiduciary requirements.

It is recommended that organizations develop a formalized trust model as part of their security architecture and risk analysis methodologies for all business systems ensuring that those systems are protected according to their stated requirements and identified risk thresholds. Leveraging the concepts of criticality and impact mentioned earlier will further ensure a common vocabulary and standard used across all of the business systems when measuring risk.

It is also recommended that security be viewed holistically rather than as functionality that can be bolted onto an existing design. A key principle of effective security design and implementation states that security should be integrated into every layer and perspective of a solution (at varying degrees depending upon the threat profile). Security is not a product or feature that can simply be added to a design to make it "secure," but rather an architectural perspective that seeks to embed the use of trustworthy capabilities and security controls as needed throughout the design.

Trust is particularly important in distributed and federated environments and plays a critical role in ensuring and enhancing overall system security and thus privacy. For the sake of defining trust and security maturity modeling relative to security architecture, the following set of principles are offered:

- Trust is a characteristic and quality of a holistic and comprehensive security effort in that it must be represented in all facets of that effort including the physical, operational, and technical components.

- Trust is a balancing of liability and due diligence. For example, you must decide how much effort to expend to reduce liability to an acceptable level for a particular business proposition and stated security policy. You must establish an equilibrium of trust.

- Trust is the enabling of confidence that something will or will not occur in a predictable or promised manner. The enabling of confidence is supported by identification, authentication, accountability, authorization, and availability.

- This confidence is ensured in part through the binding of unique attributes to a unique identity.

It is also important to note what a trust model is not. A trust model is not the particular security mechanisms utilized within a particular security architecture. Rather, it is the combination of those security mechanisms in conjunction with the security policy when they address all business, technical, legal, regulatory, and fiduciary requirements to the satisfaction of a relying entity.

A security architecture based on an acceptable trust model provides a framework for delivering security mechanisms that are then used to ensure the privacy of PII. Trust modeling is the process performed by the security architect to define a complementary threat profile and trust model based on a use-case-driven analysis of processes and data flows. The result of the exercise integrates information about the threats, vulnerabilities, and risk of a particular IT architecture. Further, trust modeling identifies the specific controls that are necessary to respond to a specific threat profile. Trust modeling allows for the design and development of a systemically secure architecture that responds cost-effectively to risks, including risks to privacy.

2.3.2   Utilize an Integrated and Holistic Approach to Security and Governance

A holistic approach to security means that an organization takes a total view to their overall security effort. Such a comprehensive view must also consider the overall needs of the business, compliance, and regulatory requirements and most importantly, be cost effective such that the cost of security does not outweigh the overall benefit to the organization. Specifically good security policies and practices are adopted and consistently followed, security awareness is reinforced, security training is provided, strong security governance is driven by executive management, and security is considered as an integrated component of every-thing that occurs within the organization (i.e., for all organizational, techni-cal, operational, and physical aspects). Governance increases the visibility of decision-making at lower managerial levels to ensure oversight exists at an appropriate level within the enterprise.

For federated systems that function between disparate organizations, it is important that the security policy between these different entities be well-defined and understood, and that the security controls supporting the agreed-to policy be implemented consistently and verified regularly.

Utilizing a holistic approach to security is predicated upon the implemen-tation of an overall corporate security governance effort. The intent of a security governance program is to ensure that an organization's data security and privacy effort has CxO–level support and that the program aligns with the business objectives while at the same time, is in compliance with applicable laws, regula-tions, standards, and best practices. A comprehensive security governance pro-gram should include the following characteristics:

- An information security strategy that exists and supports of organiza-tion's overall business plan;
- An executive management commitment;
- Specific roles and responsibilities that are articulated to ensure accountability;

- Open communication channels exist between management tiers;

- Documented set of all regulatory and compliance requirements;

- Documented and maintained information security policy, appropriate privacy, and other data asset policies;

- Developed and maintained procedures and guidelines to support business goals and objectives;

- Regular review of the security architecture and verification of the effectiveness of implemented controls.

The benefits of a holistic security architecture and strong security governance are many. A holistic security architecture is first and foremost a comprehensive set of security services that work in conjunction to satisfy an organization's identified security and privacy policies. For that reason it is critical that these policies properly and accurately reflect the security, risk, and privacy positions of the organization. Considering the current regulatory and compliance environment that most organizations exist in, it is also important to view the security architecture with the applicable requirements in mind. It is the success of the security architecture that will dictate, to a large extent, one's ability to address those requirements.

The benefits noted here intentionally map to more than just technical issues but to all aspects of one's business. For example, where good security practices are used in change control and patch management, outages and system downtime should be minimized and thus operational efficiencies improved. Likewise, reducing downtime will increase the availability of one's systems and thus better enable their usefulness to the enterprise.

Finally, we note that a secure system will enable the security and integrity of data and processing resources within the enterprise. Ultimately, it is the business that relies upon the accuracy of its data and processing resources to support the business and in making critical business decisions.

Some of the primary benefits of a comprehensive security architecture include:

- Increased transparency of accountability and informed delegation of authority.

- Controlled and agile risk management.

- Protection of the existing asset base through maximizing re-use of existing architectural components.

- Proactive control, monitoring, and management mechanisms.

- Process, concept, and component reuse across all organizational business units.
- Compliance with applicable legal and regulatory mandates.
- A more efficient IT operation:
  - Lower software development, support, and maintenance costs;
  - Increased portability of applications;
  - Improved interoperability and easier system and network management;
  - Improved ability to address critical enterprise-wide issues such as security;
  - Easier upgrade and exchange of system components.
- Better return on existing investment; reduced risk for future investment:
  - Reduced complexity in IT infrastructure;
  - Maximum return on investment in existing IT infrastructure;
  - The flexibility to make, buy, or outsource IT solutions;
  - Reduced risk overall in new investment, and the costs of IT ownership.
- Faster, simpler, and cheaper procurement:
  - Buying decisions are simpler, because the information governing procurement is readily available in a coherent plan.

The procurement process is faster—maximizing procurement speed and flexibility without sacrificing architectural coherence.

2.3.3 Implement a Risk-Based Systemic Security Architecture

Systemic security is a means to develop, implement, and manage a holistic security architecture. It addresses the need for strong security guarantees in increasingly dynamic and flexible IT environments. The systemic security approach applies time-tested security principles, iterative refinement of policies, and other means to weave security controls and assurances more systemically throughout an IT environment. With a focus on iterative refinement, organizations can transform their existing legacy deployments into resilient architectures that meet not only their security, privacy, and compliance needs, but also satisfy other business goals, such as increased agility, flexibility, efficiency, and availability.

The convergence and availability of greater numbers of computers, mobile phones, PDAs, and other devices are fueling new opportunities and new styles of sharing, participation, and commerce; and these opportunities likewise place a burden on protecting the privacy of PII. Traditional organizational and network boundaries continue to blur and fade as organizations find new ways of engaging their customers, partners, suppliers, and employees. Furthermore, the delivery of services is becoming more streamlined, as associations among components and data become more dynamic in response to "just in time" business decisions. As such, it is our view that ensuring the security of data assets is becoming increasingly more difficult if organizations do not take a more proactive and holistic approach to security.

Managing risk, cost, and complexity effectively to ensure the security and privacy of data, requires achieving a careful balance across business, operational, and technical boundaries. Architectures must be sufficiently flexible to respond to ever-changing business opportunities, policies, and regulatory pressures, and evolving threat profiles. They must also be sufficiently resilient, reliable, and predictable to support the most demanding, mission-critical environments. Using a systemic security approach addresses the challenge of designing, implementing, and managing IT environments in which everything and everyone is securely connected to the network.

The common architectural security principles that comprise systemic security will be discussed below and include:

- Self-preservation,
- Defense in depth,
- Least privilege,
- Compartmentalization,
- Proportionality.

2.3.3.1 Self-Preservation

Self-preservation is defined as "protection of oneself from harm or destruction" and "the innate desire to stay alive."[3] Applied to the topic of IT architecture, the principle of self-preservation dictates that an object must be configured, used, and managed in such a way that it protects itself from unauthorized external influence. Self-preservation, as applied to IT architecture, typically means that organizations should, at a minimum:

- Reduce the attack surface of objects, as well as the potential for undue exposure.
- Ensure, as best one can, that objects are in a known and trustworthy state, are free of vulnerabilities (for example, patched), and are configured appropriately for the environment in which they are used.

---

3. "Self-preservation," http://www.dictionary.com

- Protect management and administrative interfaces from unauthorized access.

- Prefer the use of open and vetted protocols that implement strong authentication, confidentiality, and integrity protections.

2.3.3.2 Defense in Depth

Defense in depth mandates the use of multiple, independent, and mutually reinforcing security controls. Simply put, an IT architecture should strive to eliminate, where possible, single points of security failure. The number, placement, and type of security controls used will vary based on the threat profile of the architecture (and its published services), as well as organizational policies and preferences. Regardless of the actual controls or methods used to implement defense in depth throughout an architecture, the goal remains the same—namely, to defend an IT environment in the event that a single security control fails. More and more in modern architectures there is a growing need for security architectures that can survive and recover from multiple simultaneous and random failures.

2.3.3.3 Least Privilege

The principle of least privilege states that "every program and every user of the system should operate using the least set of privileges necessary to complete the job." More generally, when discussing IT architecture, this principle is applied to the export, use, and control of services and interfaces. Fundamentally, you should not offer what you do not want others to take. Only by establishing clear and unambiguous interfaces and privileges can it be possible to decide who may use them and under what conditions.

For example, the principle of least privilege can be applied in the following ways:

- Users may be given rights to access certain systems, networks, and applications based on their organizational role;

- Applications may be started and run as unprivileged accounts with very limited access to the underlying operating system;

- Services running on an operating system may not be able to establish outbound network connections to other systems;

- Hosts residing on a given network may be restricted to communicate only with other hosts on the same network, and even then perhaps using only approved protocols.

Each of these examples shows how the principle of least privilege can be applied to different aspects of IT infrastructure and services. In each of these cases, interfaces and privileges were clearly defined, along with rules for how those interfaces and privileges could be used.

2.3.3.4 Compartmentalization

Compartmentalization is defined as the act of separating something into distinct parts, categories, or compartments.[4] Compartmentalization is a very useful approach for keeping separate (or isolated) unrelated interfaces, services, data sets, systems, networks, and user communities. It is reminiscent of the old adage, "a place for everything and everything in its place." By viewing architecture in this way, it is possible to group and isolate objects in order to manage risk, including the potential for and impact of damage in the event that an object is compromised.

Just as with the principle of least privilege, compartmentalization can be applied across the typical IT environment in various ways, including:

- Isolate or group communities of services, networks, systems, and users;
- Provide a sandbox within which applications and services can be run;
- Enforce isolation between users, data, and objects operating in different security roles, zones, or risk profiles.

2.3.3.5 Proportionality

The principle of proportionality states that "information security controls must be proportionate to the risks of modification, denial of use, or the disclosure of information." Put another way, proportionality means that the cost of protecting a given asset should not exceed its value. This is especially true when all of the various costs are considered: initial acquisition or purchase, customization and integration, ongoing support and maintenance, administration and trouble-shooting, training and education, and so on. It is essential, therefore, that organizations work to achieve a balance between security and cost in how they architect, implement, and manage their environment.

Security does not need to be expensive to be effective. Security can be dramatically improved, in many cases, simply by understanding and leveraging a few basic security principles, such as those discussed in this section. Integrating security systemically throughout an environment will offer organizations greater opportunities to not only manage their risk but also reduce their costs. For example, by bounding the selection and use of security controls (according to

---

4. "Compartmentalization," http://www.dictionary.com

the principle of proportionality), organizations can better understand what assets are most critical and deserve the most protection. Similarly, it will also help organizations better select the baseline level of security that is required throughout their environment.

The degree to which these principles can be implemented will depend on the specifics such as the architecture in which it is being used, and any applicable business or technical requirements. Taken collectively and used carefully, the implementation of IT architectures based on these security principles will help drive higher levels of security and compliance throughout an organization.

2.3.4   Support an Adaptive Security Approach to Security

The reduction in threats to data assets is accomplished by utilizing an adaptive security architecture in conjunction with a security maturity model. An adaptive security architecture can be realized by implementing an architecture in accordance with the systemic security characteristics noted above. What differentiates an adaptive security architecture is its ability to more easily or dynamically adapt to new threats. The specific recommendation for directly addressing threats to privacy is through the use of adaptive security techniques coupled with a systemic security architecture and security maturity model.

Adaptive security is an integral security effort that allows an organization to implement controls that are capable of responding to new and different threats over time. The primary differentiators of an adaptive approach to security (versus say, a prescriptive or checklist approach) are agility and resilience. In addition, adaptive security implements a security architecture that can improve and mature over time to better anticipate evolving threats. The security architecture is designed, implemented, and managed within the context of a continuous improvement schema so that the above noted characteristics are reinforced and threats thus reduced. In this way, the organization utilizes security as a vehicle for innovation that focuses on driving predictive and proactive change, and utilizing a dynamic security architecture as well as operational processes and controls. Note that a security architecture can be utilized for new environments or applied to existing infrastructure.

The security controls built into an IT architecture will be designed to include such characteristics and, in particular, to providing traditional security assurances of identification, authentication, authorization, auditing and monitoring, confidentiality, integrity, and nonrepudiation. Further, such architectures naturally support time-tested security principles such as defense-in-depth, compartmentalization, least privilege, and proportionality where necessary and possible.

2.3.4.1 Modeling Information Security Maturity

A primary differentiator of an adaptive security architecture is the use of a security maturity model. The use of a security maturity model allows an organization to develop a security architecture that improves iteratively over time. This approach also allows for a roadmap to be developed to direct the elaboration of a security architecture as it responds to new threats as well as new business and technical requirements (e.g., new legal mandates, tighter service levels, availability of faster and cheaper computer platforms, terrorism, and even higher energy prices.) The security maturity model also supports a regular threat evaluation process that monitors the overall architecture and determines its ability to defend against and respond to new and previously unanticipated threats. In this way, an adaptive security architecture functions in a continuous improvement cycle.

The goal of security maturity modeling is to help organizations move from more basic security structures to those that are more sophisticated, agile, and responsive in order to better manage risk, cost, and complexity while at the same time improving availability, performance, integration and, of course, compliance and security. Organizations at a fundamentally immature stage (e.g., levels 1 or 2) are typically at much greater risk than their peers who may be operating at more advanced (e.g., levels 2 or 3) or strategic phases (e.g., levels 4 or 5) where a comprehensive security architecture and process structure are firmly in place and is well-functioning and continuously improving over time. See Figure 2.1 for an example of such a maturity model.

2.3.5 Build Systems, Applications, Networks, Protocols, and Others Using Accepted Standards

Standardization is a necessary component for higher levels of IT operational maturity and an important enabler for interoperability, security, and privacy. Implemented effectively, standardization defines expectations and provides guarantees about what kinds of IT services, functions, protocols, and interfaces exist across an IT environment. Without these guarantees, each and every system, service or component could be installed, configured, or managed differently making it not only more difficult and time-consuming to maintain but also equally difficult to audit. For example, how difficult would it be for an organization to measure the security of its web servers if each and every one was configured and managed in different ways?

Recognizing this challenge, many organizations have adopted or plan to adopt more rigorous IT practices that enable them to implement baseline standards more effectively across their IT environment. From a security and privacy standpoint, such standardization efforts have a significant impact on an organization's ability to manage and audit its resources. Through the consistent application of standards in their environment, organizations are able to more easily

- Level 1—Chaotic Security

At Level 1, an organization's security capability is best characterized as immature or chaotic. The organization is exposed to substantial liability.

At this level, there has been little effort completed towards creating and sustaining a secure and compliant IT environment. Investment has been minimal and any organization IT security success thus far has been solely achieved through the efforts of heroes. Activities, if any, are focused on the security needs of individual projects or elements within the IT infrastructure. The organization is reactive and often is relegated to fire fighting activities after security, privacy or compliance problems are discovered by IT users, auditors, or customers. Level 1 is reached when IT shows up for work in the morning.

- Level 2—Basic Security

At Level 2, some investment has been made in the area of IT security, although such investments tend to be focused on specific projects or problems often utilizing point solutions that are not guided by an overall integrated vision and strategy. The organization is still exposed to substantial liability.

When needed, IT security policies, processes, standards, and controls can be found although often they are not widely and consistently developed, communicated, implemented, or managed. Core IT security policy, processes, and controls are beginning to be formalized in some fashion, but this effort is still in the very formative stages. The level of IT security throughout the environment is still inconsistent due to the fact that most of the policies and processes are not defined, and those that are defined may not be consistently implemented and audited. Most organizations reach Level 2 without structured, systemic efforts to address IT security and compliance problems.

- Level 3—Effective Security

At Level 3, the organization has begun to realize the strategic, competitive, and regulatory advantages for developing and maintaining a consistent IT security posture throughout their environment.

Organizations will develop a security, privacy, and compliance vision and strategy as well as a plan that will serve as a transformational roadmap to help the organization achieve its IT security and compliance goals. Organizations at Level 3 are characterized by a more proactive approach to IT security with respect to infrastructure, applications, and services. Such organizations have developed and applied (more systemically) product, capability, and configuration standards. The organization may have also started to streamline their IT security management practices through the use of automation technologies for both control and assessment. The security of the environment also strengthens as IT security processes become more repeatable and audited for compliance. Reaching Level 3 requires an organization to have an epiphany regarding the nature of, and solutions for, its IT security and compliance problems. The realization is that ensuring the secure delivery of services and the protection of IT assets requires a holistic approach that addresses the environment systemically from the perspective of policy, people, process, and technology.

- Level 4—Optimized Security

At Level 4, the IT security capabilities of the organization are measurable, predictable and repeatable, liability management is in equilibrium, and all security requirements have been addressed, where appropriate, through the implementation of an integrated security architecture.

There is a clear IT security and compliance vision and strategy from which projects, policies, processes, and control are derived. There is a well defined governance process for engaging IT security in the service development and information protection lifecycle. IT security can be consistently measured and managed in accordance with well-defined metrics, policies and service agreements. Greater levels of efficiency and optimization are achieved through the use of automation and continuous refinement practices. Failures as well as lessons learned are viewed as an opportunity to improve IT security and are consistently used in the development and refinement of policy, processes, and controls. Reaching Level 4 generally occurs when the organization shifts from being an IT security operations organization to being a secure, compliant service delivery organization. Liability

Figure 2.1 An example of a security maturity model.

management is in equilibrium (i.e., one has achieved compliance, to all applicable legal, regulatory and other mandates as necessary). In addition, one has obtained accreditation and/or certification with applicable standards and industry best practices (e.g., NIST, Common Criteria, FIPS 140-2, ISO 27001, and so forth.)

• Level 5 – Adaptive / Dynamic Security

At Level 5, the IT security organization has moved beyond addressing liability issues and the implementation of an integrated and holistic security architecture, and is focused on continuous process improvement adding quantifiable value to the business.

The data available from the management and support infrastructures is used to modify processes in order to gain efficiencies. With each security challenge or failure, the organization learns and grows safer, stronger, and more compliant. Traceability from the business metrics to the IT security metrics allows decisions and process improvement in one area to be based on information from another. Security, risk, and compliance decisions are now more grounded in facts rather than conjecture, leading organizations to more wisely and efficiently use and secure their IT assets. Further, innovation is now more readily possible. IT security, at Level 5, is already leveraging automation and has been optimized for the business. IT security innovation will therefore often focus on driving predictive and proactive change through the use of adaptive and dynamic security architectures, processes, and controls. Adaptive architectures allow the organization to respond in a more agile manner to "just in time" business opportunities all the while ensuring that a compliant IT security posture is maintained throughout service development and delivery lifecycles. Adaptive security can be used to construct self-defending architectures that are not only resilient to attack but can also adapt in response to new security requirements or threats.

Figure 2.1 (continued)

automate key tasks which in turn can be used to more easily detect anomalous behavior and transactions as well as focus in on violations. Across a more uniform IT landscape, standards violations are more easily detected.

Uniform in this sense is not the same as homogeneous. IT will forever be blessed or doomed, depending on your view, with heterogeneous processes and products. The goal of standardization is to ensure that heterogeneity is managed to a level appropriate for the organization. Further, it is important that the heterogeneous components are used as consistently as possible, and that collections of homogeneous products are configured, used and managed in a more consistent and standardized way.

One of the important side effects of standardization is that organizations are forced to consider, explicitly or not, what governing policies should be defined that dictate how their processes and products will be implemented, managed, and audited. While many organizations have developed security and privacy policies, an alarming number still have incomplete or unused policies that are not contributing value to the organization. As organizations begin to think about how their policies, standards, processes and products interrelate, it is important to think about the place for standardization in their IT environment.

Standardization is not just about product configuration. It is not just about following the same process for adding or removing user accounts in your environment. Standardization occurs at many levels and, depending on the sophistication of the organization, can be used to define interfaces for components at every level of IT. These interfaces dictate what services are exposed, the method by which those services are accessed, and how data are shared between components. By taking the time to define these relationships through standardization, organizations can more easily bring new services to market, identify standards violations, and understand the relationships between their services. Further, a side effect of this use of interfaces means that organizations can free themselves from binding too tightly to specific implementations. In an interface-driven environment, organizations can more easily substitute technologies, products and services for newer, faster, cheaper, more secure versions as long as the interface commitments are maintained. Without such standardization, organizations would need to fully vet each and every component for each new service that is being deployed, modified, and so forth. Without standards implemented at this level, IT infrastructure can easily become fragile, rigid, and easily broken.

2.4 Future Trends

Organizations that want to begin this journey are not alone. For decades, governments, industry, and standards bodies, as well as focused communities, have developed standards, best practices, and other guidance that can be used to help them define process and product standards. Further, technology adoption throughout the world has led to other forms of de facto standardization as protocols (e.g., TCP/IP), formats (e.g., OpenDocument Format) and technologies (e.g., Java) gain momentum. Choices of standards are in this way shaped by market forces and economics. Vendors want to develop products that they can sell to the largest pool of customers. Organizations have a role to play in shaping these standards however through their active participation in industry groups and standards bodies as well as through their own individual IT requirements and procurement decisions. Regardless of the method used, it is essential for organizations to understand the importance of standardization to heightened IT security and privacy.

The use of common industry best practices and nationally and internationally recognized standards also will help reduce threats to privacy. For example, the use of standardized hardware and software protocols, interfaces, and computing languages will reduce threats by allowing for the use of abstraction layers. By abstracting protocols and interfaces, virtualization can occur at all levels resulting in cost reductions, simplification of operational processes, and more optimal use of resources.

3

IT Operational Pressures on Information Security

Gene Kim, Paul Love, George Spafford, and Julia Allen

As security is a tool for management control over IT, there are few CIOs who do not appreciate its utility. However, between the CIO and the operating system, there are many layers of management of differing skill levels. To many of them, security mechanisms are just another layer of complexity in an already opaque operating environment. Gene Kim and his colleagues have spent years studying the way operations managers use security, and (not too surprisingly) discovered that those operations managers who know how to leverage security also have fewer difficulties with other types of IT service levels.

—J.L.B.

3.1 Background

Because of recent high-profile information security failures, business management will probably need little (if any) convincing that the achievement of business goals requires the effective management of information security and privacy risks. There continues to be an ever increasing number of external forces mandating security in the IT environment: the Sarbanes-Oxley (SOX) Act of 2002, the Gramm-Leach-Bliley Act, Health Insurance Portability and Accountability Act (HIPAA), emerging privacy laws, and the Payment Card Industry Data

Security Standard (PCI DSS) are just a few examples of external regulatory and contractual requirements with a compulsory security component.

Failure to have adequate information security controls in place can put the organization at risk of losing confidentiality, integrity, and availability of data and IT services. This can then put the organization at risk for financial penalties, brand damage, and lawsuits.

But, even when the business need for information security is understood and adequately funded (or perhaps even over-funded), the question remains: why are there still so many instances of information security failures, such as data privacy breaches, unauthorized access to data and IT systems, compliance failures, financial penalties, and so forth?

The problem usually lies in failed attempts to integrate information security into other functional groups. When things go wrong in IT, information security, IT operations, and development tend to blame each other. Information security may blame IT operations or development, who may blame information security in return. Each group believes the other is obstructing its efforts because their interactions are often limited to situations in which one group is demanding something of the other. To make matters worse, often, each group perceives that there is a long history of the other groups obstructing or undoing its work. Described below are three typical categories of challenges that we found during our research of high- and low-performing IT organizations.[1]

3.1.1   IT Operations and IT Service Development Impede Information Security Goals

The first category of problems includes cases wherein typical service development and IT operational practices complicate life for information security. For example:

- IT service and infrastructure components may be deployed to production in an inherently insecure and unsupportable state. Information security must then address deficiencies after the fact, when the cost of remediating the deficiencies is higher than if they had been discovered and addressed earlier in the life cycle. If not addressed, both information security and IT operations, and ultimately the organization, suffer

---

1. *Visible Ops Handbook: Implementing ITIL in 4 Practical And Auditable Steps;* Kevin Behr, George Spafford, Gene Kim; 2004, and *Visible Ops Security: Achieving Common Security and IT Operations Objectives in 4 Practical Steps;* Gene Kim, George Spafford, Paul Love; 2008. These works were supported by the study of the common practices of high-performing IT organizations, including the benchmarking of over 850 IT organizations to gain deeper insights into what enables high performers to excel, and the codifications of their transformations.

the consequences over time in higher operating costs, information security incidents, audit findings, brand damage, and so forth.

- Development projects may be constantly behind schedule, in part because information security requirements are added late in the project life cycle. To preserve project due date and budget commitments, the information security requirements may be ignored or marginalized. And this is even assuming that information security is even aware that the project exists!

- The state of the production IT infrastructure is often complex and not well understood. The lack of a preproduction test environment that adequately mirrors production makes predicting outcomes of both information security and operational changes difficult, if not impossible. As a result, IT personnel may operate in a patch-and-pray mode, where no one knows with any certainty what the outcomes of their changes will be in production.

- Portions of the IT infrastructure in the production environment are known to be fragile, so implementing any changes to these services is likely to cause an incident. To "secure" these components, information security typically resorts to Google, tribal knowledge, and best guesses to identify stop-gap measures. These fragile artifacts are rarely, if ever, replaced or patched due to fear of the unknown.

- IT operations people are busy with their own issues, and do not address known information security vulnerabilities at the rate that information security wants. When IT operations and information security staff are constantly in firefighting mode, neither have time to complete planned work—such as replacing fragile artifacts, fixing information security vulnerabilities, or otherwise moving the organization towards its goal.

3.1.2   Information Security Impedes IT Operations and IT Service Development Goals

The second category of problems includes cases when information security impedes the achievement of the goals of IT operations and development. For example:

- Information security controls often have a reputation for creating bureaucracy that hampers the completion of new projects. When doing things correctly takes too long or information security requirements are considered too late in the project life cycle, the business survival instinct forces everyone to go around the information security requirements to meet the budget and schedule needs.

- When information security has a sufficiently large backlog of reviews of changes and projects, information security becomes part of the critical path for projects to complete. Often, large, high-profile projects are ready to be deployed, but a last-minute firewall change request delays the project two weeks while it goes through the information security review and change management process. Suddenly, information security is viewed as an obstacle and a bottleneck that is slowing the business down.

- Implementation of information security requirements introduces delays in project timelines, reinforcing the perception by the business that information security lacks a sense of urgency and does not appreciate date and cost targets.

- Business and other functional groups complain that correcting issues identified during information security reviews costs too much, takes too long, and reduces the feature sets needed by the business. Information security is then viewed as a constant liability to the business, instead of a contributing asset.

- When security fixes are actually implemented (either project related or urgent patches), they often adversely impact production systems. For instance, a security patch is deployed that causes 20% of the systems to crash and 5% of the systems to no longer reboot. The political ramifications are significant.

- Lack of information security standards increases project effort and cost, because previous security work cannot be reused and leveraged. This increases the effort required for information security, development, and IT operations to design, develop, review, test, approve, and maintain these IT services.

3.1.3   Information Security Using a Technology-Centric, Bottom-Up Risk Model

The third category of problems includes cases wherein information security does not use a top-down, risk-based approach to scope, design and verify the effectiveness of controls. For example:

- A technology-centric and bottom-up approach is taken, which focuses first on technology risks and threats, then focusing on the necessary corrective actions for the "IT risks." The mistake in this approach is that, as Jay Taylor states, "there is no such thing as IT risk."[2] When IT risks are viewed outside the context of the end-to-end business risks, there is tremendous potential for the considerable errors in scoping.

---

2. "GAIT For Business and IT Risk (GAIT-R)," Institute of Internal Auditors, March 2008.

- During the first several years of SOX-404, when external auditors started testing against newly designed SOX-404 audit plans, IT findings represented the largest category of findings, totaling more than the combined findings in the revenue, procure-to-pay, and tax categories.[3] It's estimated that as much as $3 billion was spent in the first year of SOX-404 to fix IT controls to remediate these findings. Ultimately, most of these findings were found not to be direct risks to accurate financial reports and did not result in a material weakness. One of the primary conclusions of the GAIT[4] task team formed by the Institute of Internal Auditors was that, in the previous example, the IT control testing activities should not have been tested. In other words, they constituted a scoping error on the front end of the audit process.

- The proliferation of security tests wherein IP network address ranges are entered into a vulnerability scanning tool, followed by panic at the 2,000 pages of vulnerabilities which result, followed by frantic efforts to prioritize our corrective actions based on what the tool recommends, which sorts the findings by the technology vulnerabilities that are easiest to exploit.

3.2 Observations

Technology fulfils its mission by meeting two organizational goals:

1. Developing new capabilities and functionality to achieve business objectives;
2. Operating and maintaining existing IT services to safeguard business commitments.

The first objective is typically owned by application development, and the second objective is typically owned by IT operations. To help both groups achieve their goals, information security and audit help verify that controls are properly designed and operating effectively.

Development objectives are primarily around delivering enhancements or additions to functionality that align with the changing needs of the business. On

---

3. KPMG study: "Sarbanes-Oxley 404: Lessons Learned," ISACA Luncheon Sessions, April 20, 2005.

4. GAIT stands for Guide to the Assessment of IT General Controls Scope Based on Risk. "The GAIT Principles," The Institute of Internal Auditors, January 2007 (http://www.theiia.org/guidance/technology/gait/). One of the authors (Kim) was part of the GAIT team, which released guidance on how to scope the IT portions of SOX-404 in January 2007.

the other hand, IT operations objectives are primarily around assuring stable, predictable, and secure IT services.

In this type of an environment, a core and chronic conflict between these two groups almost always develops. To respond to urgent business needs, development is pressured to do work and make changes faster. On the other hand, to provide a stable, secure, and reliable IT service, IT operations is pressured to do work and make changes more slowly and carefully—or even make no changes at all (to reduce or avoid risk).

The authors have been studying the common practices of high-performing IT organizations since early 2000. These organizations were simultaneously achieving world-class results in IT operations as measured by high-service availability, information security as measured by early and consistent integration into the IT service delivery life cycle, and compliance as measured by the fewest number of repeat audit findings. Astoundingly, these organizations were also the most efficient as measured by server-to-system administrator ratio and the amount of time spent on unplanned work. The provocative conclusion is that integrating controls into daily operations results not only in effectiveness, but also efficiency. Three cultural elements that were common among the high-performing IT organizations were:[5]

- *A culture of change management.* In each of the high-performing IT organizations, the first step when IT staff implements changes is not to first log into the infrastructure. Instead, it is to go to some change advisory board and get authorization that the change should be made. Surprisingly, this process is not viewed as bureaucratic, needlessly slowing things down, lowering productivity, and decreasing the quality of life. Instead, these organizations view change management as absolutely critical to the organization for maintaining its high performance.

- *A culture of causality.* Each of the high-performing IT organizations has a common way to resolve service outages and impairments. They realize that 80% of their outages are due to changes, and that 80% of their mean time to repair (MTTR) is spent trying to find what changed. Consequently, when working problems, they look at changes first in the repair cycle. Evidence of this can be seen in the incident management systems of the high performers: Inside the incident record for an outage are all the scheduled and authorized changes for the affected assets, as well as the actual detected changes on the asset. By looking at this information, problem managers can recommend a fix to the problem more

---

5. *Visible Ops Handbook,* Ibid.

than 80% of the time, with a first fix rate exceeding 90% (i.e., 90% of the recommended fixes work the first time).

- *A culture of planned work and continuous improvement.* In each of the high-performing IT organizations, there is a continual desire to find production variance early before it causes a production outage or an episode of unplanned work. The difference is analogous to paying attention to the low-fuel warning light on an automobile to avoid running out of gas on the highway. In the first case, the organization can fix the problem in a planned manner, without much urgency or disruption to other scheduled work. In the second case, the organization must fix the problem in a highly urgent way, often requiring an all-hands-on- deck situation (e.g., six staff members must drop everything they are doing and run down the highway with gas cans to refuel the stranded truck).

A series of research projects conducted in conjunction with organizations such as the Software Engineering Institute at Carnegie Mellon University and the Institute of Internal Auditors Research Foundation have since concentrated on identifying the practices and performance that distinguish high-performers across more than 850 IT organizations studied. A 2006 and 2007 IT Process Institute IT Controls Performance Study was conducted to establish the link between controls and operational performance.[6] A 2007 Change Configuration and Release Performance Study was conducted to determine which best practices in these areas drive performance improvement.[7] The studies revealed that, in comparison with low-performing organizations, high-performing organizations enjoy the following efficiency advantages:

- Production system changes fail half as often;
- Releases cause unintended failures half as often;
- One-quarter of the frequency of emergency change requests;
- One-quarter the frequency of repeat audit findings;
- One-half the amount of unplanned work and firefighting;
- Server-to-system-administrator ratios are two times higher.

These differences validate that the hypothesis that IT controls and basic change and configuration practices improve IT operations effectiveness and efficiency. Moreover, the studies also determined that the same high performers

---

6. "IT Controls Performance Study," IT Process Institute, 2006.
7. "Change, Configuration, and Release Study," IT Process Institute, 2007.

have superior information security effectiveness. The 2007 IT controls study found that when high performers had security breaches:

- The security breaches are far less likely to result in loss events (e.g., financial, reputational, and customer). High performers are half as likely as medium performers and one-fifth as likely as low performers to experience security breaches that result in loss.
- The security breaches are far more likely to be detected using automated controls (as opposed to an external source such as the newspaper headlines or a customer). High performers automatically detect security breaches 15% more often than medium performers and twice as often as low performers.
- Security access breaches are detected far more quickly. High performers have a mean time to detect measured in minutes, compared with hours for medium performers and days for low performers.

These studies confirmed that high-performing IT organizations have figured out how to simultaneously advance the goals of information security and IT operations. They take proactive and decisive steps to promote teamwork. Information security works with IT operations to manage production systems efficiently and securely. Information security integrates with development to streamline the introduction of new systems into production, maintaining the security of these systems without introducing unnecessary controls or impeding development efforts significantly while still making sure that risks are properly managed.

In other words, the value of information security controls is not just loss avoidance and better information security incident handling. Instead, implementing the right information security controls helps advance the goals not only of information security, but also of IT operations and development as well!

In these high-performing organizations, all three groups—information security, IT operations, and development—collaborate to deliver highly available, cost-effective, and secure services. These organizations have moved beyond a focus on technology to address the core operational aspects of information security by building information security into key development and production processes. They have come to the realization that information security isn't just about technology; it's about process integration and managing people as well.

3.3 Recommendations

The way to resolve the core chronic conflict between development and IT operations is to enable the business to simultaneously respond more quickly to urgent business needs and provide stable, secure, and predictable IT services.[8] As described above, information security is a key enabler of stable, secure, and predictable IT services. When information security sufficiently integrates into development, development can understand and implement information security requirements earlier and complete projects more quickly with less rework, resulting in faster time to market and lower costs. This results in development being better able to quickly respond to urgent business needs.

When information security sufficiently integrates into IT operations, IT operations can better manage risks, preventing incidents from occurring and quickly detecting and correcting incidents when they do occur (ideally before anyone is affected). By doing this, IT operations is better able to protect organizational commitments.

To make this a reality, information security must help the other groups recognize that this core, chronic conflict exists, and then work with them to resolve the conflict. The goal is to have IT operations, development, and information security working together to achieve common objectives, as illustrated in Figure 3.1.[9]

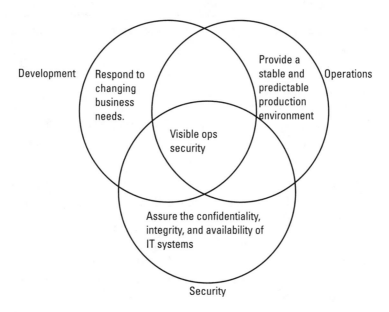

Figure 3.1 Common organizational objectives.

---

8. The authors acknowledge Dr. Eliyahu Goldratt, creator of the Theory of Constraints and author of *The Goal,* who has written extensively on the theory and practice of identifying and resolving core, chronic conflicts.

9. *Visible Ops Security,* Ibid.

How do we know this is possible? Because high-performing IT operations and information security organizations have done it already.

When information security is considered a method of controlling the IT environment, IT professionals acquire high-performer attributes, which include:

- *Business aligned.* High-performing information security teams understand how security advances and protects business goals.

- *Plugged in.* High performing information security teams are integrated into the right functional groups even though they don't have direct operational responsibility.

- *Adding value.* High performing information security teams provide value to business and IT process owners, and they know what they need from them in return.

- *Prioritized.* High-performing information security teams understand priorities and optimize the deployment of limited IT resources.

- *People savvy.* High performing information security teams leverage people and organizational skills to build effective working relationships with development and IT operations groups that make security sustainable.

By contrast, low performers:

- Focus on things the business doesn't care about. They are obsessed with the improbable or irrelevant and are mired in technological minutia. Other groups may consider them hysterical.

- Aren't present where the work is done and they're not helping the right people when they are needed. This reinforces the perception that information security is irrelevant.

- Don't offer anything to advance the operational objectives of their colleagues, nor do they clearly articulate what they want people to do differently to meet information security requirements. Consequently, they are often viewed as incompetent.

- Insist on being involved, and then over commit resources causing project delays. Other groups see them as bottlenecks to meeting project and operational objectives.

- Focus on technology risk, but cannot work through group dynamics to offer alternatives and find viable solutions. As a result, they frequently seem immature and they are ineffective in cross-functional group settings.

Our work is focused on what specific activities are required to gain situational awareness, and to create an ongoing value exchange where the other functional groups viewed information security as a critical and value-adding function, where their goals were simultaneously being achieved with information security goals.

We observed four distinct behaviors that we conclude are required to integrate information security into IT development and IT operations. The first is a necessary building block for the next, and so on. We present them in order:

3.3.1 Stabilize the Patient and Get Plugged into Production

The information security professional must gain meaningful situational awareness and integrate into daily IT operational processes. Security must integrate with change management, reduce access, and develop information security incident handling procedures that are integrated with the IT operations incident management process. The goal is to gain visibility and begin to reduce risks in IT operations. This allows quicker detection and correction of information security incidents, reduces the likelihood of information security incidents, and helps IT operations increase availability and reduce unplanned work. Security should:

- Influence daily IT operations by integrating information security into existing control points and approval processes;

- Provide value to IT operations so that the IT operations staff will continue to want to work with information security;

- Reduce the amount of reactive work for IT operations and information security.

Information security and change management have similar missions: Both groups are trying to manage risk. Information security needs change management to gain situational awareness of production changes and to influence decisions and outcomes (as opposed to being constantly managed solely by IT operations). Even if the organization achieved the mythical "perfectly secure state," any change can quickly take us out of that secure state. One of the high-performing IT organizations studied in *The Visible Ops Handbook* observed that, "Enforcing our change management processes is critical, because we are always only one change away from being a low performer." Similarly, we know that we are always only "one change away from an information security incident that puts us on the front pages of the newspapers."

Information security would restrict access to production systems, with the intent of reducing the likelihood of errors, fraud, and security incidents. In the typical IT organization, many staff members will often have greater access to production systems than they need to do their jobs. Excessive access creates the potential risk for people to make uncontrolled changes to critical systems. This not only exposes IT systems to human error that can disrupt service, but also creates unnecessary vulnerabilities for malicious and criminal acts that jeopardize the organization. To address this, one should reduce access wherever possible and ensure that some form of effective access control exists, and ensure that information enforces the effective administration of user accounts.

Lastly, we must integrate information security into the IT operations resolution processes to ensure that information security is brought in appropriately when needed. We will also define how to declare information security incidents, so that they may be resolved efficiently and effectively. Our goal is to codify with the business and IT operations how information security incidents should be declared and managed. Ideally, this will be through the existing IT operations incident management system, so we can leverage all of the existing operational bookkeeping and configuration management information, as well escalation procedures, reporting, and so forth.

As security integrates into the change, access, incident, and problem management processes, it also significantly improves the effectiveness of how information security performs incident handling. By doing so, it becomes more effective at quickly detecting and recovering from information security incidents, specifically unauthorized access and unauthorized change. The following list of information security functions are part of the overall "stabilize and plug-in" requirement.

- Gain situational awareness:
  - Find out what senior mangement and the business want from information security;
  - Find out how the business units are organized and operate;
  - Find out what the IT process and technology landscapes are;
  - Find the high-level risk indicators.
- Integrate into change management:
  - Get invited to Change Advisory Board (CAB) meetings;
  - Build and electrify the fence;
  - Ensure tone from the top and define the consequences;
  - Substantiate that the electric fence is working;
  - Look for red flags;
  - Address failed changes.
- Reduce and control access:
  - Reduce unnecessary access;
  - Establish an account management process;

- Eliminate ghost accounts;
- Reaccredit accounts routinely.

- Codify information security incident handling procedures and modify first response:
  - Define when and how to engage information security;
  - Confirm scope of detective change controls;
  - Formalize information security incident response.

3.3.2 Find Business Risks, Identify Controls, and Fix Fragile Artifacts

Where security has established situational awareness and inserted information security controls into IT operations, the problem remains that the information security risks to the organization are potentially limitless, but information security has finite time and resources to address them. To make the best use of available resources, information security must identify where the highest business risks are, discover where the business is relying most upon critical IT functionality, and take steps to ensure that adequate controls exist and are effective.

Information security should create a focusing mechanism by taking a top-down, risk-based approach to understand where the business has placed reliance on critical IT functionality, and then identifying what information security controls are needed to protect critical functionality and data. Resources should find and fix any information security control gaps, in order of priority.

As information security practitioners, many may have been exposed to top-down, risk-based approaches in support of audits. High-performing information security practitioners take the lead in defining and protecting what matters using the same risk-based approach. They do not wait until the next audit cycle to find out if things are done incorrectly, because then it's already too late. They may have missed a critical area of risk that went completely unaddressed, or, just as bad, they may have spent valuable time and resources securing IT services and systems that did not really matter.

High-performing information security professionals have confidence that they are focusing on the right things, have controls integrated into daily operations, and can leverage those controls so that they can quickly detect and correct information security incidents. They will also have evidence that controls are working when the auditors show up, and are able to map all IT services to regulatory requirements and required supporting control objectives across the enterprise.

To apply the top-down, risk-based approach, it is possible to use the GAIT[10] principles and methodology, developed by the Institute of Internal

---

10. GAIT stands for Guide to the Assessment of IT General Controls Scope Based on Risk.

Auditors. GAIT is a set of four principles and an accompanying methodology that can be used to scope IT general control processes that need to be included in the assessment of internal controls over financial reporting. The GAIT-R principles expand GAIT to allow its use for analyzing how IT affects the achievement of all business goals and objectives.

The GAIT-R Principles are:

- *Principle 1.* The failure of technology is just another risk that needs to be assessed, managed, and audited if it represents a risk to the business.

- *Principle 2.* Key controls should be identified as the result of a top-down assessment of business risk, risk tolerance, and the controls (including automated controls and IT general controls) required to manage or mitigate business risk.

- *Principle 3.* Business risks are mitigated by a combination of manual and automated key controls. To assess the system of internal controls to manage/mitigate business risks, key automated controls need to be assessed.

- *Principle 4.* IT general controls may be relied upon to provide assurance of the continued and proper operation of automated key controls (e.g., change management, access information security, and operations).[11]
  - *Principle 4a.* The IT general control process risks that need to be identified are those that affect critical IT functionality in significant applications and related data.
  - *Principle 4b.* The IT general control process risks that need to be identified exist in processes and at various IT layers: application program code, databases, operating systems, and network.
  - *Principle 4c.* Risks in IT general control processes are mitigated by the achievement of IT control objectives, not individual controls.

The specific steps are:

- Establish a business process worry list:
  - Cover the periphery by considering externally facing systems;
  - Discover and understand externally facing IT systems;
  - Verify the business process worry list.

---

11. GAIT defines operations as the responsibility to deliver IT services and the ability to restore service when interrupted at inopportune times. This would include the ITIL processes of incident and problem management, service continuity and disaster recovery, service design, and so forth.

- Work the list, zoom out to rule out:
  - Get help to zoom out to rule out;
  - Get confirmation of business process significance and complexity;
  - Get documentation on where reliance on critical IT functionality is placed in the business process;
  - Zoom in for a better view.
- Find and fix IT control issues:
  - Prepare key IT general control processes;
  - Initiate corrective action.
- Streamline IT controls for regulatory compliance:
  - Establish the high-water mark;
  - Document the IT controls and their monitoring.

3.3.3 Implement Development and Release Controls

One objective of a high-performing information security professional is to improve the quality of releases to ensure that information security standards are integrated into projects and builds. This is done by integrating into internal audit, software, and service development lifecycle, project management, development, and release management. It may also be necessary to work with accounting and purchasing to increase situational awareness and ensure that the controls are working.

Whether development is done in-house, outsourced or both, the goal is to integrate security requirements at the earliest stages of development projects. This can include providing developers with expertise and training required to help them establish secure coding practices for requirements definition, development and testing. This can be done through training or by assigning a security liaison to the development team. The biggest value that can be provided is to help establish secure coding and testing practices.

Release management owns the testing environment, and is one of the key IT service management quality processes. Information security's goal here is to ensure that the production environment matches the preproduction test environment. If it does not, results are impossible to predict. Software released to customers without this match puts them in a vulnerable position.

Internal audit and information security already share many similar goals and care about many of the same things: reliability and integrity of financial and operational information; safeguarding of assets; and compliance with laws, regulations and contracts. Security can provide auditing with expertise and education, and can share organizational information and security policies, as well as ensure adherence to daily operational procedures.

Project management tracks the overall health of IT projects, ensuring the right resources are available. Information security can provide value to this team by helping with approval processes, and being the key control gate on projects that have security implications. By becoming involved in projects early in the process, security can help influence requirements and budget decisions that have relevance to security issues. Detailed behaviors supporting the overall control implementation behavior are:

- Integrate with internal audit:
  - Formalize the relationship with audit;
  - Demonstrate value.
- Integrate into project management:
  - Participate in PMO approval meetings;
  - Determine information security relevance;
  - Integrate into project review and approval;
  - Leverage detective controls in change management;
  - Link to detective controls in purchasing and accounting.
- Integrate into the development life cycle:
  - Begin a dialog with development;
  - Establish requirements definition and secure coding practices;
  - Establish secure testing practices.
- Integrate into release management:
  - Formalize the relationship with release management;
  - Ensure standards for secure builds;
  - Integrate with release testing protocols;
  - Integrate into production acceptance;
  - Ensure adherence to release implementation instructions;
  - Ensure production matches known and trusted states.

3.3.4   Continually Improve

Any continual improvement hinges on measurement, control, and focused improvement. An information security professional must have some objective measures of the performance of the security program. The high performer will focus on those metrics that are directly correlated to the confidentiality, integrity, and availability of information as opposed to any management process that has attempted to achieve those goals. That is, metrics should measure the effect of the security program activities, not the process by which it is being integrated with the rest of the organization. The goal is to focus on the IT controls that simultaneously improve the achievement of information security goals, as well as IT operational and IT service delivery goals.

3.4   Future Trends

Effectively balancing risk with controls is made even more difficult by the constant pressure on IT to respond quickly to urgent business needs. Most business functions now require IT in order to conduct operations. In fact, almost every business decision requires at least one change by IT—a trend that continues to grow.

The resulting need for increased agility and the increasing cost and complexity of IT has contributed to the rapid adoption of virtualization technologies. Virtualization is the ability to use one physical machine to manage a wide variety of application platforms without fear of operating system incompatibilities. As such, it makes it possible to build and deploy IT releases and changes into production faster and more economically than ever before.

Some virtualization experts claim that virtualized computing environments are fundamentally no less secure than physical computing environments. Others claim that virtualization can enable better security. Both claims can be correct, but only where the management of the physical machine is secure and the configuration of each virtual machine is secured in a standardized fashion. However, the reality is that when information security controls are improperly implemented or neglected in virtualized environments, real security risks and exposures are created faster than ever. This is the potential dark side of virtualization, and the information security controls that adequately controlled risks before virtualization may no longer suffice.

Virtualization enables rapid deployment, potentially allowing an insecure IT infrastructure to be deployed throughout the organization faster than ever. The unfortunate truth is that the people who deploy this infrastructure often circumvent existing security and compliance controls when doing so. Unfortunately, the risk these deployments introduce is only discovered when a security breach occurs, an audit finding is made, or the organization loses confidential data or critical functionality.

For better or for worse, virtualization is here. Tripwire recently surveyed 219 IT organizations and found that 85% were already using virtualization, with half of the remaining organizations planning to use virtualization in the near future. Furthermore, VMware found that 85% of their customers are using virtualization for mission-critical production services. In other words, inadequate information security controls may already be jeopardizing critical IT services with risk introduced by virtualization.

Most information security practitioners now attribute the majority of security failures to misconfiguration resulting from human error. According to Gartner, "the security issues related to vulnerability and configuration management get worse, not better, when virtualized."[12] Also according to Gartner, "Like their physical counterparts, most security vulnerabilities will be introduced through misconfiguration and mismanagement.[13] Why is this the case, we ask? Among other reasons, insecure virtual server images can be replicated far more easily than before, and once deployed, require great effort to discover and bring back to a known and trusted state. Analysts have published some startling predictions on these information security implications: Gartner predicts that "Through 2009, 60 percent of production VMs will be less secure than their physical counterparts"[14] and that "30 percent of deployments [will be associated] with a VM-related security incident."[15]

The good news is that it doesn't have to be this way. If the principles of visible security ops can be acknowledged to be valid in any technology domain, then it should not matter how pervasive an inherently unsecure new technology may be, whether it be virtualization or the next as yet unforeseen major technology productivity enhancement. Where information security is seen as a key enabler of stable, secure, and predictable IT services, confidentiality, integrity, and availability will result.

---

12. Gartner, Inc. "Security Considerations and Best Practices for Securing Virtual Machines," by Neil MacDonald, March 2007.
13. Gartner, Inc. "How To Securely Implement Virtualization" by Neil MacDonald, November 2007.
14. Ibid.
15. Ibid.

4

Information Classification

Jennifer Bayuk

Information classification, related to information security, is concerned with placing information into categories related to how securely it should be handled with respect to access control and confidentiality protection. This section deals with the issues associated with classifying information with respect to its security handling. First is the issue of who is qualified to make this determination. The next issue deals with the sense that this decision is often context and content dependent, and can change with time and circumstances. For example, a seemingly innocuous piece of information may not seem very revealing, but taken in combination with other information may become much more sensitive. For example there are many women who may be characterized as blonde and 5-feet tall. Linking some financial information to the fact that the person is a blonde female who is 5-feet tall may not be very revealing, but if I add that the woman lives on Montgomery Sreet in Cleveland, Ohio, we may have reduced the possibilities down to a single individual. So the context within which a piece of information is known can be very important and change the sensitivity of the information. The content is also important. It may not be terribly important to know that John Smith has a $100 dollars in his checking account, but if it were known that John Smith has over $100,000 in his checking account, we might decide that this information is extremely sensitive. Over time, as new types of attacks and fraudulent patterns appear, we might change our minds about the sensitivity of a piece of information; for example phishing has made it much more sensitive to know the email address or phone number of a customer of your bank than it was some 10 years ago. So, classification systems should be dynamically changing in terms of context, content, and past history. The determination of the correct classification of an item of information might well involve the input of business and security professionals as well as data provided by data center resource managers.

—D.S.

4.1 Background

Information classification is the act of labeling information. A label on a piece of information enables it to be treated as an object. It may be reasoned about without concentration on its composition. It enables different information with the same label to be treated as a set, as one object. In the field of information security, information labeling is a prerequisite for providing appropriate *handling procedures.* Information handling procedures are instructions on how to deal with information when it is stored as data in computers or as text on printed materials. The basic process is depicted in Figure 4.1.

A common and well-understood example of information classification comes from the military. Military information labels include: *top secret, secret,* and *unclassified.* Before information was stored in computers, it was stored in documents, file cabinets, and locked rooms that were stamped with these labels. For several decades in the early days of computers, the military classification was the basis of general study into how to secure data in a computing environment, and also the basis of specific algorithms used to secure operating system files.

The military information classification approach was hierarchical. *Top secret* was a higher level classification than *secret, unclassified* was lower than *secret.* When applied to sets of information on computers, the hierarchical labeling system presented issues to be addressed. For example: how to prevent people who should only have access to *unclassified* data from having access to *secret* data while still allowing those with *secret* access to have *unclassified* data on the same computer. In an attempt to resolve such issues, labels were assigned to sets of people as well as the data. The same labels were used and a person was assumed to be on the same level in the hierarchy as the data they accessed. A *secret* person could read *secret* and *unclassified* data while a *top secret* person could read *top secret, secret* and *unclassified* data. Any information produced by a *top secret*

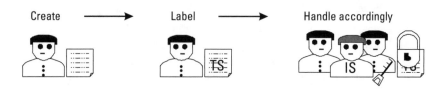

Create ⟶ Label ⟶ Handle accordingly

Figure 4.1 Information classification activity.

person was assumed by the computer to be labeled *top secret* and no *unclassified* person would be able to read it.

Implementation issues with the hierarchy quickly arose. For example: if any *unclassified* person produced data that was subsequently labeled *secret* using a computer, the individual could no longer read it, nor even to have a copy to edit after having written it. This seems a simple problem to solve by today's standards, where individual file object ownership and role-based entitlements are commonplace, but unless one can assume system administrators are all cleared at the *top secret* level, it is still not as technically easy to resolve as it sounds.

Though the military was the first to recognize the value of creating classes of data to receive special handling, privacy and intellectual property advocates soon caught up. Confidentiality in computing required information classification schemes to be applied to nonmilitary scenarios. Information security analysts tried to map confidentiality requirements onto information classifications schemes designed for military use. They devised similar hierarchical data classification models.

For example, a typical organization may have between three and five labels for information, following a hierarchy such as:

- Public;
- Proprietary;
- Proprietary Restricted.

At such an organization, procedures would be created for handling data at each classification level. Often called a *protection profile*, this set of procedures would be designed to keep data at a higher level more secure than data on a lower level. Illustrated in Figure 4.2, the assumption is that maintaining a consistent protection profile around information of a given class meets requirements for information security.

For example, all documents in the organization may be required to be stamped with one of the three labels or have the label embedded in the document itself. The protection profiles may allow *public* documents to be left about,

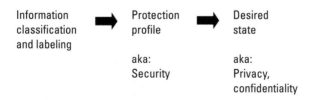

Figure 4.2 Information classification assumption.

whereas *proprietary* documents may be shared only with employees, and documents labeled *proprietary restricted* may be shared only with those who have a need to know and are not to be left unattended. Procedures designed to keep *proprietary* and *proprietary restricted* information confidential may include desktop audits wherein any unattended desktop that has information labeled *proprietary restricted* fails audit. Metrics might be kept by department and departments required to be 100% compliant.

4.2   Observations

Organizations that use this type of hierarchical classification scheme typically have a common struggle in achieving confidentiality goals. It is often the case that guidelines for determining what information should be stamped with which label are not straightforward and thus not easily understood. Inaccurate judgment on whether information is *proprietary* or not leads to mislabeling. Mislabeling leads to mishandling. The fatal flaw in most conventional information classification programs is that they lack procedures for the *labeler*.

Where information classification is focused on the end result of the labeling process—information handling, the *labeler* is left without any guidance. This focus is so prevalent that it is common in information security literature to see information classified with words that specify the handling criteria, as opposed to any attribute of the information itself. For example, here is a common textbook description of information classification labels:[1]

1. Information that does not need safeguarding;
2. Information that must be safeguarded against loss or threats to integrity;
3. Information that, if disclosed to unauthorized parties, could result in reputation or financial damage;
4. Information that, if changed by or disclosed to unauthorized parties, could result in threats to an organization's existence.

From these labels, information-handling procedures are trivial to derive, for example:

A. No need to protect;
B. Need to prevent write-access by unauthorized individuals;

---

1. To avoid direct criticism of any specific textbook which may contain otherwise sound information security education, I will omit reference to any one volume.

C. Need to prevent read-access by unauthorized individuals;

D. Need to control and trace accountability for each instance of read- and write–access.

Textbooks advocate that procedures subsequently developed to safely handle information (e.g., the clear desk and nightly audits) should be designed to be extremely simple to follow. Once information is classified as information that must be safeguarded against loss or threats to integrity, an ideal infomation security classification program will have provisions that a group of *authorized individuals* be configured in every system that contains information of that type, and methods to ensure that access to data of that type is restricted to users in that *authorized* group. There would be an auditable authorization process to add group members whereby documentation trails provide accountability for changes to membership. It would be assumed that the actual data handler (i.e., member of the *authorized* group) need not know much if anything about the information classification in order to correctly protect it. Rather, the system configuration in itself would be designed to enforce the information protection requirements.

Where information security professionals are totally occupied with controls within the systems environment, the assumption that the person performing the labeling function (the *labeler*) is qualified to do so, is critical to the success of any information classification program. The labeling function, however, is left to the end user. Information security curriculums overlook the fact that, where the derivation of handling procedures is automatic from the definition of the information itself, the labeling process itself is extremely difficult. In order for *the labeler to perform the labeling,* he or she must first understand the content of the data, and be cognizant of the risk of data exposure to threats. These include not only threats to the enterprise data owner, but consequences resulting from unmet regulatory requirements. The person would have to survey the data in the custody of the enterprise and utilize his or her understanding of its content to perform analysis to identify the distinct types of data which either by itself or in combination with data of other types, would, in his or her informed judgment, justify the assignment of one the labels (1 to 4, 1 to 5, or 1 to 3), depending how many levels an organization has chosen to adopt.

The activity described above, as that required for *the labeler to perform the labeling,* is the core of any information classification effort. Yet textbooks continue to present the last step, the analysis which leads to the conclusion that A to D are appropriate requirements given 1 to 4, as the infomation security professional practice with respect to information classification. The elementary presentation of information classification levels prior to the instruction on how to do information analysis makes it easy for an information security professional to derive information-handling procedures and masks the true complexity of the analysis leading up to the label. The omission of the actual core classification process often creates a disconnect between those who understand the content of the data and the infomation security professional assigned to protect it.

This type of classification process seems to have its roots in information security risk analysis efforts that focus on disclosure consequences. A typical risk analysis is concerned with the impact to the organization from potential harm to confidentiality, integrity, and availability of data. Such analysis also assumes that there is an omniscient business person, like the data labeler, who can make the decisions on how the business would be affected by confidentiality, integrity, and availability lapses with no guidance. Like the textbook information classification process, the textbook risk analysis process assumes that the information security professional is handed the outcome of the business decision and need only develop corresponding handling procedures.

The leap from disclosure consequences to handling mechanisms suffers from a fundamental omission, one that often leaves decisions concerning actual information classification out of the information security curriculum. The fact that the decision on how to label information is outside the realm of the information security curriculum takes the information protection responsibility away from the realm of the security professional and leaves it in the hands of the end user. End users are usually given guidelines such as 1 to 4 above and asked to classify their data. In any organization where multiple individuals may have control of similar and very specific fields of information, and also more than one data storage area, this could easily result in the inconsistent application of controls.

To make it easy on themselves, information security professionals facing choices in data handling procedures often fall back to the principle of least privilege. That is, all individuals should only have the minimum privileges to read or write data to the extent these are absolutely necessary to continue the smooth operation of the organization. It then becomes a question of how hard the InfoSec controls make it for a person who is not authorized to see the data and to actually get to it. It is also a question of where the controls are placed. Application users, for example, have got to be able to view the data in the clear (i.e., not encrypted). Database administrators do not have to actually view it, but have to have access to view it in order to troubleshoot the jobs that retrieve and load it. Job control professionals need to actually run the jobs (so by transitive trust have access to any encryption keys that are used by those jobs).

Note that the principle of least privilege itself is subject to interpretation. One organization will argue with clear conscience that job control administrators need access to data to troubleshoot jobs, while another organization will insist that no administrators should have access on a day-to-day basis, but that access to troubleshoot should only be granted at the point jobs fail. This continuum between easy access to support operations and absolute minimum need to know creates an economic argument for detective security measures rather than preventive. Where access controls are left flexible, but alerts may be devised upon potentially unauthorized data access, the unexpected access can be justified by reference to operational situations.

Despite the wide variety of choices in implementing least-privilege data handling procedures, information security professionals and auditors routinely determine whether information is appropriately handled without giving IT operations job responsibilities more than a cursory glance. They instead concentrate on whether the information security program is appropriately managed, whether risks are reported to upper management, and whether documentation on appropriate policies and procedures exist. Actual verification of who really has access to what type data is way beyond the expertise of even the above average IT control professional.

The result is that information security literature and educational materials have not been focused on securing specific classes of information, but instead have been caught up with organizational risk reduction measures. Historical approaches to information classification within the information security profession have resulted in information-handling countermeasures focused on:

- Aggregated data and infrastructure securing them;
- Enterprise-wide processes rather than data protection goals;
- Weighing threat and vulnerabilities against business acceptance of risk.

This thousand-foot view of information handling almost completely ignores actual data content. Within such organizations, there has not been much executive management reflection on the fact that enterprise-scale security programs have been using hierarchical approaches to data classification. Where approaches pass "internal control" audits year after year, there is not much call for enterprise-wide change. So the burden for actual information classification efforts and handling requirements, where they exist, have fallen into the hands of application developers meeting specific business requirements for a given set of data.

4.3 Recommendations

The information security information classification landscape is changing. With the advent of the payment card industry's data security standards for securing credit card data (PCI DSS), the real analysis required by proper information classification has entered the realm of the information security literature.[2] Figure 4.3

---

2. Payment Card Industry Data Security Standard, PCI DSS Version 1.1.

Applicable if a Primary Account Number (PAN) is stored, processed, or transmitted.

	Data Element	Storage Permitted	Protection Required	PCI DSS Req. 3.4
Cardholder Data	Primary Account Number (PAN)	YES	YES	YES
	Cardholder Name*	YES	YES*	NO
	Service Code*	YES	YES*	NO
	Expiration Date*	YES	YES*	NO
Sensitive Authentication Data**	Full Magnetic Stripe	NO	N/A	N/A
	CVC2/CVV2/CID	NO	N/A	N/A
	PIN / PIN Block	NO	N/A	N/A

* These data elements must be protected if stored in conjunction with the PAN.
**Sensitive authentication data must not be stored subsequent to authorization (even if encrypted).

Figure 4.3   Excerpt from PCI Data Security Standards, Version 1.1.

indicates the prescriptive nature of PCI DSS requirements with respect to labeling certain fields of data as *protection required*. It indicates, for example, that certain data fields may be unprotected in isolation, but are considered *protection required* when stored in conjunction with other fields. These are labeling requirements at the semantic level. They require assignment of labels to information as opposed to data.

Information that is properly labeled allows the handling requirements to be specified as network, operating system, and application security requirements surrounding the end-to-end transmission and storage of data within the organization. In the case of PCI DSS, these requirements are quite specific:[3]

1. Install and maintain a firewall configuration to protect cardholder data.
2. Do not use vendor-supplied defaults for security parameters.
3. Protect stored cardholder data (see detail with respect to PAN).
4. Encrypt transmission of cardholder data across open, public networks.
5. Use and regularly update antivirus software.
6. Develop and maintain secure systems and applications.

---

3. Ibid.

7. Restrict access to cardholder data by business need-to-know.

8. Assign a unique ID to each person with computer access.

9. Restrict physical access to cardholder data.

10. Track and monitor all access to network resources and cardholder data.

11. Regularly test security systems and processes.

12. Maintain a policy that addresses information security.

Further detail in the standard reveals that requirement three, in conjunction with the definitions in Figure 4.3, means that certain data fields may be *unencrypted* in isolation, but must be *encrypted* when stored in conjunction with other fields. The information label *protection required* is supplemented with the handling procedure *encryption.*

Though privacy laws and similar field-specific counterparty minimum-security requirements existed before PCI DSS,[4] they were not perceived as requirements for businesses to take detailed technical measures. Nevertheless, these requirements have for some time been coming from customers and business partners in the form of legal contracts and service agreements. Other sources of requirements, such as industry associations and independent standards setting organizations, also influence any individual company's information classification exercises (see Figure 4.4). It is not uncommon to see InfoSec professionals claim to be compliant with a myriad of regulations and requirements without ever having begun a true internal information classification effort.

It took the low-level technical detail of PCI DSS to confront those regulated with the level of analysis required to perform information classification and map it to associated information-handling procedures. In this model, information-handling procedures are directly derived from the definition of the information data fields themselves, no matter what the end user labels them or where they sit in the organization's infrastructure. In this model, a clear semantic definition for data fields, pursued at an industry level, makes information protection choices more obvious. Infosec professionals should embrace labeling processes that originate in industry consensus on data modeling. Because the handling requirements are clearly mapped to the data label, there are clear criteria for evaluating technical alternatives, and thus clear measures for success in achieving goals, notably that of protecting privacy.

---

4. For example, GLBA and EU Data Privacy Laws.

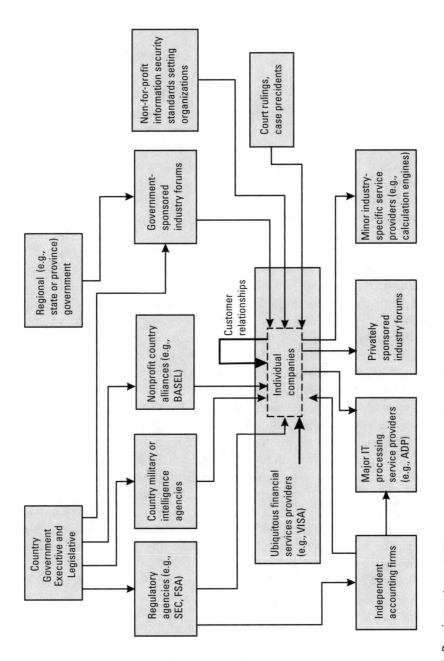

Figure 4.4 Requirements sources.

4.4 Future Trends

The technical expectations that accompany the PCI DSS have set a new bar for information classification exercises. It is no longer best practice to assume a hierarchical set of labels and place similar labels on information storage infrastructure. For an information security organization to embark on the new best practice, information security professionals must become cognizant of data modeling. Control points of the future will be cogs on very large enterprise-wide architectural wheels. The architecture will include the same infrastructure components it does today, but it will have an overlay of a data model.

At the core of any information handling process is an information model. Where data are stored electronically, they may be divided in many ways. Most people are familiar with files and directories in hierarchical structures. In highly technical environments, it is more common to think of data in relational models, that is, to identify interdependencies among data concerning different types of object in the enterprise environment. There are also object-oriented models, wherein data are either completely encapsulated by hierarchical parent-child relationships, or via links that allow multiple objects to include the same individual object as part of its own definition.[5] Each model will have its own technical implementation that takes advantage of the relationships between the data as depicted in the model.

Figure 4.5 shows the same basic set of data on customer accounts stored in a few different ways. It also illustrates that the ways in which permissions and procedures may be developed around information handling will often depend on the data structure in which the information is stored. For example, customer information in the hierarchical model may be protected at the folder level, in the relational model at the table level, and in the object model, at the object level.

In all models, it may be possible to expose account information when it is linked only to descriptions or balances without disclosing the name of the customer to whom the account belongs. However, information security technologies such as encryption and data masking may have serious performance impacts when applied to certain fields accessed via one technical implementation and less in another. As information classification becomes more field-driven and associated handling procedures more proscriptive, the average information security professional will by necessity be more and more involved in data architecture and technical implementation strategies. Verification that implementation meets requirements will no longer be a matter of maintaining generic protection profiles, but also involve architecture and design review, infrastructure configuration strategies, and source code vulnerability testing. As discussed above, this is

---

5. Note that these are three widely used models, but there many other ways of depicting data.

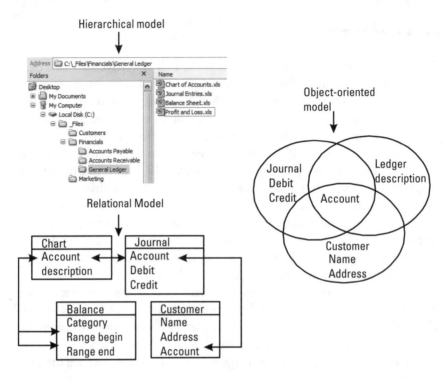

Figure 4.5 Data models.

already being done by application development teams as specific technical protection requirements become more prevalent. Economies of scale dictate that this activity be elevated to the level of the organizational information security program.

5

Human Factors

Mahi Dontamsetti

Security deals with the protection of information and is concerned with maintaining confidentiality (preventing unauthorized eavesdropping) and integrity of the source and content of the information (preventing tampering), and providing access control (restricting access to only those entitled and authorized). Privacy deals with how you use information you gain access to, whom you share it with, and for what purposes. Good privacy protection also involves providing visibility of this to the individual whose information you are using. In this chapter we learn that good security can serve as a tool to help ensure privacy, but it can also involve a loss of privacy, such as when you monitor employees and customers in an attempt to observe and stop fraudulent behavior (such as money laundering). Thus there is often a delicate balancing act with respect to protecting privacy and monitoring for fraudulent behavior. In the case of financial services, this concern for privacy is generally related to damages occurring as a result of a privacy violation, such as incidents of identity theft. The recent increase in incidents of identity theft and related fraud has increased the concern for privacy of sensitive customer financial information, and has increased regulation in this area. Other sensitive financial information includes trade secrets and intellectual property. Privacy used to be ensured through obscurity and the general difficulty in finding and correlating information that was largely in paper form, and stored in physical files and on microfiche. Today with increasingly large amounts of data available online and accessible to powerful computers able to correlate these mountains of information, concern for privacy and information protection has magnified many-fold.

—D.S.

5.1 Background

Mention privacy and it evokes very strong emotions in individuals. Most will say that privacy is under attack. They will cite numerous instances from personal experiences and from the press, of instances where someone's privacy was invaded. They will state categorically that our privacy is being invaded by telemarketers, identify thieves, press, government, and so forth. People believe it is a fundamental right. Here is a quick test, "Which amendment in the bill of rights in the United States Constitution mentions privacy?" Most will choose the fourth amendment which details the right to be secure in our homes and protected against unreasonable searches and seizures. In fact, the word privacy appears nowhere in the U.S. Constitution! Why is it that individuals have such strong feelings about privacy and are surprised that it has no mention in the U.S. Constitution or subsequent amendments?

Privacy is exceedingly difficult to define. It means different things to different people. Even the English language dictionaries differ on the definition of privacy. Merriam-Webster's defines it as, "The quality or state of being apart from company or observation" and alternatively as, "freedom from unauthorized intrusion." The American Heritage Dictionary adds to the above by defining privacy to include, "the state of being concealed." The Oxford English Dictionary defines it as "state or condition of being withdrawn from the society of others, or from public interest." Most people, when asked to define privacy, will define it is as the "right to be left alone," first mentioned by future Supreme Court justice Louis Brandeis in 1890. Historically an individual's definition of privacy has evolved with the times. Most common definitions in the middle of the twentieth century for privacy were established around the ability to have a place where one is not disturbed, any intrusions of this place being viewed as invasions of privacy; others may have defined it as being able to have private communications (phone conversations, mail, and so forth) that could not be intercepted or eavesdropped upon. This definition evolved in the latter part of the twentieth century to include protection against unsolicited telemarketing calls, unsolicited messaging—junk mail, e-mail, SMS, and so forth. In the twenty-first century privacy has focused around protection of, or lack of control over personal information such as names, Social Security numbers, and health and financial information from unauthorized access.

The common theme in all these definitions is the existence of a personal or human element. Privacy is an individual or personal right. Since individuals differ in what is important to them, so does their definition of privacy. Invasion of privacy will mean different things to different individuals. Adding to the complexity surrounding privacy is the fact that, since it is an ill-defined right, it is difficult to enforce in a court of law. Lacking consensus on the definition of privacy results in a lack of clarity on what constitutes an invasion of privacy or a privacy violation. Additionally, the right to privacy is often at odds with other rights. For instance, the right to be secure in our homes conflicts with the right of law enforcement for lawful search or seizure; the right to private communications conflicts with the right of government to protect its citizens; and the right to keeping personal information secret conflicts with the freedom of press, as well as a business's right to conduct commerce and protect its customers.

I define privacy as:

- Secluded space and uninterrupted time;
- Secret communications;
- Control of personal information.

5.1.1 Historical Perspective on Privacy

In the middle ages, privacy was primarily the domain of the rich. Rich people could afford to control the environment around them and that led indirectly to controlling encroachments on their privacy. For instance, building walls around their homes provided them seclusion of space and time. Being poor and in indentured servitude provided limited scope for privacy. The primary means of communications was the spoken word between two individuals, which did not lend itself to secrecy. In an era where individuals were owned, protection of personal information was nonexistent.

Privacy is a modern concept with its roots in the early part of the last century. Are you tired of an intrusive press and modern technology that makes it easy to invade privacy? Sound like a current day problem? In fact, an intrusive press and the advent of photography were the catalysts for the foundation of privacy in 1890. Lawyers Samuel Warren and Louis Brandeis (a future Supreme Court justice) believed that laws and government intervention were needed to protect against the unwanted public disclosure of private information. They felt that photography and communication recording devices made it impossible for individuals to protect themselves against negative publicity. Their initial work and writings laid the foundation for privacy law until the middle of the twentieth century.

Currently privacy protection in the United States is primarily under state law not Federal and differs from state to state. Privacy protection covers the areas of intrusion, disclosure of personal or private information, and usurpation of someone's name or likeness. Protection against intrusion covers private places/residences and public places where an expectation of privacy is reasonable (recent legal cases of cameras in gym locker rooms, department store changing rooms fall in this category). Interactions in purely public places do not provide an individual a basis for successful legal action claiming intrusion in most cases. Disclosure of personal and private information covers information that is either not publicly available or information that does not provide any public benefit on disclosure.

5.1.2 Impact of Technology on Privacy

Technology has led to what I call the "democratization of privacy." Privacy could be bought in the past by rich individuals by having secluded residences making it difficult to encroach. They could also control the release of their personal information. Privacy for the poor was a result of their anonymity and large numbers. Not any more. Technology has leveled the playing field for everyone. It is just as easy today to find information on the Internet about a celebrity as it is about a common man. While personal information such as social security numbers, health records, buying preferences, financial information, and political beliefs, among others, used to exist prior to the advent of the Internet, the information was primarily stored either on paper, microfiche, or nonnetworked databases or some such other media. The storage medium and technology available made it very difficult to search and retrieve information. Paper and microfiche records had to be indexed which was an expensive manual process. Thus only minimally relevant and important information was indexed. Retrieval involved searching for the keywords in the index and then retrieving the corresponding records. Paper records had limited shelf life and could be prone to environmental damage, limiting the period of their usefulness. Nonnetworked databases and the high cost of storage also led to storing of limited information as opposed to entire text or records which is prevalent today. Since most information existed in individual database silos, it made it difficult to aggregate information from these disparate databases.

Today with the proliferation of information sources (credit bureaus, local/state/federal records, court/tax documents, and so forth), digitization of information, dramatically reduced cost of storage, and ease of search and retrieval has led to easy access to previously hard to get personal information. This information is not only comprehensive, easily searchable and retrievable, but also exists in perpetuity. It is a Herculean task to delete information on the Internet. In addition, technological advances in reducing the costs and miniaturization of recording devices has led to an increase of use of video cameras, camera phones, voice recorders and other devices that record and store daily activities and conversations adding to the information repository. Tracking software keeps track of our visits to various web sites on the Internet, email sites monitor our email to better serve targeted advertisements, e-commerce web sites keep a history of our previous purchases, traffic cameras, and electronic toll booths record our travels, and credit card companies record our purchases. We live in an electronic age where many of our actions are being recorded.

Technology has one of the greatest impacts on privacy. It has had the double impact of making it easy to invade an individual's privacy while making it hard to successfully legally prosecute against an invasion of privacy. One of the bases for claiming invasion of privacy is when personal information is publicly disclosed. However, one of the tests for what is personal information used by the U.S. courts is the fact that information that is being claimed as personal did not already exist in public records. With the proliferation of public records such as property, tax, court, driving records, credit history, and others, it makes it difficult to claim information did not already exist in a public forum. Moreover with the recent tendency to publish personal details on the web via chats and blogs, to upload photographs, e-mail, as well as interact in social networking sites, all done voluntarily, we are leaving bits of personal information that make it difficult to later claim personal information was exploited.

The right to private communications has been more impacted by technological advances than any other right. It is the only privacy right that individuals cannot protect by themselves. One could go to remote regions and become a hermit to get seclusion, minimally used modern financial, medical, and transportation systems to protect private information, but if one wants to communicate with someone over long distances, the communication can be intercepted, unless specialized devices are used. Communication technology has become so complex with digitization, electronic/optical transmission, transmitting and receiving devices that it is very difficult for individuals to protect their communications without some specialized technical help. Encryption devices, secret key exchange mechanisms, and other devices are needed today to effectively secure one's communications. With the advent of globalization, long-distance communication links have extended across nations and continents, making them more than ever susceptible to eavesdropping and interception by intermediary telecom providers, countries, and governmental agencies. Even face-to-face private conversations can be eavesdropped on by parabolic antennas, tape recorders, and other devices. More and more communications use wireless (Wi-Fi, cellular phones, satellite communications) and Internet communications which are all interceptible. While one would think that the sheer volume of traffic on the Internet and voice networks would provide some level of anonymity, technological advances in real-time search and storage, ensure that is not so.

5.1.3   Privacy in a Corporate Setting

We have previously defined privacy as the right to secluded space and uninterrupted time, secret communications and control of personal information. All of these rights are impacted when an employee is at work. What is a secluded space and uninterrupted time when an employee is using office space provided by an employer and is paid for time spent at work? How should the right to secret communications be interpreted when the employee is using communication devices provided by his or her employer during work hours? What is control of personal information in a work environment? Would job title, responsibilities, name, location be considered personal information? What is control in this instance? For example, can an employee have control over who is informed about his or her salary and would that be considered personal information? How about institutions that use biometric devices? Should the fingerprint information be considered personal and should the employee have control over who has access to it? What about an employer's rights to monitor employee Internet usage to protect clients, employees and their business?

All of the above are issues that corporations deal with daily and have policies and procedures in place to address them. Suffice it to define personal information in a work environment as individual information that does not change when an employee changes jobs. Any information that remains unchanged when an employee leaves an employer's employment should be considered personal. Name, Social Security number, home address, driver's license number, bank account numbers, and medical information would all be considered personal information under this definition since they remain unchanged from job to job.

5.1.4   Evolution of Personal Information

Along with changing technology, changing human and social behaviors have also redefined what constitutes personal information. Personal information used to be relatively easily defined during the middle of the last century. With the advent of the Internet and increased online presence leading to participation in chat groups, email, and social networking sites, the scope of what constitutes personal information has expanded and become more nebulous. Use of identities (username/password) is necessary on the Internet to differentiate individual users. In social networking sites such as Facebook or MySpace, users use identities to create online personas of their personal life storing daily dairies, travels, interests, hobbies, and so forth. The medium allows individuals to describe their personal life in ways it was not possible before, to an audience not reachable before. What is the expectation of privacy, if any, with regards to the information a user voluntarily puts on the Internet?

Salvador Minuchin described human identity as consisting of the "sense of belonging and a sense of being separate." I believe this is also a good definition of human personal information. Information that separates us would be information that uniquely identifies us (Social Security numbers, driver's license numbers, and so forth) as well as medical, financial, and similar information. Information that provides a sense of belonging or grouping would be information that identifies membership in a particular religion, faith, political party, race, language, private club, and others. Individuals consider information from both categories as personal and private. Individuals are apt to consider disclosure of either their social security number or religion as invasion of privacy.

5.2 Observations

Recent trends are pushing the envelope of what is considered personal information. For example consider the instance where an individual purposely builds an online persona that is different from his or her real world personality. Would disclosure of this information be considered a violation of personal privacy laws? In a recent case, Wikipedia had to block certain IP addresses of congressional staffers since they were creating overly flattering, untrue bios of their congressmen. Since individuals were being prevented control of their personal information (however untrue), would this be a violation of privacy rights?[1] Should untrue personal information self-created by a user be afforded the same protection as true personal information?

An identity on eBay, which has an excellent reputation that eBay users trust and conduct business with, may be more valuable to an individual than say a driver's license number. That individual may classify his or her eBay identity as key personal information, since it may take years to build back the trust once the identity is stolen and misused.

5.2.1 Privacy Trade-offs—Human Behavioral Impact on Privacy

Since privacy is personal, it is subject to idiosyncrasies of human behavior. While a telemarketing call promoting a product you have no interest in would be considered an invasion of privacy, another call highlighting the experience of a political candidate you support may be considered otherwise. A request for personal information from a consumer products company would offend many of us and we may decline considering it private information, whereas many of us gladly provide the same information if not more, for supermarket frequent customer cards, entry into sweepstakes, and other gifts of monetary value. In other instances, such as when we are booking an airplane flight, we have to enter

---

1. Holtzman, H. David, *Privacy Lost: How Technology is Endangering Your Privacy,* Jossey-Bass, 2006, p. 81.

personal information. At the end of the transaction, our information may be automatically forwarded to a hotel or car rental agency site. In most cases we do not mind, since it is convenient. Contrast the previous scenario with several social situations where a friend or acquaintance asks our permission to send our personal information to either his or her friend. We may have questions that we will ask that may have to be addressed prior to giving permission to our friend to release our information.

As the examples above demonstrate, the following affects how individuals perceive or react to situations which, in some circumstances, present privacy issues:

- Potential for personal gain;
- Potential for convenience;
- Perception (not real) of control over personal information.

These are privacy tradeoffs. Individuals make privacy tradeoffs consciously or unconsciously everyday, when faced with a decision that requires them to divulge personal information. The higher the potential for personal gain or convenience or the stronger the perception of control over the information, the more likely it is that individuals will divulge personal information.

Figure 5.1 demonstrates the probability of personal information being provided. It is interesting to note that personal gain does neither have to be substantial or actually realized. Individuals willingly part with personal information for minimal actual realized gain and in some instances even when they know the probability of realizing the gain is low.

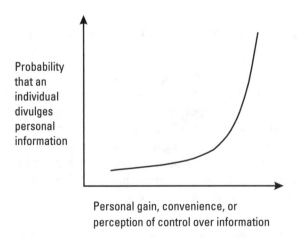

Figure 5.1 Tendency to divulge personal information versus perception of gain.

All personal information is not treated or valued equally by individuals. Individuals are more protective of certain elements of their personal information than others. One of the key drivers for this behavior is the probability of negative impact that release of the information can cause that particular individual. As depicted in Figure 5.2, the higher the perception that release of the information will cause harm—be it financial, physical, psychological, or social harm to the individual, the higher intrinsic value that individual subconsciously assigns to that information. For instance, Jewish individuals during Nazi Germany valued any personal information that could indicate religious affiliation higher than any other personal information. Prior to that period, they might not have protected that information as zealously. Similarly individuals belonging to a minority religion, race, or any other group, may value certain portions of their personal information more than individuals belonging to a majority religion, race, or group.

Another factor that affects a person's acceptance of an invasion of privacy is the level of trust individuals subconsciously assign to the party holding the personal information. For instance, individuals typically assign a high level of trust to their financial institution. They are more apt to feel strongly about loss of personal information if their credit card numbers were stolen from that financial institution than from the local gas station or restaurant. Even though the information lost is identical, people believe that the financial institution should be held to a higher standard and any loss there is more of a privacy violation than the local restaurant. Sometimes the perception of invasion of privacy is related more to who lost the information than what information was lost.

Cultural, political, and social conditions impact how individuals value personal information. Since these conditions change over time, the human

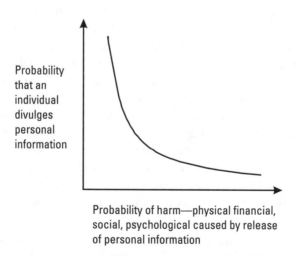

Figure 5.2   Tendency to divulge personal information versus perception of harm.

perception of importance of specific elements of personal information also changes with the times.

5.2.2   What is Risk?

There are probably as many definitions of "risk" as there are possible different things we are worried about happening. In the broadest sense risk is the notion that more than one outcome is possible in a given situation and sometimes those outcomes are bad. In information security we most often are talking about "operational risks" and "reputational risks" which are risks to the institution to which we belong manifested by breakdowns in IT controls. The Bank for International Settlements (BIS), in their work commonly called the Basel II standards, defined operational risk as: "… the risk of loss resulting from inadequate or failed internal processes, people and systems or from external events. This definition includes legal risk, but excludes strategic and reputational risk."[2]

It is important to understand the goal of the BIS was to define a way to calculate the amount of financial reserves that should be held to keep an institution from insolvency due to some operational risk being manifest and the need for capital to be drawn down to cover the losses. This has an important limitation in that if there were no direct losses their definition would not consider this an operational risk. So if an event occurred that drove customers away impacting revenue like an ATM network being offline or caused operational expenses to increase to remedy some issue like recovering from a virus outbreak, neither of these would be considered an operational risk.

Reputational risks are things that harm the value of the company's brand. The BIS was not so bold as to define how one should measure reputational risks, but yet they need to be part of our calculus to drive information protection decisions. I would proffer that a better definition of risk would be: "the risk of loss of funds, revenue, profitability, or market opportunity resulting from inadequate or failed internal processes, people and systems or from external events."

The reason we desire to define risk is we want to make rational decisions as to what we need to consider or do in a given situation and have a basis for comparison of those decisions between other situations using a model. A former CISO once described to me as the definition of success in building a risk model was not to have the model be perfect, but only be hard to disprove. The motivation here is you want something that allows you to make comparisons within a similar population set so that given the same inputs you get the same outputs. The goal was to actually build in the subjectivity to the model design not to

---

2. Bank for International Settlements, *Basel Committee on Banking Supervision International Convergence of Capital Measurement and Capital Standards, A Revised Framework,* June 2004, p. 137.

allow much subjectivity to occur on the inputs used to generate the outputs from the model.

Whenever I get into a discussion with colleagues about risk models I remember something from a grade school physics class about significant digits. This was the scientific precept that if you have some data that you only know to a certain magnitude of precision, and those data are combined with other data you measured with higher precision, then the output of the calculation must be at the same number of significant digits as the least precise data input. For example, if I am trying to calculate square area and I measure 0.5 meters on the x axis and 3.976 meters on the y axis the square area is 2 square meters. If the axis was measured as 0.50 meters the area would be 1.9 square meters. The point of the example is you can only make an assumption about the accuracy of the calculation when you know the least amount of precision that is used in any variable to that calculation, and in information security risk models we always have large chunks of imprecision.

We often try to turn our risk definition to a formula so that it feels definable.

For example, risk equals the sum of products of impact, vulnerability, threat, and likelihood.

$$R = \sum (V * T) * (L * I)$$

There are many hard problems to overcome to make this a mathematical formula rather than a semantic one. For example, the variables are not truly independent of one another. Yesterday's unlikely event that used an unknown vulnerability and therefore was low likelihood is today much more likely and more adversaries are capable of using the attack method.

Consider Vulnerability Can you force something to go wrong, or in other words is there susceptibility for a component in the environment to have a flaw that can be used by an adversary to their advantage? We have to recognize that some vulnerabilities are known and hence a scalar value could be assigned to describe their magnitude or severity. A good measurement method for this is a scheme such as the common vulnerability scoring system (CVSS) developed by the Forum of Incident Response and Security Teams (FIRST.org). This type of scheme can also be used to measure gaps in the company's information security policies using the same concept to score the vulnerability resulting from the policy gap.

It is important to realize in addition to the measured vulnerabilities above other vulnerabilities are likely present, but unknown to the observer. These need to factor into the formula if it were to be precise but, as they are difficult to enumerate with any precision and are often ignored for the sake of simplicity (also in large measure why qualitative approaches still are greatly favored).

Consider Threat   Does somebody wish to do you harm and if they wish it can they act on it? In the intelligence world this is also described as capability and intent. In the risk formulas there are very different ways of addressing threat. These are often mapped using a scenario approach to describe a given threat actor (adversary) and their capabilities to a specific attack vector.

- *Threat Actor:* Organized crime syndicate.
- *Intent:* Desire to steal cash with the minimum chance of being caught.
- *Capabilities:* Has logistical capabilities (low-level people to pull money from ATMs) and access to significant technical attack methodologies via the Internet, and possibility to subvert insiders inside the bank.
- *Attack vectors:* Bank mainframe ATM settlement, debit card issuance\distribution, ATM point-of-sale device, intermediary card processor, bank customer card holder.

In the model we often use the twinning of the threat and the vulnerability to define unique cases as not all vulnerabilities are exploitable by the different threat actors. For example bypassing a cryptographic control is probably beyond the capability of an unsophisticated insider, but not unreasonable for a well-funded highly motivated attacker like an intelligence service.

Consider Impact   What happens when something goes wrong? In information security this is often when CIA (confidentiality, integrity, or availability) are breached. When we speak about impact the key question is from who's point of view are we observing? Is it from the bank that loses $500,000 in 1,000 different fraudulent ATM transactions? Is it from the customers who cannot buy groceries because $500 is missing from their account? Is it from the merchant with a point-of-sale system that was compromised by hackers? Is it from the hacker who is worried about getting caught? Is it from the newspaper reader who sees a story stating that XYZ bank was hacked and hundreds of thousands of account numbers were stolen and wonders if their account is OK?

Consider Likelihood   What is the frequency of an occurrence of an event? Establishing likelihood is desirable in the model as we want a rationale to say we felt safe in ignoring something, or at least giving it a lighter treatment if we deemed a low chance of occurrence.

I parse the likelihood only into two macro buckets. Bucket one is events that are frequent and therefore have a known minimum rate of occurrence.

Bucket two is events that are infrequent for which you have no idea how to measure with fidelity. Operations management professionals make their living eating out of bucket one whereas the risk management professionals gorge their fill from bucket two. The classic bucket one sample is the frequency of antivirus detection by commercial products looking at user files. You can easily measure the number of files infected (and hopefully repaired) per day and be close to prediction of future days of the minimum number of detected files. (Unfortunately, it does not have much guarantee of predictability on the upper bound as over the baseline of infection rate is a factor of new attacks.) Virus events for the most part are all low-impact events as the controls manage the problem to a certain noise level. We still see from time to time high-impact virus events that the collected data does little to forecast.

The bucket two side of this is how many undetected pieces of malicious code hit your shop per day? Since they are by my definition undetected you cannot measure them. Now given what we know about threat and capabilities it is not unreasonable to assume undetectable malware exists, then the only question is how likely is it that somebody uses it against you?

All bucket one events need to be included in your risk model regardless of the impact is high or low. Since they happen a lot you need to deal with them in some way. In bucket two you really only need to worry about high-impact events. If it is unlikely to occur and has the minimal impact why worry about the case if it does occur. The area of raging debate is how to handle high-impact, but low-likelihood events from bucket two. The penultimate example of this is the tragedy of 9/11. On September 10, 2001, very few people conceived of commercial airliners being used as a weapon of mass destruction. Two days later virtually no one doubted it might happen again and many thought it was imminent. Much work was done to eliminate vulnerabilities (and we can argue how effective that has been another time), but was the reduction of vulnerability the reason the attack vector was not successfully reused or has the frequency just not recurred? So if we were trying to calculate a likelihood value for this what would we use? Count the number of flights since Kitty Hawk in 1900 to September 11, 2001 and say the frequency is 4 out of that sum?

5.3 Recommendations

So how do you handle high-impact, but low-likelihood events?

One approach that is being taken is to look at the capability and intent of the adversary groups, and look at the vulnerabilities they could exploit, and attempt to lessen the impact of those being exploited. The truly bad impacts probably only concern a minority of your assets and only a subset of your adversary groups, so spend your time on working those into the model.

A different approach to this is to just ignore the likelihood in your model since you really don't have a good way to measure it so don't try. In some cases the effort spent arguing about if a scenario was likely or unlikely is better spent just fixing a problem. This will really annoy some people in your organization who think you shouldn't try to defend from unlikely events, but it is not like they have a better answer most of the time.

In a risk model devoid of likelihood what do you do? In that case the threats and vulnerabilities play more of a role in the calculus. One workable method is to use the threat model to define the expected control sets and to make the required controls not monolithic, but a function of the asset or process criticality. The approach is to use an inherent risk (which is the risk before any controls are applied) and then use the application of controls to reduce risk to a residual level you are comfortable. In essence, the assumption about likelihood is instead the inherent risk determination.

To qualify the inherent risk of an IT application, one might come up with a scheme to collect the answer to a bunch of questions concerning inherent risk and use those to produce a calculation of a risk score. The ability to quantify is improved if inherent risks can be categorized by threats to well-known categories of controls, like confidentiality, integrity, and availability.

For example: First you provide some macro questions that describe the materiality of the application overall and the operating environment overall. For example, is there a significant customer or regulatory impact if there was a problem? For confidentiality, you might ask what classifications and volumes of data does the application contain or how many records does a single query return? For integrity, you may ask things like is this an application we use for aggregated statement of financial results or does it contain the record of customer holdings? (Say in this case financial aggregate applications get a 1, customer holding systems get a 2.) For availability, you can use measures related to business continuity. If the system cannot be down more than 1 hour without inherent risk to privacy, it gets a 4, after 24 hours it gets a 2, and so forth.

Another reason for CIA scores being independent is the controls you would apply do not all mitigate the same kinds of risks. If my application had a high score for availability risk then why would I invest in cryptographic controls to protect the data in the application unless there was also a high-confidentiality risk score? Once the inherent risk is decided, substituting it for likelihood allows the loss expectancy to drive the implementation of controls.

In the above description of impact having different points of view as to who the risk is seen from, can lead to four different measurements of impact that need to be considered in the risk model. If I am the bank I would naturally measure from my perspective, but I have to also be cognizant of the risk to the other counter parties like the customer and the merchant and to some degree to adversaries like the hacker. Coming back to the premise that risk trade-offs with respect to privacy are personal, one of the elements of human nature that anyone must address in the security model is that it acknowledge the "what's in it for me" perspective that people bring. Information security is usually about making a series of trade-offs to manage larger risks into smaller ones. This is fine in a purely academic sense, but in the real world where security matters the transference of risks for the greater good of your institution may well meet with unexpected resistance. In the ATM example above, impact is relative to different points of view, that is, whose perspective the risk is seen from can lead to four different measurements of impact required to be considered in the risk model. If I am the bank, I would measure from my perspective naturally, but I have to also be cognizant of the risk to the other counter parties like the customer and the merchant and to some degree to adversaries like the hacker. Even when controls are agreed to be justified by a risk model, there is debate over the extent of their adequacy.

For example, suppose there is a large risk with transporting sensitive data that is in clear text on magnetic tapes. As we all know, once in a while these tapes find a way to go missing. This poses some headline risks, legal or regulatory risk, and potential of customer impact as well which your institution really wants to avoid. To manage this risk you embark on a major initiative to encrypt your data as it is written on to the tapes. Problem solved right? Maybe, but the day-to-day hard problem with encryption is not the algorithm to do the enciphering, it is the management of the encryption keys. Now in the risk model you see a large enterprise risk due to the personally identifiable customer information contained in the backup tapes when they are sent off-site. You implement an encryption tool to fix this so the risk to your business units goes down. The problem is this encryption tool, despite all the great glossy marketing slides, has a few implementation problems with the key management and as a result a small number of people in the operations team have root-like access to get all the keys out of the management engine. You have reduced the risk that anyone on the planet can retrieve your data and now only a few dozen trusted operations people could access it. All in all, a seemingly good risk mitigation result for the company.

The problem is the operations group now has a segregation of duties problem and they are about to start an internal audit review of their operations. Before, when the company's data was in clear text, they did not have an issue as they did not have to manage any keys. (The business had the risk.) In the last audit no issues were raised with the management of the tape inventories, the recall and restoration processes, and so on. This time however, the somewhat glaring key management problem is looming. If your operations team's incentives (for example what makes up their bonus) is the risk mitigation for the whole company then they are in good shape. However, it is much more likely their management has told them success in their unit is measured in terms of cost, service level, and having a clean review from audit. This last objective is now directly in conflict with the thing that manages down the risk for the whole corporation. If your management scheme allows for credit when risk is transferred from one area to another, this is not really a problem. If your management scheme does not address this potential problem you will face unanticipated obstacles with the implementation of the tape encryption tool.

Perception Versus Reality Delta   In the earlier impact example of the ATM fraud, one impact noted was an erroneous report by a media outlet about XYZ bank being hacked. This sadly is becoming common place as the environments that we operate in are sufficiently complex that breakdowns or breaches in those environments surface their symptoms in a place somewhat detached from the cause. In the ATM example, the customer got a letter stating that a debit card was replaced due to a fraud or perhaps they just got a new card in the mail. The normal reaction is "well my bank must have had a problem so they replaced my card." The reality is another part of the supply chain was compromised and as a result the bank had to replace the card. (That is not to say banks are by any means immune or without the potential for fault, just that it is really hard to tell as an outside observer if that is the case.)

A second example is perceived risks versus the real risks in online banking. Make no mistake about it, the criminals want to take your money and the online and mobile banking channels are relatively low-risk ways for them to do it. They can act from great distances, across multiple jurisdictions, and without the chance to be shot at during the hold-up. The perception is that the only thing the bad guys can do to get your bank data is to get your password. The reality is they only started there because it was easiest. They can take over your PC, ask you to unwittingly supply you banking details, subvert some other part of the supply chain like a retailer you frequent, or redirect you to some other bogus web site that looks real to you. The change towards multifactor authentication requirements of the online banking channels were positioned as solving the security problem. Well sorry to say the reality is it did not solve it, and it only forced changes to the tactics the bad guys had to use to succeed. If you take a step back the real problem is banks don't really know what customer behavior is going to be with these channels as there is scant history and as a result a 90-year-old retiree asking to perform their first ever wire transfer to send the sum total of their account balance to Kazakhstan did not seem abnormal.

When Risks Collide   The intersection between the "perception versus reality delta" and the "risk to who parallax" subtexts also provides interesting areas for risk analysis. This is best shown by the risk to the customer as advocated by a set of regulatory bodies or the risk to the financial sector as advocated by multiple others. (As an observation, these are often different teams in the same agency.)

If I am a consumer advocate my point of view is from the risk to the customer and I am working from the perception that ID theft is the main problem, you might conclude that protection of personally identifiable information is the paramount concern. Conversely, if I am a central banker my point of view is keeping the financial sector working and my perception is that a terrorist group or natural disaster is the greatest threat, then I might conclude that managing the availability of systems is the paramount concern. Alternatively, if I am the external auditor of a financial institution I am working with the perception that financial impropriety is the paramount concern and my perception is that insiders are trying to cook the books, so I might conclude that managing integrity is the paramount concern.

5.4 Future Trends

Privacy is a modern concept and extremely difficult to protect. Being very personal, it also means different things to different people. We looked at the evolution of privacy, its modern definition, and its applicability in corporate, social and group settings. While there are a lot of things that are nebulous about privacy, things that are clear are that it is under attack every day, its definition evolves with technology, and while it is held very dear, in reality it is relinquished for the most miniscule of benefits.

The traditional definition of risk with respect to information security is inadequate and any adequate new definition must factor in perceived trade-offs with respect to privacy considerations and reputational risk. The traditional formula for defining risk as a product of impact, likelihood, threat, and vulnerability is flawed because likelihood is very a difficult measure to estimate, and is in fact a perception. Though a definitive replacement for traditional methods of risk assessment, it is still elusive, any new definition should also consider the difference between the perception and reality of impact.

Acknowledgments

There are many contributors to this chapter, some of whom are unaware of their role in bringing shape to the ideas in this chapter. Most of the thoughts presented in this chapter have formed over years of discussion and debate with my colleagues and industry veterans. They share most of the credit for this chapter.

One person whom I would like to acknowledge specifically is Mark Clancy, executive vice president, Citigroup. He has been a tremendous source of input for this chapter and played a critical role in its definition. An industry veteran, he is always willing to assist and has been a great sounding board for me personally. One the leading industry experts on operational risk, this chapter would not have been complete but for his assistance.

Part II: Risks

Risk management professionals traditionally have been businesspersons concerned with market risk, credit risk, and operational risk in that order. Market risk is concerned with the possibility that there will be no market for a company's product, or that a product may not be properly designed to meet the needs of the marketplace. Without due consideration of market risk, business is likely to be severely impacted. Credit risk is concerned with the ability of a business to handle its cash flow. If a business extends credit to customers who do not pay, business may be severely impacted. Operations risk is concerned with whether management can succeed in operating the business. If a company cannot supply goods and services, or maintain an on-going concern, the business will fail. In the context of this traditional hierarchy, risk management with respect to information security is a subset of information technology (IT) risk, which is itself a subset of operations risk. That is, as business risks go, InfoSec seems a poor and often neglected cousin.

Nevertheless, within IT, the term *risk management* is used to refer almost exclusively to security measures. This reflects the pervasiveness of information security controls as an increasingly common means of achieving management objectives with respect to IT. The authors review the fundamental assumptions on which risk management with respect to information processing is based, and provide insights into how it should be viewed to maintain concentration on objectives of confidentiality, integrity, and availability. In so doing, they reveal a tacit acknowledgement that infomation security forms the basis of management control over information technology, and hence, as reflected in the automation prevalent in this age, over company operations. The chapters in this section make a case that it is not possible to minimize operations risks without some concentration on information security risk.

6

Making the Case for Replacing
Risk-Based Security

Donn B. Parker

In my mind, Donn Parker is the grandfather of applied information security and I have always admired his clear thinking and easily understood writing style. His definitive book *Fighting Computer Crime* introduced me to the basic concepts of security and was extremely influential in my pursuing a career in information security. In fact, my first publication specifically on security described Donn's six security functions, namely, avoidance, deterrence, prevention, detection, recovery, and correction. I have used this model many times in subsequent publications. In the second edition of his book, he expands the number of steps to eleven and adds mitigation, transference, investigation, sanction or credit, and education to the list.

In November 2001, *Information Security Magazine* published columns that were written by some twenty leading practitioners regarding what we thought would be the most important issues confronting us in the upcoming year or two. My column was all about complying with laws and regulations. Unfortunately, my prediction came to pass and we entered a period where many security-related decisions are mandated by legislators and regulators. This is right in line with Donn's assertions.

I was personally very honored when Donn agreed to write this chapter and the preface to the book. Donn's experience in the field spans some 35 years, while mine is a mere dozen years, although I have been involved in information technology much longer than that. Many information-security professionals, especially among those who cling to the old formulations, consider Donn's views contrarian and controversial. However, this book is meant to debunk the old tired security myths and point us in a more realistic direction, which is precisely why I asked Donn to contribute this chapter. Fortunately, the other editors and I agree with most of Donn's views, which is a sign of their progressiveness also. It is often necessary to take an extreme position, as Donn has done in this case, in order to get people to think about the issues and take action on them. Donn does this so well, and we are all beneficiaries of his wisdom and experience.

—C.W.A.

6.1 Introduction

Information security is mostly based quite naturally and obviously on reducing and eliminating risk of loss. Security is justified and prioritized by managing the risk that we attempt to measure by risk assessment. We also seek to be diligent by using good practices; achieve compliance with regulations, laws, contracts, standards, and auditors; and enable our computer applications to function or be more competitive by using sufficient security. Unfortunately, this idealized approach of justifying and prioritizing security based on risk is not valid because security risk cannot be effectively measured, and you can't control what you can't measure, and you can't effectively manage what you can't control. Therefore, risk management becomes an oxymoron. Fortunately, we can abandon failed and intangible risk-based security by improving, justifying, and prioritizing security by measurable and manageable diligence, compliance, and enablement without the need to measure security risk.

The lack of management support to achieve adequate security is caused by our flawed risk-based approach to security. Management takes risks in the normal course of business every day, and it is easily expedient for them to accept security risk rather than reducing it when security with its constraints and cost is inconvenient and interferes with business. We need to make it imperative and unavoidable that management supports reasonable levels of security. We can do this by emphasizing diligence and compliance to avoid negligence and penalties, and emphasizing enablement to securely use computer applications, stay within budgets, and be competitive. I have found that these are more effective and powerful justifications for better security than security risk reduction that then likely becomes serendipitously achieved.

6.1.1 Understanding Security Risk

To understand the need for this fundamental change of our basic concepts, we must first understand security risk. Security risk in its most basic form is a prediction of the frequency and impact of one or more adversities. It is often numerically predicted as annual loss expectancy (ALE) or as high, medium, or low. Abstract scales such as 1 to 10 are often used as well to quantify the estimation of the frequency and impact. Frequency usually is predicted in occurrences per time period such as two per year and occurs at three levels:

1. There are adversities that are impossible to assess with frequency near or equal to zero;
2. At the other extreme there are adversities where perpetrators are currently engaged in causing adversities with high frequency;
3. Inbetween zero frequency (1) and high frequency (2) there are rare adversities that happen only occasionally.

Rare adversities (3) are the only events subject to risk. Certainties (2) are not risks and we can justify and prioritize improved security to control and manage them in a measurable, straightforward manner. By rare, I mean possible adversities that haven't happened or haven't happened frequently enough to be able to validly predict what will happen in the future. By certainties or frequent adversities, I mean that enough of them are being experienced currently to know what the frequencies and impacts are now and will be in the near future with a high degree of certainty. With certainties we can directly justify, prioritize, and apply controls and see the results in a timely manner. With rare adversities we can apply controls but are unable to know the results for a long time, if at all, since the adversities may rarely or never happen.

The debate about validity of security risk assessment is obscured and confused because rare adversities and certainties that are not risks are mixed together and estimated the same way. Supporters of risk-based security often falsely claim that risks are measurable because certainties are measurable. Certainties such as many kinds of malware attacks, credit card fraud, identity theft, data entry errors, and phishing require no risk assessment to justify increased security. They can be counted, measured, and tolerated because the cost of ending or reducing them by applying more security is greater than the cost of the impact, or active efforts are being applied or planned to preclude or reduce them to a tolerable level. We can relatively easily obtain support from management to deal with this real certain and current loss experience in a straightforward manner. The challenge that we face is what to do about the rare adversities such as many kinds of sabotage, theft, denial of service, extortion, and espionage that could have large impacts but occur only occasionally. These are the only kinds of threats where risk management would apply by assessing the risks of future adversities if that were possible.

For example, suppose we install a safeguard against a rare type of hacker intrusion. If the attempted or actual intrusions don't occur, change, or become even less frequent, has our investment in the safeguard prevented or changed the attempts and intrusions and reduced or eliminated the loss? We cannot be certain unless we capture and obtain truthful confessions of all the malicious hackers about their practices. Cause and effect in security and abuse and misuse are complex. We cannot ask unknown adversaries how they reacted to safeguards. The losses could have ended for a variety of reasons, rational or irrational. The adversaries might have gone back to school, begun to attack our systems in more effective ways, or become busy developing or waiting for more powerful attack tools to cause more ingenious and larger losses.

Security risk assessment requires that we must estimate potential impacts. But the only valid estimate would be more than the net worth of the entire organization since we don't know all of the ramifications of an incident, such as civil litigation, lost equity value, liability, or what the perpetrators may do with their gain to cause additional harm. For example consider the total failure of Barings Bank in London resulting from a failure of one simple segregation of duties in the Singapore office coupled with a stock market upheaval resulting from the Kobe, Japan earthquake. In short, we can determine neither the amount we could lose in the future nor the savings that we will obtain if our investment in security is a success.

Confusion exists as well by combining security risk with business risk. They are fundamentally different concepts. Business risk is a desirable voluntary investment to return a profit or a return on investment (ROI). Security risk is undesirable and involuntary. It has no ROI, only a possible but unknown future savings. We are motivated to reduce it as much as possible. Business risk affects the profit and loss ledger, and security risk, and the cost of security to reduce it is noted in the expense ledger as a cost of doing business. Table 6.1 summarizes some of the differences between security risks and business risks.

All information and information systems are at security risk at all times, and the frequencies and impacts are estimates that are based on extrapolations of past loss experience of the organization and others, and current vulnerabilities and potential threats. Unfortunately, statistically sufficient loss experience and many vulnerabilities and threats are not known. And, there is no one-to-one relationship between risks, perpetrators, threats, vulnerabilities, and losses, on the one hand, and safeguards on the other. Each influences the value of all the others in often hidden and complex ways and to varying degrees. Many safeguards may affect one risk, and one safeguard may affect many risks. And, we are not sure if the safeguards chosen by risk assessment reduce the risk, because the future potential perpetrators and their plans that determine our risks are unknown. In addition, past loss experience, even if we know what it is, does not adequately predict the future in our fast-changing e-commerce and technology. Many statistics of others' loss experience such as surveys produced by the CSI/FBI annually and trade journals are not valid for risk estimating purposes because they are based on self-selected samples and general questions asked of

Table 6.1
Differences Between Security Risks and Business Risks

Security Risk	Business Risk
Involuntary risk of unknown value, cannot be avoided.	Voluntary discretionary investment decision can be made.
Explicit sources of risk are not identifiable.	Competitors are known.
Perpetrators' SKRAMO* is unknown.	Competitors' SKRAMO* is known.
Adversaries normally lie, cheat, deceive, and act irrationally.	Predictable competitors normally follow ethical practices.
ROI is negative, unknown, and not demonstrable.	ROI is zero or positive and can be easily demonstrated.
Positive benefit is absence of unknown possible loss.	Positive benefit is measurable profit.
Negative result is unlimited, unknown loss.	Negative result is limited to investment.
Risk assessment is not verifiable because results are obscure.	Risk assessment is verifiable by obvious results.
Amateurs perform risk assessment.	Professional risk managers perform risk assessment.
Limited resources tend to be allocated for risk assessment.	Generous resources tend to be allocated for risk assessment.

* SKRAMO means skills, knowledge, resources, authority, motives, and objectives.

people that often don't know the real or complete facts. In addition, statistics of many organizations' losses, while possibly valuable for actuarial purposes pertaining to most of an insurance company's customers, do not necessarily apply to any one organization with its special circumstances. One special situation such as a labor dispute, conspiracy, drug addicted or disgruntled employee or former employee, a malicious hacker, or business problem may change the risk dramatically at any time.

6.2 Why Risk Assessment and Risk Management Fail

CISOs have tried to justify spending resources on security by claiming that they can manage and reduce security risks by assessing, reporting, and controlling them. They try to measure the benefits of information security "scientifically" based on risk reduction. After all, risk management is popularly used successfully for many projects in IT. But for security, this doesn't work.

Methods for attempting to evaluate security risks are the emperor's new clothes. In my experience many efforts to use such methods (e.g., NIST Annual Loss Expectancy) as those recommended throughout the information security literature have faded away when the high cost of doing thorough assessments, complexity, easily disputable results, and rapidly changing environments are taken into account. Many small businesses selling automated risk assessment products and services quickly fail.

It is not possible to know the effectiveness of safeguards that have little or no detection capabilities associated with them. Howard Schmidt was quoted in *ComputerWorld*, on September 26, 2005 at an ISACA Conference in Las Vegas, as saying that: "...often you can measure a negative event but not a positive one. As a result, it becomes very difficult to demonstrate the business value of security programs." (The confidential nature of a risk assessment usually would preclude publicly reporting the results as a violation of an organization's security.) Good security is when nothing bad happens, but with nothing bad happening, there is nothing to measure. Therefore, the goodness of security against rare adversities can't be measured since you don't know what or who you may have stopped. I have never heard of a study to determine the validity of a risk assessment after its completion and new security measures have been taken or not taken. Proof of concept has never been performed.

It should be obvious to anybody familiar with computer and information misuse and abuse losses that information defenders can apply many good controls that through experience they have found effective against rare adversities in many cases. However, experience was under the control of unknown, and often irrational, perpetrators. They have unknown skills, knowledge, resources, authority, motives, and objectives while attacking from unknown locations at unknown future times, or attacking known but untreated vulnerabilities, or vulnerabilities that are known to the attackers but unknown to the defenders (a constant problem in our technologically complex environments). In addition, when perpetrators fail in attacking one possible vulnerability, they often attempt attacks on other vulnerabilities to accomplish their goals. Therefore, risks may be related in unknown complex ways so that reducing one risk may increase or decrease other risks. This latter point alone precludes the effective use of risk assessment methods.

The other factor in risk is impact. Impact may be minimal in major attacks and major in limited or minor attacks. The complete failure of Barings Bank in London and the huge penalties imposed on TJX in their identity theft and privacy violation are examples of this. You never know what amount of liability, litigation, or secondary effects may ensue after even a minor incident or violation of an obscure vulnerability. The conclusion is easily seen to be that there are too many interrelated unknown variables and too many interrelated known variables with unknown values. And they all change in unknown ways over time depending on unknown future circumstances such as system changes, litigation events and costs, lost talent, labor disputes, social and political changes, business changes, perpetrators' plans and intent, and failures, successes, and frailties on the part of perpetrators and defenders.

6.2.1   Misplaced Support for Risk-Based Security in Practice

Some supporters of security risk management and risk assessment in debates with me (CISSPs are referred to the risk threads in the CISSP Forum) often admit that there are not enough valid data to make security risk assessment a straightforward and successful method. However, they argue that this is not a reason to abandon it. They say that we must continue to strive to obtain the necessary valid data, and it will be possible ultimately to attain the goal. I suggest that with the increasing number of computer users worldwide, increasing dependency on growing numbers of computers, complexity of systems and networks, and advancing sophistication and effectiveness of criminal attacks, there is no hope of catching up nor achieving ultimate success of risk management and assessment.

Expert Dan Geer, with a Ph.D. in statistics, in a statement that he made at the 2006 RSA Conference, believes that the problem of insufficient data is researchable and solvable in about ten years if we start major, organized efforts now. In the meantime he suggests that we should continue trying, expanding our data bases and stick to a coarse granularity level of ordinals (estimating in terms of ones followed by lots of zeros). Others claim they can do it quantitatively now. These are CISOs who are strongly committed to risk-based security by having significant ongoing risk management functions, and job titles and descriptions that include risk management. Some of them explain that the numbers simply constitute a language to express opinions and intangibles that CISOs, business units, and top management understand to justify their decisions that they have already reached concerning their security requirements.

One CISO told me that he performs risk assessment backwards. He says that he already knows what he needs to do for the next five years to develop adequate security. So he creates some risk numbers that support his contention. Then he works backwards to create types of loss incidents, frequencies, and impacts that produce those numbers. He then refines the input and output to make it all seem plausible. I suggested that his efforts are unethical since his input data and calculations are fake. He was offended and said that top management understands the numbers to be a convenient way to express only the CISO's and stakeholders' expert opinions of security needs.

Supporters of risk-based security also point out that risk assessments are required in much recent legislation such as in GLBA and SOX. My inquiries about how CISOs go about performing risk assessments to meet the requirements lead me to conclude that regulatory requirements easily can be met by performing a "very high level" assessment that in a few paragraphs describes the dangers that a corporation is most concerned about with appropriate caveats that much is unknown. Some risk assessments now consist of prioritizing which applications, systems, and networks are in most need of security attention because of their critical role in the business of the organization, especially in meeting the requirements of SOX.

Dave Cullinane, while he was CISO at Washington Mutual, on June 3, 2004 presented an ISSA chapter talk on meeting the SOX requirements. With his approval I paraphrase from my notes as follows:

> Risk assessment consists of identifying all applications in four levels of sensitivity relative to financial reporting and business records. The highest level consists of applications producing the final net value and performance of the bank. He found 85 applications at that level based on the advice of business managers. The other levels are for applications that feed into the next level. The lowest level consists of applications that process transactions and input data. New applications are being created throughout the bank continuously and represent an almost impossible challenge to keep up. He uses a diligence approach and spends time visiting and communicating with other CISOs and using benchmarking to determine generally accepted practices that he must have. He does no formal quantification of frequency and impact of incidents, and he explains the security needs to management in terms of diligence in meeting the requirements since SOX holds management responsible for the integrity and authenticity of the financial records.

"Security's Shaky State" in *Information Week*, December 5, 2005 stated that their latest survey of 1,522 responses from IT security administrators, managers, midlevel executives, and corporate executives indicates that IT security is underfunded, understaffed, and underrepresented. The top five drivers in that year's survey were improving business practices, auditing regulations, industry standards, security breaches from external sources (these are mostly certainties, not risks), and legislated regulations. The publication reported that the most pronounced shift from last year's survey is the increasing importance of compliance issues for assessing risk before information security purchases. Compliance hit the top spot as a risk assessment driver. CISOs must learn to "talk the talk" of compliance and move security from a technical control to a business control, and they don't see internal threats within the organization as their problem according to the article. The Computer Security Institute (CSI) *Alert* newsletter for December, 2005, in an article reporting on a panel of CISOs at the CSI 32nd annual conference, generally agreed that regulatory compliance, particularly in regard to Sarbanes-Oxley (SOX), is still the major driver of security efforts, despite being a hindrance to more thoughtful, comprehensive security management.

6.2.2 Alternatives to Security Risk Assessment

Justifying increased support for security by reporting to management that a security risk is measured to be a certain value (quantitatively or qualitatively) is folly. Management's business is risk-taking, and when a security risk is presented to them, they are able to respond that they take risks every day. And they simply accept the risk presented to them and refuse to support the security that is claimed may reduce it, especially when they see the negative impact and inconvenience that security has on the organization and their business goals. Everybody hates the constraints of security. When the reputed risk doesn't materialize into an adversity or some other larger unpredicted risk or adversity materializes instead, there is a justified loss of trust and belief in the validity of security risk assessment and those presenting it. Also, management is generally insightful and experienced enough to know that security people may exaggerate their findings or resort to unsupported guessing to justify their recommendations. These presumptions remain to be proved in the general case, but I have seen examples of all of them in my own experience.

On the other hand, if we present to top management (as I have in many security reviews for clients) that they should support security for reasons of achieving diligence to avoid negligence; compliance with law, audits, regulations, and contracts; and enablement; they have little reason to resist, and I find that they are more likely to approve recommendations based on my experience and the following reasoning:

Diligence

We can show management the results of our threat and vulnerability analyses by giving examples of the existence of similar threats and vulnerabilities that others have experienced and their solutions. Then we can show them easily researched benchmark comparisons of the state of their security relative to other well-run enterprises, and especially their competitors, under similar circumstances. We then show them what would have to be done to adopt others' good practices and safeguards to assure that they exceed, or are within the range of the other enterprises. This is based on 35 years of experience from the beginnings of information security of what others have done, and from what is available from the multibillion-dollar information security products and services industry. We also identify standards and well-accepted guides as the sources of good practices and safeguards. If management spurns any of our recommendations, we document this and the good business reasons for it to limit our and management's liability.

The ultimate motive here is avoiding management negligence (and possibly litigation) to achieve diligence and serendipitously possibly reduce risk as well.

Diligence need not result in mediocrity and failure to advance security by using old solutions. Every organization does some security well and some security poorly. Diligence takes the good that some do as a source of good practice and therefore spreads a higher level of security than would otherwise be obtained. We develop new security for new technology and against new adversities, and it also comes from the research and development in the information security industry motivated by profits, competition, existence of loss experience, and meeting customer needs. Diligence also need not be proven valid since the final results prove themselves from good or bad experience. And, the results are direct solutions. This is different from risk assessment where solutions don't come from assessment but must be chosen by diligence anyway and then tested again by further risk assessments.

Compliance

We are finding that the growing body of security compliance legislation such as SOX, GLBA, the Foreign Corrupt Practices Act, and HIPAA, and the associated personal and corporate liability of managers is rapidly becoming a strong and dominant security motivation. The FTC has already demonstrated their intent to regulate by applying significant penalties in a number of cases. (The current legislation is poorly written and has a sledge-hammer effect as written by unknowing legislative assistants but will improve with experience as has computer crime legislation.)

Enablement

It is easily shown in products and services planning that security is required for obvious and competitive purposes, such as the Microsoft experience of being forced by market and government pressures and litigation to build security into their products.

I find among my clients that top management is relieved by not having to deal with quantitative and qualitative risk assessments that are easily subject to question. They more readily accept, sometimes with resignation, the recommendations and demands required of them by the new tangible and measurable objectives of diligence, compliance, and enablement. This is especially the case when they hear about the deficiencies and requirements from internal and external auditors and regulators as well (who are also held to account in the legislation) and recognize the personal and corporate liability involved.

6.3   Conclusion

The bottom line is that no matter how elaborate or scientific the risk assessment methodology is, whether it is OCTAVE, FAIR, FRAP, NIST, or even Dr. Kevin Soo Hoo's approach, which is the most complete mathematical model of risk assessment methods ever developed, there are no sufficiently valid frequency and impact data that will make the results valid. Business managers can guess the frequency and impact of a rare adversity, but an event, vulnerability, circumstance, or perpetrator unknown to them can materially change the risk making any security decisions, or their implementations, the wrong ones done in the wrong ways at the wrong times. And the situation will get worse because of increasing complexity and change of technology, opportunities for crime, numbers and types of perpetrators, and potential for loss. We must not base our security on chance.

There is only one solution available to us. Replace intangible and unmanageable risk-based information security with security management based on diligence, compliance, and enablement. This can be accomplished without loss of integrity or reputation by rejecting the weak risk-based security guidance in trade and professional publications, perform only high-level general risk assessments when they are required, gradually eliminate the risk motivation and risk assessment requirements in our policies and practices, and emphasize and practice diligence, compliance, and enablement.

7

The Economics of Loss

Scott Borg

Risk and return on security investment (ROSI) are controversial topics. Donn Parker debunks the use of risk-based methods to evaluate and improve security. Others propound the concepts without really understanding them. I myself have written a fair amount on these topics and tend to take a middle path. That is to say, I think that the traditional methods are useful for determining security priorities and spending, but there are considerable deficiencies in the measuring and gathering of input data and these deficiencies need to be addressed head on.

Scott Borg takes an interesting approach in this chapter. He supports the risk-based approach but claims that, while the mathematics of risk analysis is fine, the calculations of the costs of security incidents often are way off. He propounds using a comprehensive "loss of value" approach. It is gratifying to see such a recommendation as I have been a proponent of value loss as the most meaningful measure of the cost of using, or not being able to use, economic goods and services ever since I wrote my dissertation on the effective use of computer resources.

What is particularly useful in this chapter is the way in which the author takes on a number of the most commonly held, but mistaken, beliefs and assumptions relating to loss of value. He contends that fixations on assets, market value, and productivity are all misguided. For example, it is common to consider the specific value of an asset when prioritizing which assets to protect most assiduously. However, an asset's intrinsic value may not relate to its value to the overall system and the value lost (or not created) were it to fail. The author gives some examples of this. I was reminded of the proverb (later quoted by Benjamin Franklin) about "for want of a nail, the kingdom was lost." It is so true that seemingly trivial omissions or failures can precipitate major disasters. Similar logic is applied to market value, which may not reflect the true value of an asset or facility to a particular individual in that its loss would cost much more than its price. Regarding productivity, we see how the value created by the same object, here a telephone, can vary greatly depending on context.

The net result is that the author shoots down many of the basic assumptions that many use when attempting to assign value to security and privacy, and suggests realistic concepts in their place.

—C.W.A.

7.1   Security as the Prevention of Loss

Security is ultimately about preventing losses. In fact, security could be defined as any measures people carry out to reduce their losses from illegal or abnormal events.

Economics drives security. It is the tool we use, with varying degrees of success, to quantify security decisions. We decide if a given security expenditure is warranted by comparing it to the scale of the losses it is expected to prevent. If a security measure costs more than the losses it is expected to prevent, then it isn't worth the expenditure. If a security measure costs less than the losses it is expected to prevent, and we place a high degree of confidence in its efficacy, then it probably is worth the expenditure. We choose among different security expenditures by deciding which ones we think will prevent the most losses per dollar spent. We try to achieve the greatest possible reduction in losses per dollar spent.

Anyone who makes reasonable decisions about security is making those decisions on economic grounds. When people fail to recognize this, it is generally because they think economics is limited to discussions of money and markets. But, economics is also concerned with production, its costs, and its benefits. The estimates of costs and benefits need not be monetary. They might, for example, be stated in terms of lives lost and lives saved. They might involve the quality of life.

Loss of privacy causes a loss of value from an economic standpoint. This is because privacy creates value, both directly and indirectly. It contributes directly to our quality of experience and our ability to make free choices. It contributes indirectly to our financial and personal security, since losing control of personal information makes us vulnerable to other crimes.

While economics does aspire to precision, it can also deal with situations where little precision is possible. The assessments of the quantities involved in the costs and benefits might be vague and intuitive. They might, for example, involve only a rough distinction between massive, unacceptable losses and moderate, acceptable losses. But, if security decisions are justified, they will always be founded on estimates that are quantitative and economic. They will involve weighing one set of costs or losses against another set of costs or losses.

7.2 Quantifying the Risk of Loss

The key to quantifying security is the concept of expected losses. We can calculate these expected losses:

1. By estimating the likelihood of a given type of security event in a given period of time (the *threat*);

2. By estimating the losses that could arise from that security event (the *consequence*); and,

3. By estimating the extent to which the event will cause those losses, given the existing security measures (the *vulnerability*).

These are risk factors in a mathematical sense. We can multiply them together to get the expected loss or risk. This gives us the classic risk equation:

$$\text{threat} \times \text{consequence} \times \text{vulnerability} = \text{risk}$$

In this equation, the threat will generally be stated as a probable number of incidents per year. The consequence will be stated as the possible cost per incident. The vulnerability will be stated as the probable extent to which the consequence will take place, given the defensive or mitigating measures that have been put into place. The risk will then be the annualized expected loss.

This basic risk equation can be formulated in a number of other ways that are mathematically and conceptually equivalent. In place of vulnerability, for example, some people like to substitute "1 minus mitigation," where the mitigation is the percentage by which the expected loss has been reduced. In place of three basic factors or categories, some people like to make two basic factors by multiplying one of the pairs together, before multiplying it by the third. Threat and consequence, for example, are sometimes multiplied together to yield hazard, which is then multiplied by vulnerability to yield risk. Alternatively, consequence and vulnerability can be multiplied together to yield expected loss per incident, which is then multiplied by the threat to yield risk. There are also various systems for allocating subordinate factors between the three categories, so that everything relevant is taken into account somewhere in the equation.

7.3 Refining the Basic Risk Equation

The basic risk equation usually needs to be refined a bit before it can be used to make practical budget decisions. This is mainly because in addition to estimating the probable loss, we need to have some idea of how probable it is that our estimate is correct. There are various methods of keeping track of our degree of confidence in our estimates. These methods result in a range of outcomes for each factor in the risk equation, with a probability assigned to each outcome.

There are also various methods of adjusting for the future value of money, so that costs today can be weighed against costs at different times in the future. These adjustments usually take account of the various interest charges that would be required to spend the same sum of money at various times. The interest rates employed in these calculations need to be adjusted for inflation, since it's the future purchasing power that the company cares about, not the nominal quantity of future dollars. Adjustments for the future value of money can also take account of probable changes in the value of money due to other factors. Some companies, for example, will want to consider the future value of money in the light of future exchange rates between currencies. The exact ways in which a company needs to adjust for the date at which it will spend money will ultimately depend on the nature of that company's cash flows.

Despite these possible refinements, the basic formula for making sense of risk is still essentially the same. It still comes down to an estimate of our expected losses over a given period of time, for different threats, under different policies.

7.4 The Problem of Quantifying Loss Itself

The core of the risk equation is the estimate of loss or "consequence." This is the number we most need in order to turn intuitive security assessments into actual economic calculations. Without some idea of how large the consequence would be, it is not worthwhile to talk about how frequently that consequence will occur or how much it can be reduced by security measures.

The key problem, then, is how to quantify this loss of value. Many publications on security economics get the basic risk equation right, although sometimes using different terminology. Once people know their expected losses under various conditions, it is not too hard to calculate the return-on-investment for various security measures. But, most of the existing literature on security economics doesn't explain how to calculate the costs or losses correctly. This is why when people try to make the case for increased security expenditures by quoting some amazingly high loss statistic, they get little response: most such claims have no credibility, because hardly anyone trusts the methods used to produce them.

When these calculations of cost go wrong, they tend to go wrong at the very beginning. The mathematics that's employed is fine. When there are relevant empirical data, the statistical analysis of those data is usually done correctly. But, the people doing the calculations frequently formulate the problem incorrectly, look at the wrong data, and have serious misconceptions about what their results will represent.

To avoid these mistakes, it is necessary to begin by talking about loss of value in a relatively comprehensive sense, rather than jumping directly to something like loss of profits, loss of assets, loss of customers, or loss of capitalization. By starting with a more comprehensive picture, we can take account of all the ways in which losses could be inflicted. Once we have identified the loss in value more broadly, we can then look at how that loss is felt by different parts of a business operation.

7.5   Confronting the Reality of Hypothetical Actions

From a business standpoint, any event that prevents a business from actively creating value needs to be counted as causing a loss of value. If a business is expected to create a certain amount of value in the next financial period, and a security event prevents it from doing so, then the loss involved is the reduction in value creation caused by that security event.

Security professionals sometimes complain that any estimates of the gains or losses from security measures need to be based on comparisons of what happened with what didn't happen. How is it possible, they say, to quantify what didn't happen? How can security professionals show how much they have contributed, when their entire contribution was simply to prevent something?

But this complaint is caused by a misconception about how business decisions are made. All business judgments are based on quantitative comparisons of what happened with what didn't happen. We judge the effectiveness of a marketing plan, a CEO, a product innovation, or any other business measure by comparing how the business did after employing that measure with how we expected the business to do if it hadn't employed that measure. We assess all business measures by quantifying things that didn't happen.

The problem with most of the methods currently employed for estimating loss of value is not that they deal with hypothetical events. The problem is that they are measuring the wrong things in the wrong places. By stopping to look at some of the mistakes that people habitually make when they try to estimate the losses from cyber and physical attacks, we can put this subject on a sounder foundation. Four of these mistakes that people make are especially illuminating.

Each mistake, once its fallacies are understood, leads directly to an indispensable component of the correct method.

7.6 Overcoming the Fixation on Assets

One of the biggest and most widespread mistakes is to think that what people lose, when they suffer a loss of value, are "assets." This is the notion behind the widespread belief that security programs should be designed to protect a company's assets. Indeed, the idea that security professionals should be protecting assets seems so self-evident that most security planners fail to notice the extent to which this policy ignores most what matters to a business.

In fact, there is little correlation between the value of an asset and the extent to which a business would be hurt by an attack on that asset. Often a large business operation can be shut down for weeks or caused to have huge liabilities by an attack on a piece of equipment that is in itself of little value. Imagine a physical attack that ruptures an inexpensive piece of piping or a cyber attack that causes a low-cost pressure gauge to give a false reading. If this attack causes a toxic gas to be released upwind of a large city, the result could be harm to thousands of people and bankruptcy for the company. Yet, the asset involved might be of little value.

The way to avoid this kind of mistake is to begin by looking at activities a business carries out to create value, not its static assets. Closely related to these activities are the ways a business could be caused to destroy value if it operated defectively. Instead of imagining that value resides in static assets, it is vital to understand that value is something created by the operations that a business carries out to turn inputs into outputs. Except in certain parts of the financial industry, what matters most is the value being created, not the value being stored.

7.7 Overcoming the Fixation on Market Value

Another of the biggest and most widespread mistakes is thinking that the value someone loses when they are deprived of something is the "market value" of that thing. This is another misconception that sounds so reasonable to people, they rarely stop to consider how rarely it is true.

Consider what the losses would be to you personally or to your company if you were deprived for a month of some basic product that you ordinarily take for granted, such as your telecommunications, your heating or air conditioning, your computers, your transportation, your medical care, or your food. Would the losses that you suffer be equal to the amount that you ordinarily pay each month for that type of product? Does the amount you pay each month for something like your telephone service represent even a good first approximation of what that service is worth to you? Of course not! Does the fact that diamonds are expensive mean that you would suffer a great loss if you were deprived of them? Unless your main activity is modeling jewelry, it's not likely. The fact is that market value of something has almost no relation to the losses that we would suffer if we were deprived of that thing.

What, then, do we use as a measuring point if we can't use the market value? The secret is to start with the "indifference points" that people use to decide whether a deal is worth doing.

For a customer, the indifference point is that customer's willingness-to-pay. If the customer is offered a price that is lower than his or her willingness-to-pay, the customer will make the purchase. If the customer is offered a price that is higher, then the customer won't make the purchase.

For a supplier, the indifference point is that supplier's opportunity cost. If the supplier is offered a price that is higher than its opportunity cost, then the supplier will make the sale. If the supplier is offered a price that is lower, then the supplier won't make the sale.

Both the customer's and the supplier's indifference points are determined by the best available alternative to the deal currently being offered. The customer's willingness-to-pay is determined by what that customer could do with the same resources if the customer didn't make that purchase. The supplier's opportunity cost is determined by what that supplier could do with the same resources if the supplier didn't make that sale. This means that both the willingness-to-pay and the opportunity cost are usually definite numbers. If there is a negotiation involved, the customer and the supplier will usually each go into the negotiation with a pretty definite idea of the maximum or minimum price that would be acceptable.

These indifference points mark the endpoints of a unified business activity that turns inputs into outputs. They determine whether that activity is worth carrying out. The fact that we can usually tell whether an activity is worth carrying out means we are already able to estimate, at least roughly, the amount of value created by a business activity.

This business activity is the core of economics. All of the other economic components are defined, at least implicitly, in relation to this business activity. The customers are whoever receives the outputs of that business activity and pays for those outputs. The suppliers are whoever supplies the inputs to that business activity and is paid for those inputs. Markets are the forums in which suppliers are matched with customers, and in which alternative suppliers or alternative customers can be substituted.

The precise value created by any business activity is the willingness-to-pay of the customers, minus the opportunity costs of the suppliers.

The actual price in any deal is the point at which the value created is divided between the supplier and the customer. Price isn't as fundamental as willingness-to-pay and opportunity cost. But, it is still vitally important, because an individual company's share of the value being created is determined by the way prices divide up that value. The value captured by the supplier is the price, minus the opportunity cost. The value captured by the customer is the willingness-to-pay, minus the price.

Although companies will be most concerned with the value that they are capturing, they also need to have some idea of how much overall value they and their trading partners together are creating by their deals. Without this knowledge, companies will not be able to foresee the way prices could change as a result of security events. Hence, without the broader picture of value creation, companies will not be able to estimate their own potential losses.

7.8   Overcoming the Fixation on Productivity

Yet another big and widespread mistake is to think that value creation and value destruction can be understood in terms of the productivity of individual components. Those taking this approach usually try to assign a productivity rate to a given type of equipment or system. Next, they measure how long that equipment was shut down as a result of the security event. Then they multiply the productivity rate times the length of time the equipment was shut down. If the people applying this method incorporate a lot of empirical data, they can make it sound as though they are doing something reasonable until someone asks a "dumb question," such as, "how much value is that piece of equipment over there actually creating?"

Suppose the piece of equipment is a telephone. The amount of value that telephone is being used to create depends entirely on who is using it and what that person is using it for. A telephone that is used by the company president to negotiate the company's biggest deals has a very different level of productivity than a telephone in a storage room that people have forgotten is there. A telephone in the trading room of a financial services firm has a very different level of productivity than a phone in the office that sells money orders and travelers' checks.

In addition, the amount of value created by a piece of equipment depends on its marginal productivity. If a telephone is the last one put in service or the first one taken out of service, its marginal productivity might be scarcely more than zero. If that telephone is unavailable, another can easily substitute. On the other hand, if the telephone is the last one the company has that is still working, its marginal value might be enormous. In fact, in certain circumstances, the very survival of the company could depend on it.

And that brings up another condition: the value created by a piece of equipment depends entirely on the market environment in which it is being operated. If there is no demand at that moment for whatever the company produces, then the value being created at that moment by every piece of equipment in the company might be almost nothing. A telephone can't create any value if no one needs to call in or out. Alternatively, if the market conditions are such that every company in that market can sell everything it can produce, then the slightest reduction of capacity caused by any piece of equipment being unavailable might have an immediate impact on the company's total profits.

These points might sound obvious, but people who try to calculate the value lost or created by adding up the productivity of individual pieces of equipment are ignoring every one of them.

The remedy is to start with the value created by the entire business operation, rather than trying to figure out the value created by adding up the parts. Then, after assessing the larger business operation, it is possible to determine how much that larger operation would be disrupted by damage to one of its contributing parts.

7.9   Overcoming the Neglect of Substitutes

A final big and widespread mistake is to forget to pay adequate attention to what substitutes. This is the mistake that is being committed every time someone states what system or activity was lost without also stating what system or activity replaced it. Often a piece of equipment will be put out of commission, but the people responsible for the operations will find an ingenious work-around that will allow them to continue the operations anyway. Even when the larger operation needs to be shut down for a period of time, the people and equipment will often do something else useful, such as catching up on maintenance, stock inventories, or clerical work. The substitute activities may create considerably less value than the normal activities that were interrupted. But, the value they create is usually far from negligible, and it may be a large portion of the value that would have been created ordinarily.

Any estimate of loss that doesn't take account of the substitute activities is likely to be highly inaccurate. Something always substitutes, even though it may be very different from whatever it is replacing.

The remedy is to assume that the loss calculation will always be a relative one. The value lost as a result of an attack can only be calculated by taking the value created before the attack and subtracting the value created after. If this isn't a central part of the loss calculation, then that calculation must be regarded as incomplete.

Interestingly enough, it is often possible to estimate the drop in the value created without knowing the absolute quantity of value created before or after the attack. This is because there will often be an unknown portion of value created that remains essentially unaffected by the attack. In such cases, subtracting the value created after the attack will also subtract the portion of the value created that is unknown.

7.10 Taking Account of the Duration and Extent of the Effects

The principles already described give us most of the guidance we need for calculating the value destroyed by an attack. We know how to estimate the value being created before the attack, and how to subtract the value created after the attack.

The total value that is lost, both at the level of the individual company and at the level of the market, depends not just on the degree to which the value ordinarily created by a business is being destroyed, but also on the duration of the destruction. This means that it is vital to identify all the effects that would have lasting consequences: irrevocably lost opportunities, possible damage to business relationships, or lasting damage to production capabilities.

For an individual business, one of the effects of a security event that is especially likely to cause persisting losses is damage to business relationships. The strength of these relationships can be measured by the total switching costs that a trading partner would need to pay in order to replace that customer or supplier with another one. Switching costs for customers include things like researching a new product, establishing a new account, educating the new supplier about the company's special needs, training employees in the somewhat different procedures necessary to utilize the new product, adapting or replacing other products and systems that need to be made compatible with the new product, and accepting the risks of a less familiar supplier. There is a similar, partially symmetrical list of switching costs for a supplier.

A security event causes lasting damages to relationships by forcing the company's trading partners to pay part or all of the switching costs that would allow them to move their business to a new customer or supplier. Even the threat of losing a customer or supplier will cause companies to spend part of the switching costs, so that they will be ready if their previous customer or supplier becomes unavailable to them. If a company needs to shut down its operations for a significant period of time, its trading partners may need to start doing business with an alternative customer or supplier. This may force the trading partners to pay out most of the total switching costs.

Once business relationships have been lost or damaged, the consequent losses can be very long term. Even a slightly damaged business relationship may force the company deemed unreliable to lower its prices. Meanwhile, a lost business relationship may cause the company to lose the total value it would have captured from doing business with that trading partner over the entire period of that relationship. This is a loss that can be estimated by assessing the probable life span of such relationships without any significant security events.

In addition to considering the duration of the destruction, it is also important to trace how far the damage extends. For the individual business, this means looking at potential liabilities. For the larger economy, this means looking at the knock-on effects. It is easy, in assessing losses, to consider too narrow a range of effects and to overlook consequences that are less direct.

7.11 Distinguishing Between the Different Business Categories of Attacks

This entire analysis of costs needs to be founded on a clear understanding of what security events can do to a business. Here, it is necessary to distinguish sharply between indiscriminant, natural events and highly discriminant, malicious events. Indiscriminant, natural events usually interrupt operations and require extra expenditures to put things back in order. Discriminant, malicious events can harm businesses in a wider variety of ways.

From a business standpoint, there are four things an attack can do:

1. The attack can interrupt the business operations;
2. The attack can cause the business operations to be carried out in a defective way;
3. The attack can discredit certain business operations, so that they are abandoned;
4. The attack can undermine the basis for the business operations so that they can no longer be carried out profitably.

In practice, each of these four business effects of attacks needs to be analyzed somewhat differently, and each results in very different cost curves over time.

The classic information assurance categories (availability, confidentiality, integrity) are not useful categories for understanding the business effect of cyber attacks, because they only identify the mechanism, not the consequences. With a bit of imagination, it is possible to see how a breakdown in any of the information assurance categories could be used to produce any of the business consequences. Breakdowns in availability, for example, could be used to discredit a business operation. Breakdowns in confidentiality could be used to interrupt a business operation. There is no close relationship between the information assurance categories and their business effects.

7.12 Putting the Proper Risk Estimates Back into the ROI Calculation

Once the quantification of consequences described here is inserted into the existing analyses of risks, it becomes possible to start calculating the ROIs for security correctly. In addition to providing the central term in the risk calculation, a clear and quantitative understanding of consequences allows the estimates of the threats and the vulnerabilities to be made much more precise. This can provide a sound economic basis for decisions and policies regarding security and privacy.

8

Legal and Regulatory Obligations

Thomas J. Smedinghoff

Although computer crime has been rampant since the dawn of the silicon age, day-to-day legal involvement in information security processes is a relatively recent phenomenon. Tom's article describes how the legal profession has developed an activist's interest in the cause of defending corporate assets as well as protecting customer privacy using the sword of due diligence. Tom's textbook knowledge of security and privacy law allows him to succinctly describe why companies need to pay attention to the evolving legislative landscape on security and privacy. The history of security and privacy concerns covered in Part I has left us with the legal and regulatory landscape he depicts. His legal advice for risk mitigation (not surprisingly) foreshadows many of the practitioner approaches in Part III.

Information security is rapidly emerging as one of the most important legal issues facing companies today. Concerns regarding corporate governance, individual privacy, accountability for financial information, the authenticity and integrity of transaction data, and the security of sensitive business data are driving the enactment of new laws and regulations designed to ensure that businesses adequately address the security of their own data. These legislative and regulatory initiatives are imposing obligations on all businesses to implement information security measures to protect their own data and to disclose breaches of security that do occur.

In particular, legal developments in three key areas are rapidly shaping the information security landscape for most companies in the United States, and are having a significant impact on international law as well. They are:

- A continuing expansion of the duty to provide security;

- The emergence of a legal standard for compliance; and

- The imposition of a duty to warn.

Although the law is still in evolving, and is often applied only in selective areas, the developments in these three areas are imposing significant new obligations and risks on most businesses.

—J.L.B.

8.1   The Expanding Duty to Provide Security

8.1.1   Where Does It Come From?

There is no single law, statute, or regulation that governs a company's obligations to provide security for its information. Corporate legal obligations to implement security measures are set forth in an ever-expanding patchwork of state, federal, and international laws, regulations, and enforcement actions, as well as common law duties and other express and implied obligations to provide "reasonable" or "appropriate" security for corporate data.

Some laws seek to protect the company and its shareholders, investors, and business partners. Others focus on the interests of individual employees, customers, and prospects. And, in other cases, governmental regulatory interests, or evidentiary requirements are at stake. Many of the requirements are industry-specific (e.g., focused on the financial industry or the healthcare industry) or data-specific (e.g., focused on personal information or financial data). Others focus only on public companies.

When viewed as a group, however, they provide ever-expanding coverage of most corporate activity. The most common sources of obligations to provide security include the following:[1]

Statutes and Regulations

Numerous statutes and regulations impose obligations to provide security. Some of the most common sources of statutes and regulations with such requirements include:

- Privacy laws and regulations that require companies to implement information security measures to protect certain personal data they maintain about individuals;

---

1. See Appendix A for a compilation of some of the key laws and regulations governing information security.

- E-transaction laws designed to ensure the enforceability and compliance of electronic documents generally;
- Corporate governance legislation and regulations designed to protect public companies and their shareholders, investors, and business partners;
- Unfair business practice laws and related government enforcement actions;
- Sector-specific regulations imposing security obligations with respect to specific categories of data (e.g., tax records).

A list of some of the more common statutes and regulations governing the security of personal data is set forth in Appendix A.

Common Law Obligations

For years, commentators have argued that there exists a common law duty to provide appropriate security for corporate data, the breach of which constitutes a tort. Courts are now beginning to accept that view.[2]

Rules of Evidence

Recent court decisions also suggest that security will increasingly be a requirement for the admissibility of digital records.[3]

Industry Standards

In some cases, companies become obligated to comply with the requirements of certain technical security standards. Examples include the Payment Card Industry Data Security Standard (PCI Standard)[4] that merchants must agree to as a condition of accepting credit cards, the EV SSL Guidelines[5] that certification authorities must agree to in order to issue EV SSL certificates, and the international ISO/IEC 27001 Standard[6] sometimes imposed on businesses by contract with trading partners. In each of these cases, the standard has no legal authority by itself, but becomes binding typically through a contractual agreement. In some cases, however, such as in Japan, compliance with a particular standard (in that case, ISO/IEC 27001) may be required by regulation.

---

2. Some of the recent cases to accept this view are listed in Appendix A, Part E.
3. See, e.g., American Express v. Vinhnee, 2005 Bankr. Lexis 2602 (9th Cir. Bk. App. Panel, 2005); Lorraine v. Markel, 2007 U.S. Dist. Lexis 33020 (D. MD. May 4, 2007).
4. Available at www.pcisecuritystandards.org.
5. Available at www.cabforum.org
6. ISO/IEC 27001, Information Technology—Security Techniques—Information Security Management Systems—Requirements (Oct. 2005) (hereinafter "ISO/IEC 27001"), available for purchase at http://www.standards-online.net/InformationSecurityStandard.htm.

Contractual Obligations

As businesses increasingly become aware of the need to protect the security of their own data, they frequently try to satisfy their obligation (at least in part) by contract in those situations where third parties will have possession of, or access to, their business data. This is particularly common, for example, in outsourcing agreements where a company's data will be processed by a third party.

Self-Imposed Obligations

In many cases, security obligations are self-imposed. Through statements in privacy policies, on websites, or in advertising materials, for example, companies often make representations regarding the level of security they provide for their data (particularly the personal data they collect from the persons to whom the statements are made). By making such statements, companies impose on themselves an obligation to comply with the standard they have represented to the public that they meet. If those statements are not true, or if they are misleading, such statements may become, in effect, deceptive trade practices under Section 5 of the FTC Act, or under equivalent state laws.

The bottom line is that a company's duty to provide security may come from several different sources—each perhaps regulating a different aspect of corporate information—but the net result (and certainly the trend) is the imposition of a general obligation to provide security for all corporate data and information systems.

8.1.2 What Is Covered?

When addressing the security of corporate information, all types of information need be considered. This includes financial information, personal information, tax-related records, employee information, transaction information, and trade secret and other confidential information.

8.1.2.1 Personal Data

The obligation to provide adequate security for personal data collected, used, and/or maintained by a business is a critical component of all privacy laws.

In Europe, the legal duty to provide security for the protection of personal information is one of the key principles set forth in the EU Data Protection Directive.[7] It recognizes that the protection of the rights of data subjects with respect to the processing of their personal data require the implementation of appropriate security measures.[8] Accordingly, the directive requires that EU

---

7. Directive 95/46/EC of the European Parliament and of the Council of 24 October 1995 on the protection of individuals with regard to the processing of personal data and on the free movement of such data (hereinafter "EU Data Protection Directive").

member states enact legislation obligating the controllers of personal data to "implement appropriate technical and organizational measures to protect personal data against accidental or unlawful destruction or accidental loss, alteration, unauthorized disclosure or access, in particular where the processing involves the transmission of data over a network, and against all other unlawful forms of processing."[9]

Subsequent EU country implementations of the directive generally impose such a requirement for security.[10] Numerous other country privacy laws (which also tend to take on omnibus approach to privacy, like the EU) also impose a general duty on all companies to protect the security of personal information. Examples include Canada, Japan, Argentina, South Korea, Hong Kong, and Australia.[11]

Likewise, in the United States protecting personal information is the focus of numerous federal and state laws. These include sector-specific privacy laws such as the Gramm-Leach-Bliley Act (GLB Act) in the financial sector, the Health Insurance Portability and Accountability Act (HIPAA) in the healthcare sector, and the Privacy Act of 1974 applicable to the federal government, as well as numerous more general state laws as outlined in the Appendix.

8.1.2.2 Most Other Corporate Data

Security obligations are also expanding to cover most other types of corporate data. These include, for example

- *Corporate Financial Data:* Corporate governance legislation and caselaw designed to protect the company and its shareholders, investors, and business partners, such as Sarbanes-Oxley and implementing regulations, require public companies to ensure that they have implemented appropriate information security controls with respect to their financial information.[12] Similarly, several SEC regulations impose a variety of requirements for internal controls over information systems.

- *Transaction Records:* E-transaction laws designed to ensure the enforceability and compliance of electronic documents generally—both the federal and state electronic transaction statutes (E-SIGN and

---

8. EU Data Protection Directive, Preamble at Para. 46.

9. EU Data Protection Directive, Article 17(1).

10. See statutes listed in Appendix A, at Part I

11. See statutes listed in Appendix A, at Part J.

12. See generally, Bruce H. Nearon, Jon Stanley, Steven W. Teppler, and Joseph Burton, Life after Sarbanes-Oxley: The Merger of Information Security and Accountability, 45 Jurimetrics Journal 379-412 (2005).

UETA) require all companies to provide security for storage of electronic records relating to online transactions.

- *Tax Records:* IRS regulations require companies to implement information security to protect electronic tax records, and as a condition to engaging in certain electronic transactions.
- *E-Mail:* SEC regulations address security in a variety of contexts, such as retention of e-mail.

8.1.2.3 All Digital Evidence

Providing appropriate security to ensure the integrity of electronic records will likely be critical to securing the admission of the electronic record in evidence in a future dispute.

The Federal Court of Appeals decision in the case of *American Express v. Vinhnee* [13] suggests that appropriate security is a condition for the admissibility in evidence of electronic records. In that case, the court refused to admit electronic records into evidence because American Express did not adequately establish that they were "authentic."

According to the court, the primary authenticity issue for admissibility is establishing "what has, or may have, happened to the record in the interval between when it was placed in the files and the time of trial." And to do this, the court said, "one must demonstrate that the record that has been retrieved from the file, be it paper or electronic, is the same as the record that was originally placed into the file."[14] Thus, the Court required a showing that appropriate security was in place to ensure the integrity of the electronic records from the time they were created until the time that they were introduced in court.

8.2 The Emergence of a Legal Standard for Compliance

The general legal obligation to provide security for data is often simply as an obligation to provide "reasonable" or "appropriate" security designed to achieve certain objectives. In some cases, statutes and regulations define those objectives in terms of positive results to be achieved, such as ensuring the *availability* of systems and information, controlling *access* to systems and information, and ensuring the *confidentiality, integrity,* and *authenticity* of information.[15] In other

---

13. American Express v. Vinhnee, 336 B.R. 437; 2005 Bankr. Lexis 2602 (9th Cir. December 16, 2006).

14. Id. at p. 444.

15. See, e.g., Homeland Security Act of 2002 (Federal Information Security Management Act of 2002) 44 U.S.C. Section 3542(b)(1); GLBA Security Regulations (OCC), 12 C.F.R. Part 30

cases, they define those objectives in terms of the harms to be avoided (e.g., to protect systems and information against unauthorized access, use, disclosure or transfer, modification or alteration, unlawful processing, and accidental loss or destruction).[16] And in some cases, no objectives are stated.

Laws and regulations rarely specify what specific security measures a business should implement to satisfy those legal obligations.[17] Most laws simply obligate the company to establish and maintain internal security "procedures," "controls," "safeguards," or "measures"[18] directed toward achieving the goals or objectives identified above, but often without any further direction or guidance.

In Europe, for example, the EU Data Protection Directive requires the controllers of personal data to:

> implement *appropriate* technical and organizational measures to protect personal data against accidental or unlawful destruction or accidental loss, alteration, unauthorized disclosure or access, in particular where the processing involves the transmission of data over a network, and against all other unlawful forms of processing.[19]

Thus, country implementations of the EU Data Protection Directive generally require the use of security measures that are *appropriate* to protect the personal data[20] or that are *necessary* to protect the personal data.[21]

Appendix B, Part II.B; HIPAA Security Regulations, 45 C.F.R. Section 164.306(a)(1); Microsoft Consent Decree at II, p. 4.

16. See, e.g., FISMA, 44 U.S.C. Section 3542(b)(1). Most of the foreign privacy laws also focus their security requirements from this perspective. This includes, for example, the EU Privacy Directive, and the privacy laws of Canada, Finland, Italy, and the UK.

17. Although they often focus on categories of security measures to address. See, e.g., HIPAA Security Regulations, 45 C.F.R. Part 164.

18. See, e.g., FDA regulations at 21 C.F.R. Part 11 (procedures and controls); SEC regulations at 17 C.F.R. 257.1(e)(3) (procedures); SEC regulations at 17 C.F.R. 240.17a-4 (controls); GLB regulations (FTC) 16 C.F.R. Part 314 (safeguards); Canada, Personal Information Protection and Electronic Documents Act, Schedule I, Section 4.7 (safeguards); EU Data Privacy Directive, Article 17(1) (measures).

19. EU Data Protection Directive, Article 17(1) (emphasis added).

20. See, e.g., the privacy laws listed in Appendix A, Part I for Belgium, Chapter IV, Article 16(4); Denmark, Title IV, Part 11, Section 41(3); Estonia, Chapter 3, Sections 19(2); Greece, Article 10(3); Ireland, Section 2.-(1)(d) and First Schedule Article 7; Lithuania, Article 24(1); Netherlands, Article 13; Portugal, Article 14(1); Slovakia, Section 15(1); Sweden, Section 31; and the UK, Schedule 1, Part I, Seventh Principle.

21. See, e.g., the privacy laws listed in Appendix A, Part I for Finland, Section 32(1); Germany, Section 9; Hungary, Article 10(1); Italy, Sections 31 and 33; and Spain, Article 9.

In the United States, HIPAA requires "reasonable and appropriate" security,[22] and the GLBA security regulations require covered financial institutions to "implement a comprehensive written information security program that includes administrative, technical, and physical safeguards *appropriate* to the size and complexity of the bank and the nature and scope of its activities."[23] Likewise, state personal information security laws, such as in California, generally require "reasonable security procedures and practices."[24]

8.2.1 The Developing Legal Definition of "Reasonable Security"

Although laws requiring that companies implement "reasonable" or "appropriate" security leave businesses with little or no guidance as to what is required for legal compliance, developments over the past few years suggest that a legal standard for "reasonable" security is clearly emerging. That standard rejects requirements for specific security measures (such as firewalls, passwords, antivirus software, or the like), and instead adopts a fact-specific approach to corporate security obligations that requires a "process" applied to the unique facts of each case.

Rather than telling companies what specific security measures they must implement, the legal trend is to require companies to implement a comprehensive information security program based on an ongoing and repetitive process that is designed to assess risks, and then identify and implement appropriate security measures responsive to those risks. The decision regarding the specific security measures is then left up to the company.

The essence of this risk-based process-oriented approach to security compliance is implementation of a comprehensive program that requires a company to:

- Identify its information assets;
- Conduct periodic risk assessments to identify the specific threats and vulnerabilities the company faces;
- Develop and implement a security program to manage and control the risks identified;
- Address employee training and education;

---

22. 42 U.S.C. 1320d-2(d)(2).

23. See, Gramm-Leach-Bliley Act ("GLBA"), Public Law 106-102, §§ 501 and 505(b), 15 U.S.C. §§ 6801, 6805, and implementing regulations at 12 C.F.R. Part 30, Appendix B (OCC), 12 C.F.R. Part 208, Appendix D (Federal Reserve System), 12 C.F.R. Part 364, Appendix B (FDIC), 12 C.F.R. Part 568 (Office of Thrift Supervision) and 16 C.F.R. Part 314 (FTC) (emphasis added).

24. Cal. Civil Code § 1798.81.5(b).

- Monitor and test the program to ensure that it is effective;
- Continually review and adjust the program in light of ongoing changes, including obtaining regular independent audits and reporting where appropriate; and
- Oversee third party service provider arrangements.

A key aspect of this process is recognition that it is never completed. It is ongoing, and must be continually reviewed, revised, and updated. The process for "reasonable" security can be summarized as follows:

8.2.1.1 Identification of Information Assets

The first step in implementing a comprehensive security program is to define the scope of the effort. What information, communications, and processes are to be protected? What information systems are involved? Where are they located? What laws potentially apply to them? As is often the case, little known but sensitive data files are found in a variety of places within the company. Deciding "how" to protect information begins with determining "what" needs to be protected.

8.2.1.2 Periodic Risk Assessment

Determining how to protect these information assets requires a thorough assessment of the potential risks to a company's information systems and data. This involves identifying all reasonably foreseeable internal and external threats to the information assets to be protected.

For each identified threat, the company should then evaluate the risk posed by the threat by:

- Assessing the likelihood that the threat will materialize;
- Evaluating the potential damage that will result if it materializes;
- Assessing the sufficiency of the policies, procedures, and safeguards in place to guard against the threat.[25]

Such risk should be evaluated in light of the nature of the organization, its transactional capabilities, the sensitivity and value of the stored information to the organization and its trading partners, and the size and volume of its transactions.[26]

---

25. See, e.g., FISMA, 44 U.S.C. Sections 3544(a)(2)(A) and 3544(b)(1); GLB Security Regulations, 12 C.F.R. Part 30, Appendix B, Part III.B(2)

26. See, e.g., Authentication In An Electronic Banking Environment, July 30, 2001, Federal Financial Institutions Examination Council, page 2; available at www.occ.treas.gov/ftp/advisory/2001-8a.pdf.

This process will be the baseline against which security measures can be selected, implemented, measured, and validated. The goal is to understand the risks the business faces, and determine what level of risk is acceptable, in order to identify appropriate and cost-effective safeguards to combat that risk.

This risk assessment process plays a key role in determining whether a duty will be imposed and liability found. In *Wolfe v. MBNA America Bank,* for example, a federal court held that where injury resulting from negligent issuance of a credit card (to someone who applied using the plaintiff's identity) is foreseeable and preventable, "the defendant has a duty to verify the authenticity and accuracy of a credit account application."[27] In *Bell v. Michigan Council,* the court held that where a harm was foreseeable, and the potential severity of the risk was high, the defendant was liable for failure to provide appropriate security to address the potential harm.[28] On the other hand, in *Guin v. Brazos Education,* the court held that where a proper risk assessment was done, but a particular harm was not reasonably foreseeable, the defendant would not be liable for failure to defend against it.[29]

The law does not generally specify what is required for a risk assessment. But, the federal banking regulators have referred financial institutions seeking general information on risk assessments to:[30] (1) the "Small Entity Compliance Guide for the Interagency Guidelines Establishing Information Security Standards,"[31] and (2) the "FFIEC IT Examination Handbook, Information Security Booklet."[32] The National Institute of Standards and Technology (NIST) also offers guidance on conducting risk assessments.[33]

---

27. Wolfe v. MBNA America Bank, 485 F.Supp.2d 874, 882 (W.D. Tenn. 2007).

28. See Bell v. Michigan Council, 2005 Mich. App. Lexis 353 (Mich. App. February 15, 2005).

29. See Guin v. Brazos Higher Education Service, Civ. No. 05-668, 2006 U.S. Dist. Lexis 4846 at *13 (D. Minn. Feb. 7, 2006) (finding that where a proper risk assessment was done, the inability to foresee and deter a specific burglary of a laptop was not a breach of a duty of reasonable care).

30. "Frequently Asked Questions on FFIEC Guidance on Authentication in an Internet Banking Environment," August 8, 2006 at p. 5, available at www.ffiec.gov/pdf/authentication_faq.pdf. The Federal Financial Institutions Examinations Counsel (FFIEC) is a group of U.S. federal regulatory agencies, that include the Board of Governor's of the Federal Reserve System, Federal Deposit Insurance Corporation, the National Credit Union Administration, the Office of the Comptroller of the Currency, and the Office of Thrift Supervision.

31. Small Entity Compliance Guide for the Interagency Guidelines Establishing Information Security Standards, December 14, 2005, available at www.federalreserve.gov/boarddocs/press/bcreg/2005/20051214/default.htm.

32. FFIEC IT Examination Handbook, Information Security Booklet, July 2006, available at www.ffiec.gov/ffiecinfobase/booklets/information_security/information_security.pdf.

33. See National Institute of Standards and Technology, "Risk Management Guide for Information Technology Systems," NIST Special Publication No. 800-30; available at http://csrc.nist.gov/publications/nistpubs/800-30/sp800-30.pdf.

8.2.1.3 Develop Security Program to Manage and Control Risk

Based on the results of the risk assessment, the law requires a business to design and implement a security program consisting of appropriate physical, technical, and administrative security measures to manage and control the risks identified during the risk assessment.[34] The security program should be in writing,[35] and should be coordinated among all parts of the organization. It should be designed to provide reasonable safeguards to control the identified risks (i.e., to protect against any anticipated threats or hazards to the security or integrity of the information and systems to be protected). The goal is to reduce the risks and vulnerabilities to a reasonable and appropriate level.[36]

In other words, it is not enough merely to implement impressive-sounding security measures. Posting armed guards around a building, or requiring key-card access, for example, may give the appearance of security. But, if the primary threat the company faces is unauthorized remote access to its data via the Internet, these physical security measures are of little value. Likewise, firewalls and intrusion detection software are often effective ways to stop hackers and protect sensitive databases, but if a company's major vulnerability is careless (or malicious) employees who inadvertently (or intentionally) disclose passwords or protected information, then even those sophisticated technical security measures, although important, will not adequately address the problem.

In determining what security measures should be implemented within a particular organization, virtually all of the existing precedent recognizes that there is no "one size fits all" approach. Which security measures are appropriate for a particular organization will vary, depending upon a variety of factors, including:

- The probability and criticality of potential risks;

- The company's size, complexity, and capabilities;

- The nature and scope of the business activities;

- The nature and sensitivity of the information to be protected;

---

34. See, e.g., GLB Security Regulations (OCC), 12 C.F.R. Part 30 Appendix B, Part II.A; Eli Lilly Decision at II.B; HIPAA Security Regulations, 45 C.F.R. Section 164.308(a)(1)(i); Federal Information Security Management Act of 2002 (FISMA), 44 U.S.C. Section 3544(b); Microsoft Consent Decree at II, p. 4 (cited in Appendix at Part F).

35. See, e.g., GLB Security Regulations, 12 C.F.R. Part 30 Appendix B, Part II.A; HIPAA Security Regulations, 45 C.F.R. Section 164.316(b)(1); Federal Information Security Management Act of 2002 (FISMA), 44 U.S.C. Section 3544(b); Microsoft Consent Decree at II, p. 4 (cited in Appendix at Part F).

36. See, e.g., HIPAA Security Regulations, 45 C.F.R. Section 164.308(a)(1)(ii)(B).

- The company's technical infrastructure, hardware, and software security capabilities;

- The state-of-the art technology and security;

- The costs of the security measures.

This focus on flexibility means that, ensuring compliance may ultimately become more difficult, as there are unlikely to be any safe-harbors for security. As stated in the HIPAA security regulations, for example, companies "may use any security measures" reasonably designed to achieve the objectives specified in the regulations.[37]

8.2.1.4   Awareness, Training, and Education

Training and education for employees is a critical component of any security program. Newer statutes and regulations clearly recognize that even the very best physical, technical, and administrative security measures are of little value if employees do not understand their roles and responsibilities with respect to security. For example, installing heavy duty doors with state of the art locks (whether of the physical or virtual variety), will not provide the intended protection if the employees authorized to have access leave the doors open and unlocked for unauthorized persons to pass through.

Security education begins with communication to employees of applicable security policies, procedures, standards, and guidelines. It also includes implementing a security awareness program,[38] periodic security reminders, and developing and maintaining relevant employee training materials,[39] such as user education concerning virus protection, password management, and how to report discrepancies. Applying appropriate sanctions against employees who fail to comply with security policies and procedures is also important.[40]

8.2.1.5   Monitoring and Testing

Merely implementing security measures is not sufficient. Companies must also ensure that the security measures have been properly put in place and are effective. This includes conducting an assessment of the sufficiency of the security measures and conducting regular testing or monitoring of the effectiveness of

---

37. HIPAA Security Regulations, 45 CFR Section 164.306(b)(1).

38. See, e.g., FISMA, 44 U.S.C. Section 3544(b)(4); HIPAA Security Regulations, 45 C.F.R. Section 164.308(a)(5)(i); Ziff Davis Assurance of Discontinuance, Para. 24(d), p. 5 (cited in Appendix at Part F).

39. Ziff Davis Assurance of Discontinuance, Para. 27(c), p. 7.

40. HIPAA Security Regulations, 45 C.F.R. Section 164.308(a)(1)(ii)(C).

those measures.[41] Existing precedent also suggests that a company must monitor compliance with its security program.[42] To that end, a regular review of records of system activity, such as audit logs, access reports, and security incident tracking reports[43] is also important.

8.2.1.6 Review and Adjustment

Perhaps most significantly, the legal standard for information security recognizes that security is a moving target. Businesses must constantly keep up with every changing threats, risks and vulnerabilities, as well as with the security measures available to respond to them. It is a never-ending process. As a consequence, businesses must conduct periodic internal reviews to evaluate and adjust the information security program[44] in light of:

- The results of the testing and monitoring;
- Any material changes to the business or arrangements;
- Any changes in technology;
- Any changes in internal or external threats;
- Any environmental or operational changes;
- Any other circumstances that may have a material impact.[45]

In addition to periodic internal reviews, best practices and the developing legal standard may require that businesses obtain a periodic review and assessment (audit) by qualified independent third-party professionals using procedures and standards generally accepted in the profession to certify that the security program meets or exceeds applicable requirements, and is operating with sufficient effectiveness to provide reasonable assurances that the security, confidentiality, and integrity of information is protected.[46]

---

41. FISMA, 44 U.S.C. Section 3544(b)(5); Eli Lilly Decision at II.C; GLB Security Regulations, 12 C.F.R. Part 30, Appendix B, Part III(c)(3).

42. Ziff Davis Assurance of Discontinuance, Para. 27(e) and (f), p. 7; Eli Lilly Decision at II.C (cited in Appendix at Part F).

43. HIPAA Security Regulations, 45 C.F.R. Section 164.308(a)(1)(ii)(D).

44. GLB Security Regulations, 12 C.F.R. Part 30, Appendix B, Part III.E; HIPAA Security Regulations, 45 C.F.R. Section 164.306(e) and 164.308(a)(8); and Microsoft Consent Decree at II, p. 4; Ziff Davis Assurance of Discontinuance, Para. 27(e) and (f), p. 7; Eli Lilly Decision at II.D (cited in Appendix at Part F).

45. GLB Security Regulations, 12 C.F.R. Part 30 Appendix B, Part II.E; HIPAA Security Regulations, 45 C.F.R. Section 164.308(a)(8); and Microsoft Consent Decree at II, p. 4; and Eli Lilly Decision at II.D (cited in Appendix at Part F).

46. Microsoft Consent Decree at III, p. 5 (cited in Appendix at Part F).

It should then adjust the security program in light of the findings or recommendations that come from such reviews.[47]

8.2.1.7   Oversee Third-Party Service Provider Arrangements

Finally, because companies often rely on third parties, such as outsource providers, to handle much of their data, laws and regulations imposing information security obligations often expressly address requirements with respect to the use of third-party outsource providers. First and foremost, they make clear that regardless of who performs the work, the legal obligation to provide the security itself remains with the company. As it is often said, "you can outsource the work, but not the responsibility." Thus, third-party relationships should be subject to the same risk management, security, privacy, and other protection policies that would be expected if a business were conducting the activities directly.[48]

Accordingly, the developing legal standard for security imposes three basic requirements on businesses that outsource: (1) they must exercise due diligence in selecting service providers,[49] (2) they must contractually require outsource providers to implement appropriate security measures,[50] and (3) they must monitor the performance of the outsource providers.[51]

8.2.2   An Increasing Focus on Specific Data Elements and Controls

In addition to laws imposing general security obligations with respect to personal information, developing law is also beginning to include specific rules for certain categories of data elements, and certain types of security controls.

8.2.2.1   Sensitive Data

From its inception, the EU Data Protection Directive has required special treatment for particularly sensitive personal information. Specifically, the directive prohibits "the processing of personal data revealing racial or ethnic origin, political opinions, religious or philosophical beliefs, trade-union membership, and the processing of data concerning health or sex life," unless certain exceptions apply.[52]

---

47. Ziff Davis Assurance of Discontinuance, Para. 27(h), p. 7(cited in Appendix at Part F).

48. See, e.g., Office of the Comptroller of the Currency, Administrator of National Banks, OCC Bulletin 2001-47 on Third Party Relationships, November 21, 2001 (available at www.OCC.treas.gov/ftp/bulletin/2001-47.doc).

49. See, e.g., GLB Security Regulations, 12 C.F.R. Part 30 Appendix B, Part II.D(1).

50. See, e.g., GLB Security Regulations, 12 C.F.R. Part 30 Appendix B, Part II.D(2); HIPAA Security Regulations, 45 C.F.R. Section 164.308(b)(1) and 164.314(a)(2)

51. GLB Security Regulations, 12 C.F.R. Part 30 Appendix B, Part II.D(3).

52. EU Data Protection Directive, Article 8.

Those exceptions include "explicit consent" by the data subject, and carrying out obligations under applicable employment laws.

But, even with consent, processing such sensitive data, according to EU interpretation, requires that "special attention" be given to data security aspects to avoid risks of unauthorized disclosure. In particular, "[a]ccess by unauthorized persons must be virtually impossible and prevented."[53]

In the United States, a de facto category of sensitive information has been defined by the various state security breach notification laws (discussed below). These laws require special action (i.e., disclosure) in the event of a breach of security with respect to a subcategory of personal data generally considered to be sensitive because of its potential role in facilitating identity theft.

8.2.2.2 Social Security Numbers

Separately, the security of social security numbers has also been the focus of numerous state laws enacted during the past few years.[54] The scope of these laws range from restrictions on the manner in which social security numbers can be used, to express requirements for security with respect to the communication and/or storage of social security numbers. Some states prohibit initiating any transmission of an individual's social security number over the Internet unless the connection is secure or the social security number is encrypted.[55]

The bottom line is that if a company wants to continue collecting, maintaining, and transferring data with SSNs, it will have provide special treatment for the protection of that data (at least for the SSN number portion), such as encryption, using secure communications media, controlling access, and adopting special security policies.

8.2.2.3 Credit Card Data

For businesses that accept credit card transactions, the Payment Card Industry Data Security Standards (PCI Standards)[56] impose significant security obligations with respect to credit card data captured as part of any credit card transaction. The PCI Standards, jointly created by the major credit card associations, require businesses that accept MasterCard, Visa, American Express, Discover,

---

53. Article 29 Data Protection Working Party, Working Document on the processing of personal data relating to health in electronic health records (EHR), 00323/07/EN, WP 131, February 15, 2007, at pp. 19-20; available at http://ec.europa.eu/justice_home/fsj/privacy/docs/wpdocs/2007/wp131_en.pdf (emphasis in original).

54. See list of state laws in GAO Report, Social Security Numbers: Federal and State Laws Restrict Use of SSN's, Yet Gaps Remain, September 15, 2005 at Appendix III; available at www.gao.gov/new.items/d051016t.pdf.

55. Maryland Commercial Code, § 14-3402(a)(4); Nevada Rev. Stat. 597.970.

56. Available at www.pcisecuritystandards.org.

and Diner's Club cards to comply. Some states are also beginning to enact laws to address security of credit card data.[57]

8.2.2.4 Data Destruction

A new trend during the past few years has been for laws and regulations to impose security requirements with respect to the manner in which personal data is destroyed. These regulations typically do not require the destruction of data, but seek to regulate the manner of destruction when companies decide to do so.

At the Federal level, both the banking regulators and the SEC have adopted regulations regarding security requirements for the destruction of personal data. Several states have adopted similar requirements.[58]

Such statutes and regulations generally require companies to properly dispose of personal information by taking reasonable measures to protect against unauthorized access to or use of the information in connection with its disposal. With respect to information in paper form, this typically requires implementing and monitoring compliance with policies and procedures that require the burning, pulverizing, or shredding of papers containing personal information so that the information cannot be read or reconstructed. With respect to electronic information, such regulations typically require implementing and monitoring compliance with policies and procedures that require the destruction or erasure of electronic media containing consumer personal information so that the information cannot practicably be read or reconstructed.[59]

8.2.2.5 Online Authentication

Satisfying a company's legal obligations to provide information security will always include an obligation to properly authenticate the identity of persons seeking access to the company's computer systems or data. Such a requirement is expressly addressed, for example, in most U.S. information security laws and regulations, including HIPAA,[60] GLBA,[61] the Homeland Security Act,[62] FDA

---

57. See, e.g., Minn. Stat. Chapter 325E.64.

58. See list in Appendix.

59. See, e.g., 16 CFR Section 682.3.

60. Health Insurance Portability and Accountability Act (HIPAA) Security Regulations, 45 C.F.R. § 164.312(d). HIPAA security regulations apply to medical records in the healthcare sector.

61. Gramm Leach Bliley Act (GLBA) Security Regulations, 12 C.F.R. Part 30 Appendix B, Part III.C(1)(a). GLBA security regulations apply to customer information in the financial sector.

62. Homeland Security Act of 2002 § 1001(b), amending 44 U.S.C. § 3532(b)(1)(D), and § 301(b)(1) amending 44 U.S.C. § 3542(b((1) ("'information security' means protecting information and information systems from unauthorized access, ...").

regulations,[63] and state information security laws.[64] Likewise, in April 2007 the Federal Communications Commission (FCC) issued an Order directed to telephone and wireless carriers to protect personal telephone records from unauthorized disclosure that imposes specific authentication requirements.[65] And, in a case involving identity theft, a court found that there was a common law duty to verify the authenticity of a credit card application.[66] In all cases, the key issue is not whether authentication is required, but rather, what form of authentication is legally appropriate.

Historically, the standard approach to authentication of identity has been to use a user ID and password. But, based on recent developments, that approach may no longer be *legally* adequate in all cases. In the United States, regulators in the financial sector were the first to formally state that reliance solely on a user ID and password—so-called single-factor authentication—is considered "to be *inadequate*" at least in the case of high-risk transactions.[67] Other countries, such as Singapore, have also adopted similar requirements.[68]

8.3   The Imposition of a Duty to Warn of Security Breaches

In addition to the legal duty to *implement security measures* to protect data, numerous laws also impose an obligation to *disclose security breaches* to the persons affected. By requiring notice to such persons, these laws seek to provide them with a warning that their personal information has been compromised, and an opportunity to take steps to protect themselves against the consequences of identity theft and unauthorized account access.[69]

---

63. Food and Drug Administration regulations, 21 C.F.R. Part 11.

64. See, e.g., Cal. Civil Code § 1798.81.5(b).

65. See FCC Order re Pretexting, April 2, 2007—In the Matter of Implementation of the Telecommunications Act of 1996: Telecommunications Carriers' Use of Customer Proprietary Network Information and Other Customer Information IP-Enabled Services, CC Docket No. 96-115, WC Docket No. 04-36, April 2, 2007, at Paragraphs 13-25; available at http://hraunfoss.fcc.gov/edocs_public/attachmatch/FCC-07-22A1.pdf (hereinafter "FCC Pretexting Order").

66. Wolfe v. MBNA America Bank, 485 F.Supp.2d 874, 882 (W.D. Tenn. 2007).

67. See, Authentication in an Internet Banking Environment , October 12, 2005, available at http://www.ffiec.gov/pdf/authentication_guidance.pdf. This was later supplemented by an FAQ titled "Frequently Asked Questions on FFIEC Guidance on Authentication in an Internet Banking Environment," August 8, 2006, available at http://www.ncua.gov/letters/2006/CU/06-CU-13_encl.pdf.

68. Monetary Authority of Singapore, Circular No. SRD TR 02/2005, November 25, 2005.

69. See, e.g., Recommended Practices on Notice of Security Breach Involving Personal Information, Office of Privacy Protection, California Department of Consumer Affairs, April, 2006 (hereinafter "California Recommended Practices"), at pp. 5-6 (available at www.pri-

A total of 44 states, plus the District of Columbia, Puerto Rico, and the Virgin Islands have enacted breach notification laws as of May 2008.[70] In addition, the federal banking regulatory agencies issued guidance for financial institutions regarding this duty to disclose breaches.[71] For the most part, these laws are a direct reaction to a series of well-publicized security breaches involving sensitive personal information over the past few years,[72] and an effort to address the problem of identity theft.

8.3.1 The Basic Obligation

Taken as a group, the state and federal security breach notification laws generally require that any business in possession of sensitive personal information about a covered individual must disclose any breach of such information to the person affected. The key requirements, which vary from state-to-state, include the following:

- *Covered information.* The statutes generally apply to breaches of unencrypted sensitive personally identified information. This is usually defined as information consisting of first name or initial and last name, plus one of the following: social security number, drivers license or other state ID number, or financial account number or credit or debit card number (along with any PIN or other access code where required for access to the account). Some state breach notification laws also cover additional data elements

- *Definition of breach.* Generally the statutes require notice to the persons who are affected following the unauthorized acquisition of computerized data that compromises the security, confidentiality, or integrity of their personal information. In some states, however, notice is not required unless there is a reasonable basis to believe that the breach will result in substantial harm or inconvenience to the individuals whose data was compromised.

---

vacy.ca.gov/recommendations/secbreach.pdf); Interagency Guidance supra note 4, at p. 15752.

70. See list in Appendix at Part B.

71. Interagency Guidance on Response Programs for Unauthorized Access to Customer Information and Customer Notice, Part III of Supplement A to Appendix, at 12 C.F.R. Part 30 (OCC), 12 C.F.R. Part 208 (Federal Reserve System), 12 C.F.R. Part 364 (FDIC), and 12 C.F.R. Part 568 (Office of Thrift Supervision), March 29, 2005, Federal Register, Vol. 70, No. 59, March 29, 2005, at p. 15736 (hereinafter "Interagency Guidance").

72. For a chronology of such breaches in the U.S., and a running total of the number of individuals affected, see Privacy Rights Clearinghouse at www.privacyrights.org/ar/ChronDataBreaches.htm.

- *Who must be notified.* Notice must be given to any residents of the state whose unencrypted personal information was the subject of the breach. Some states also require notice to the attorney general, and several states require notice to the credit agencies.

- *When notice must be provided.* Generally, persons must be notified in the most expedient time possible and without unreasonable delay; however, in most states the time for notice may be extended for the following:

  - Legitimate needs of law enforcement, if notification would impede a criminal investigation;

  - Taking necessary measures to determine the scope of the breach and restore reasonable integrity to the system.

- *Form of notice.* Notice may be provided in writing (e.g., on paper and sent by mail), in electronic form (e.g., by e-mail, but only provided the provisions of E-SIGN[73] are complied with), or by substitute notice.

- *Substitute notice options.* If the cost of providing individual notice is greater than a certain amount (e.g., $250,000) or if more than a certain number of people would have to be notified (e.g., 500,000), substitute notice may be used, consisting of:

  - E-mail when the e-mail address is available;

  - Conspicuous posting on the company's web site; and

  - Publishing notice in all major statewide media.

Several of these issues vary from state to state, however, and some have become controversial. The biggest issue revolves around the nature of the triggering event. In California, for example, notification is required whenever there has been an unauthorized access that compromises the security, confidentiality, or integrity of electronic personal data. In other states, however, unauthorized access does not trigger the notification requirement unless there is a reasonable likelihood of harm to the individuals whose personal information is involved[74] or unless the breach is material.[75]

---

73. 15 USC Section 7001 et. seq. This generally requires that companies comply with the requisite consumer consent provisions of E-SIGN at 15 USC Section 7001(c).

74. Arkansas, Connecticut, Delaware, and Louisiana are examples of states in this category.

75. Montana and Nevada are examples of states in this category.

8.3.2   International Adoption

Although the breach notification concept began in the United States, it is rapidly spreading to the international sector.

The European Commission released a Communication proposing changes to EU law that would require "electronic communications networks or services" to "notify their customers of any breach of security leading to the loss, modification or destruction of, or unauthorized access to, personal customer data."[76] In the United Kingdom, a July 2007 report by the Select Committee on Science and Technology on the Internet and Personal Safety of the House of Lords also recommended adoption of security breach notification legislation.[77]

In Canada, the Office of the Privacy Commissioner issued voluntary guidelines for responding to data breaches in August 2007. Pointing out that "notification can be an important mitigation strategy" that benefits both the organization and the individuals affected by a breach, the guidelines indicated that "if a privacy breach creates a risk of harm to the individual, those affected should be notified" in order to help them mitigate the damage by taking steps to protect themselves.[78] Shortly thereafter, the privacy commissioner in New Zealand released similar guidelines.[79] Although the New Zealand guidelines are voluntary, the privacy commissioner noted that "principle 5 of the Privacy Act (governing the way personal information is stored) does require all organizations and individuals that hold personal information to take reasonable steps to protect it. This can include notifying people of significant breaches, where necessary."[80]

The Australian privacy commissioner has also recommended that Australia consider amending its privacy legislation to include a mandatory requirement to report security breaches involving personal information. Her February 28, 2007 submission to the Australian Law Reform Commission supported "consideration of the addition of provisions to the Privacy Act to require agencies and organizations to advise affected individuals of a breach to their personal

76. See   Communication   at   http://europa.eu.int/information_society/policy/ecomm/doc/info_centre/public_consult/review/staffworkingdocument_final.pdf.

77. Science and Technology Committee, House of Lords, "Personal Internet Security" 5th Report of Session 2006–07, July 24, 2007, at Para. 5.55

78. Office of the Privacy Commissioner of Canada, Key Steps for Organizations in Responding to Privacy Breaches, August 28, 2007; available at www.privcom.gc.ca/information/guide/2007/gl_070801_02_e.asp.

79. See Privacy Breach Guidance Material, Office of the Privacy Commissioner, available at http://www.privacy.org.nz/privacy-breach-guidelines-2/.

80. Privacy Commissioner, Media Release, August 27, 2007, available at www.privacy.org.nz/filestore/docfiles/5001509.doc.

information in certain circumstances."[81] On September 12, 2007, the Australian Law Reform Commission released its *Review of Australian Privacy Law*[82] which proposed numerous changes to Australia's privacy law. Included among the proposals was a new system of data breach notification.[83]

8.4 Conclusion

Virtually all companies have a duty to provide security for all of their corporate data and information systems. In other words, information security is no longer just good business practice. It has become a legal obligation.

---

81. See, Australian Government, Office of the Privacy Commissioner, Submission to the Australian Law Reform Commission's Review of Privacy - Issues Paper 31, February 28, 2007, at paragraphs 127-129; available at www.privacy.gov.au/publications/submissions/alrc/all.pdf.

82. Available at www.austlii.edu.au/au/other/alrc/publications/dp/72/.

83. Available at www.austlii.edu.au/au/other/alrc/publications/dp/72/60.pdf

9

Telecommunications

Edward G. Amoroso

We had originally sought out Ed to contribute to the practitioner section. However, when we saw what he wrote, we quickly realized that the risks he was most concerned about were risks to telecommunications services, that is, risks that affect any user of telecommunications services, which means all of us. So we moved his contribution up to the risks section.

However, it is still possible to read Ed's chapter keeping in mind his point of view as a practitioner. As the chief information security officer at AT&T, the telecommunications security issues that seem overwhelming complex to the layman are a day-in-the-life for Ed. Ed's fact-based, lack of hype in enumerating the issues is a refreshing change from most literature on the information security risks inherent in today's telecommunications. For those interested in further reading, Ed's book, *CyberSecurity,* brings other complex aspects of the realm of information security to the layman.

At the time of this writing in 2008, the telecommunications industry is driving four major technological advances. These advances, listed below, provide an excellent framework for examining security issues that are likely to emerge in telecommunications in the coming years:

Mobility: Increased mobility in telecommunications will require security infrastructure to protect more powerful end-points in nonfixed locations.

Globalization: Globalization of telecommunications will require changes in security processes across massively diverse geographic and political ranges.

Internet Protocol (IP): IP-based telecommunications for voice, data, and video will increase flexibility, but will intensify traditional Internet security issues.

Bandwidth: Dramatic increases in throughput rates, especially for residential users, will create attractive new opportunities for malicious hackers.

Each of these technological advances is in some varying stage of completion by global carriers such as AT&T. All of them, however, are well-enough along to have already fundamentally changed the telecommunications landscape. As with any technology evolution, security professionals are obliged to analyze the threat ramifications. The discussion below provides a high-level introduction to several security threats that will arise in telecommunications as a direct result of these advances.

Two important notes are worth highlighting before we continue: First, the treatment in this chapter is not intended to be comprehensive, but rather to introduce a representative set of security issues for discussion. Second, we include mention of several security challenges for which a solution is not immediately obvious. This does not reduce our enthusiasm to raise these issues to prompt greater urgency in seeking acceptable mitigation.

—J.L.B.

9.1   Security Issues in Mobile Telecommunications

Modern mobile telecommunications are designed to support users in nonfixed locations carrying powerful portable devices. If the processing power on these portable devices continues to evolve with Moore's law, we should expect to see many tens of thousands of times the processing power in the coming decade. Such distributed power on our phones, laptops, and personal digital assistants (PDAs) will introduce new pressures on the enterprise perimeter model, and will resurface many traditional computer security threats on portable devices.

9.1.1   Pressure on the Perimeter Model

Modern network security is built on the concept of closed perimeters. Security devices such as firewalls and intrusion detection systems have evolved as a result of this model, and have since been dispatched on a massive scale to every known fixed entry point across every network on the planet. On the corporate enterprise, for example, all PCs, servers, and network elements reside within an Intranet perimeter and are managed within that perimeter as trusted entities. When these devices need to be located outside the perimeter, a VPN tunnel is used to extend the protected enclave. In short, the primary security challenge that mobility introduces, especially in the enterprise, is that tunnel extensions become no longer the exception, but rather the norm.

Business users have already begun to shift their perspective on traditional perimeter views for their handheld messaging infrastructure. RIM/Blackberry services, for example, do not easily track a perimeter model, but are in extensive use. So, it is not a stretch to assume that reliance on the perimeter model could change. Some groups, such as the Jericho Forum [1], recommend following a data-centric security approach where networks are assumed to have no perimeters. Rather, protection is provided using data-centric techniques such as cryptography, an approach that certainly could be useful in handling security for mobility evolution. Other groups, such as AT&T, have suggested that security policy-based services be centralized in carrier infrastructure outside the corporate Intranet and home network. This could also be useful in securing mobility, especially as 3G and 4G wireless connectivity to laptop computers becomes as ubiquitous as cell phone coverage.

9.1.2 Computer Security Threats for Portable Devices

More mature participants in the computing industry will remember when phones and computers were different. Computers had screens and keyboards for running software, while phones had keypads for making calls. Information security evolved separately in each case, with firewalls, intrusion detection systems, and antivirus systems for computers, and fraud detection systems for phones. With the convergence of computers and phones in mobility, portable devices unfortunately inherit the security threats of each. This conclusion is now evident in the security industry where firewalls, antivirus systems, and the like, are available for mobile devices. Similarly, fraud-avoidance services to address hijacked laptop connectivity are likely to become more generally available soon. (Whether this trend is exciting or disturbing depends on your vantage point as a user or seller of these services.)

So, the bad news is that the security industry will have to relive many of the growing pains of computer and telephony security. The good news, however, is that the industry has matured considerably in the past couple of decades. Consider, for example, that mobile operating systems such as Microsoft's Windows Mobile are less complex than their predecessor PC-based versions. This bodes well for software vulnerability management. Also, as bandwidth for traditional PC services continues to exceed wireless interfaces, hackers will most likely continue to prefer attacks that target computer systems in fixed locations. Finally, security methods that have worked perhaps less well in traditional computer system environments can be appropriately de-emphasized in the new mobility environment. Intrusion detection, with its many noisy and false positive alarms, comes to mind as a potential candidate for de-emphasis in mobility.

9.2 Security Issues in Global Telecommunications

Globalization of telecommunications service allows carriers to provide for domestic groups as they extend their businesses into distant regions. Globalization in telecommunications is clearly driven by business economics, generally with an eye toward regions experiencing growth rates in consumption. Nevertheless, ubiquitous global standards such as the Internet Protocol (IP) are also a powerful enabling factor in establishing global footprints. Two representative security issues that arise with global telecommunications are an increased demand for diverse organizations to cooperate in dealing with large-scale cyber attacks, as well as an increased motivation to address the global problem of software piracy.

9.2.1 Global Cooperation on Cyber Attack

In protecting service infrastructure, telecommunications security groups must cooperate with a variety of organizations external to their company. They need to establish relationships with other service providers, for example, so that when attacks transcend their own infrastructure, they are capable of dealing with the cross-carrier issues. Telecommunications security groups also need to cooperate with their customers when attacks cross local and wide-area networking boundaries. Furthermore, they need to cooperate with government organizations when laws are being broken, perhaps as illegal use of services or illegal acts committed using telecommunications. To date, cooperation between telecommunications security groups and local, in-country external groups has been reasonably effective, especially for traditional threats such as voice fraud. As threats have evolved toward general network security on IP-based systems, this local cooperation has also evolved, albeit more slowly, given the lack of historical experience in dealing with computer network attacks.

With the present shift to global service infrastructure, the type of cooperation necessary also shifts. One should expect more cases, for example, where security telecommunications groups in the United States must reach out to service providers or law enforcement teams in countries where such interaction has never been required in the past. As a result, language issues, cultural differences, legal interpretations, and other problems of global human interaction are likely to complicate the global security picture for some time. Furthermore, as network security attacks such as botnets draw on global resources, this cooperation will become more critical. A botnet that includes controllers or software drop locations in, say, China, is more effectively blocked if the controls reside in-country, than if the address shuns must be performed in a distributed manner across the world. To date, security interfaces between global carriers have been mostly informal and driven by social interaction rather than through a well-engineered set of interaction processes. Such loosely defined methods in areas ranging from lawful intercept activity to customer notification will have to be more carefully examined as globalization increases in intensity.

9.2.2 Global Attention to Software Piracy

The software piracy issue, especially for Microsoft operating systems and applications, has risen considerably with increasing software demand in growth regions such as Asia. A recent study by the Business Software Alliance estimates that piracy in Asia costs the software industry roughly $11 billion in 2006 [2]. Another estimate suggests that one of every three copies of Microsoft operating system software is pirated [3]. For telecommunications, this represents a serious issue because pirated operating systems cannot be properly protected. Critical patches, for example, are often not feasible on systems that have not been procured through standard channels. Microsoft, in particular, has been at the epicenter of this debate. Internal network analysis in AT&T Labs of netflow traffic on the AT&T IP backbone confirms that large numbers of bots appear to originate in growth regions where piracy is high and security updates appear to be low [4]. Nevertheless, even where software patch updates are feasible, global attentiveness to system integrity issues remains tepid.

The result is that as long as software piracy reduces the percentage of properly patched systems across the globe, so many more end-points on telecommunications services will continue to have bots and other forms of malware. In turn, these infected systems will continue to clog up networks, and will continue to threaten the global Internet-based infrastructure. This problem is best solved by improving the integrity of end-user systems in regions where usage growth is very high. Partnership and agreements between software companies and their global users to address software piracy and to increase the percentage of end-user PCs that are properly patched, will thus become more urgent than ever, if only to ensure the integrity of our global telecommunications infrastructure.

9.3 Security Issues in Internet Protocol–Based Telecommunications

Modern Internet Protocol (IP)-based telecommunications services utilize the familiar set of TCP/IP programs, interfaces, and standards. This stands in contrast to traditional time division multiplexing (TDM) services designed decades ago in the Bell System and still found in circuit switched telecommunications. Two threats that emerge from the rapid shift of modern telecommunications to IP are reduced technological diversity in global telecommunications infrastructure, and increased reliance on shared, decentralized, Internet-based systems.

9.3.1   Reduced Technological Diversity

In the last couple of decades, telecommunications has enjoyed rich innovation from its original circuit switched base. This has included advances in packet switching, high-speed data networking, mobile communications, and TCP/IP-based application internetworking. The result has been a plethora of choices for telecommunications (or home networking) decision makers, which in turn has led to a high degree of heterogeneity in most network designs. A typical modern business, for example, might utilize circuit switched voice over TDM equipment, IP-based Internet services on an Internet Service Provider (ISP) router backbone, Layer 2 frame relay or asynchronous transfer mode (ATM) on specially designed carrier switches, wireless services over cellular infrastructure, and remote access VPN over local home broadband and Wi-Fi. The resultant infrastructure is complex, expensive to maintain, and typically subject to convergence plans by CIO and telecommunications teams, if only to reduce support costs. So nearly every participant in the telecommunications industry has committed to a rapid convergence of its full suite of services to IP.

A subtle benefit that may be lost in such convergence, however, is the diversity inherent in the use of separate service infrastructures. When an enterprise has trouble handling viruses on the local LAN, for example, maintaining separate circuit switched voice services allows the phones to keep ringing. Similarly, if a local business voice switch experiences some sort of glitch or outage, IP connections are generally established using separate routers, so employees can keep using the Internet. Certainly, convergence does not imply that lost network technology diversity cannot be managed, but rather that the obligation exists for security professionals to double their efforts at addressing known and emerging threats on converged platforms. One solution is to demand high levels of availability and reliability for selected IP services. Carriers should be held to the highest quality standards if organizations and homes are to integrate their services into a common IP framework. In addition, carriers should be employed to help create high-availability backup systems with provision for business continuity services. In all cases, of course, physical layer diversity must be demanded as well.

9.3.2   Increased Reliance on Shared, Decentralized Internet-Based Systems

The shift to IP-based networking in telecommunications also introduces greater dependence on shared systems such as the domain name system (DNS) and the border gateway protocol (BGP). These systems are characterized by decentralized design and operation, with their correct usage dependent on many players across the globe agreeing to a loosely managed set of agreed upon procedures. Stated more simply, systems like DNS and BGP work because everyone agrees to follow the rules. If someone does not follow the rules, then chaos can and will ensue. This cooperative agreement among network operators has worked for the most part on the existing Internet. The vast majority of network operators are honest and diligent, and communities of operators such as the North American Network Operators Group (NANOG) [5] have formed that help promote shared learning and continued cooperation.

One must recognize, however, that as more services move to IP-based technology, and that as they are designed to coexist in Internet-space, these services will also become dependent on shared systems like DNS and BGP. Such dependence underscores the critical importance of initiatives designed to increase the security and dependability of these systems, often through the introduction of PKI-based services. Proposals for adding strong authentication to both BGP and DNS, for example, have been in the public domain for many years, albeit with only lukewarm acceptance. Considerable volumes have been written on the weaknesses of BGP [6] and DNS [7], hence we will not list them here. Nevertheless, one would expect that the importance of the security hardening of shared Internet services will only increase in coming years with continued convergence on IP-based systems.

9.4 Security Issues in Bandwidth-Increasing Telecommunications

Bandwidth increases in telecommunications services have been dramatic in recent years. This includes bidirectional broadband services in residential and small office environments, as well as modern services such as virtual private network (VPN) connections to large businesses. Two security issues that emerge as telecommunications bandwidth continues to increase are that residential users will have greater security responsibility and botnets will continue to emerge as a huge threat to the global economy.

9.4.1 Residential Users Have Greater Security Responsibility

The increase in bandwidth to residential users has enabled a new generation of computing and networking services previously considered unimaginable due to bandwidth limitations. These services include online interactive games such as *World of Warcraft*, as well as popular video sites such as YouTube.com. Since this increase in bandwidth for consumers includes both downstream and upstream processing, the end-user now becomes responsible for protecting a network connection that is much more attractive to malicious intruders. Suppose, for example, that a home network of several powerful PCs is connected to the Internet via fiber operating at multiple megabits per second in both directions. This is exciting for the residents because it enables voice, video, and data applications that require large throughput. One rarely considers, however, that this set-up is roughly akin to the computing and networking power one might have found in a highly protected data center just a few years ago! That data center was probably surrounded by perimeter defenses run by security professionals; the present home network is probably protected by no one.

It is unlikely that end-users in residences will ever become enthusiastic about security. Even if financial or service incentives were put in place to entice greater security, most consumers would not have the system administrative skills to perform the security task properly. So, security protections will need to come from some other source. One promising trend involves service providers partnering with their residential customers to install proper filters and protections into the network. This holds the great promise of allowing end-users to enjoy their computing power and bandwidth without having the corresponding responsibility for protection. Another key trend is that software providers such as Microsoft have come to recognize the huge security responsibility they hold. Systems such as auto-update for Microsoft users have been valuable in helping to ensure that critical patches are put in place in a timely manner.

9.4.2   Botnets Become a Huge Threat to the Global Economy

In spite of the potential partnerships between home users and their service providers, and in spite of advances being made by software vendors, the harsh reality is that today, most home networks are unprotected and have huge networking capacity. This situation is desirable for malicious botnet designers because it provides a fertile breeding ground for recruiting and running large numbers of bots with tremendous power. If, for example, only three PCs with 500 kbps upstream processing capability are combined into a simple botnet (and this could be the simplest botnet one might imagine), the combined upstream networking capability of 1.5 Mbps is enough to fill up an entire T1 connection [8]. The reader is encouraged to do the math to discover how easy it becomes to disrupt even larger connections with relatively modest botnets.

The result is that with the dramatic and exciting increases occurring in telecommunications bandwidth to the home, the need to reduce the threat of botnets becomes more intense. Most service providers are beginning to explore techniques for filtering upstream activity that is clearly botnet related. Furthermore, carriers continue to expand their ability to filter these types of attacks in the core of their network. In any event, as long as bandwidth continues to increase, especially to the residence, the threat of botnets will increase as well.

References

[1]   http://www.opengroup.org/jericho.

[2]   Yu, Eileen, "Revenue Loss from Piracy in Asia Up," *ZDNet Asia,* May 15, 2007, (http://www.zdnetasia.com/news/software/0,39044164,62013101,00.htm).

[3]   August, T. and Tunca, T., "Let the Pirates Patch—An Economic Analysis of Network Software Security Restrictions," Graduate School of Business, Stanford University, 2006 (digital.mit.edu/wise2006/papers/3B-2_August-Tunca-wise06.pdf).

[4]   Based on discussions with David Gross and Brian Rexroad of AT&T Labs–Security.

[5]   http://nanog.org.

[6]   Butler, K., et al, "A Survey of BGP Security," ACM Draft Version, April 2005.

[7]   Householder, A., et al., "Securing an Internet Name Server," CERT Coordination Center, August 2002.

[8]   Based on discussions with David Gross of AT&T Labs–Security.

Part III: Experience

This volume is a collection of opinions. It is important to understand that the field of information security is not a science. It is more of a collection of individual experiences with hard problems. An individual's perception of security is shaped by his or her experiences with information security requirements and how they were met by the organizations of which he or she is a part. These include judgments concerning the adequacy of security measures meant to address privacy requirements. The contributors to this section have shaped the way their organizations have responded to information security and privacy requirements with methods and procedures supported by technical security measures. Their experience collectively presents a snapshot of the practice of information security as it exists today and provides a thoughtful approach to maintenance of security measures.

When soliciting practitioners to contribute to this volume, the editors intended to cover many more industries than appear in the pages that follow. In many cases, practitioners were more than willing to share their experience, but their organization's public relations policies prevented them from contributing to this publication. This accounts for the absence of practitioner articles from major fields that would be expected to be very active in information security and privacy (to name but a few obviously missing: government, health care). Though we will not share the companies or individuals who could not contribute, we know them to be great examples of advanced thinking in the profession. Though we think their contributions would reflect well on their organizations, we are nevertheless reminded of seeing articles in *CISO Magazine* quoting

CISOs complaining about their budgets. We always wondered how those individuals kept their jobs. Perhaps this type of negative publicity has made public relations departments hesitant to commit to sharing information on information security challenges in general. Regardless, in the absence of representation on these pages, we encourage practitioners to seek out others in their fields via industry forums or local chapters of the information security professional organizations active in their communities, for example, ISACA and ISSA.

10

Financial Services

John Carlson

John Carlson has done a masterful job in explaining the security and privacy issues that financial institutions must confront in order to protect information and financial assets. He brings to bear his extensive experience at the vortex of the industry to articulate where the industry stands and where it is headed so far as security and privacy challenges are concerned.

Having been in information technology and security in financial services for most of my career, I am very much aware of the legal and regulatory requirements placed on financial institutions by government and I recognize how difficult it can be to navigate through the myriad of complex laws, regulations, and guidance. The achievement of this chapter is how it describes and explains such complexities in easy-to-understand terms.

The banking and finance sector is often the leader when it comes to information security and privacy. This is readily understood as financial institutions have custody of such huge repositories of sensitive information about individuals and organizations and their finances. In fact, the whole foundation of the financial services industry is based on its ability to maintain the trust and confidence of its customers, business partners, and other stakeholders.

While those in other industries, academia, and government might not be subject to the restrictions placed upon so highly regulated an industry, everyone has a vested interest in the continued integrity and trustworthiness of financial organizations, since the whole global economy depends on the well-protected operation of financial firms. Also, since being a primary target of malicious and/or fraudulent attacks, and to avoid intense and costly pressure from legislators and regulators, financial services are often the first to actively engage new security challenges. Other sectors frequently learn from their experiences and technology investments.

Perhaps the most important lesson of the entire chapter is the distinction between compliance with various laws and regulations versus actually being secure. While there is little question that full compliance is certainly better than being noncompliant in any respect, full compliance does not guarantee adequate security. It is only a jumping-off point. Organizations must engage in a program that goes beyond compliance and which achieves a level of security that meets the requirements of all the stakeholders. Following the premises and requirements of laws, regulations, and guidance is important in its own right, since noncompliance can bring down the wrath of legislators, regulators, and stakeholders upon the institutions that do not achieve the standard. But, again, that's only part of the job. The competent and experienced security professional will work to get the whole job done.

This chapter reviews the major security and privacy protection requirements for financial institutions in the United States. The chapter is divided into three sections. The first section covers the major laws and regulatory and supervisory requirements. The second section outlines potential trends for future regulatory and supervisory requirements. The last section describes activities within the financial industry to meet these challenges.

—C.W.A.

10.1 Laws, Regulations, and Supervisory Requirements

Financial institutions in the United States are governed by numerous regulatory and supervisory requirements pertaining to the security and privacy protection of customers. In the realm of security and privacy, the most mature regulatory enforcement mechanisms of all industries exist in the financial industry. Most financial institutions in the United States must comply with multiple regulations and therefore meet the demands of multiple regulators. These requirements are necessary by virtue of the institutions' fiduciary responsibilities to customers and shareholders and the overall safety and soundness of the financial system. Security and privacy protection is a fundamental building block for all financial services, but these requirements also are in response to changing threats and risks. Notably, the financial sector is a favorite target of cyber criminals.

The cybersecurity threat environment is constantly evolving. International crime rings that use the Internet for fraud and financial gain have propagated in recent years, and criminals are writing code to compromise systems. Phishing,[1]

---

1. Phishing is the use of technology and social engineering to entice consumers to supply personal information such as account numbers, login IDs, passwords, and other verifiable information that can then be exploited for fraudulent purposes, including identity theft. Phishing is most often perpetrated through mass emails and spoofed web sites.

cybersquatting,[2] viruses, malware, and other forms of attack are endemic. Hackers are shortening the period between the discovery of a software flaw and exploitation of that flaw. Criminals are using "social engineering" to trick consumers into providing personal information that can facilitate fraud and identity theft. Therefore, in response to concerns over the protection of personal or sensitive information stemming from highly publicized breaches, and resulting consequences including fraud, loss of consumer confidence, and identity theft, federal and state governments are imposing additional requirements on financial institutions.

Governments, and their appointed financial regulators, understand that customer trust in the security, integrity, and availability of financial information and transactions is vital to the stability of the industry and the strength of a nation's economy. In response to government action and changing threats, financial institutions are deploying stronger and broadly accepted authentication methods, applying additional security controls to detect and prevent fraudulent activities, enhancing protection of critical assets and business continuity, strengthening software applications, enhancing training of employees, developing new policies, and increasing educational programs for customers on how to protect their information and prevent identity theft. These efforts address other information security concerns including integrity, availability, accountability, and assurance.

Regulation is a double-edged sword. On the one hand, regulations such as those resulting from the Gramm-Leach-Bliley Act (GLBA) provide a level-setting mechanism by requiring all participants to abide by similar rules. On the other hand, each of these regulations adds a set of compliance requirements and costs to financial institutions. Overlap among regulations and the resulting compliance inefficiencies, and lack of flexibility around regulations that are implemented in a defined or proscriptive fashion, are commonly cited downsides. Moreover, unequal application of regulatory standards to financial and nonfinancial firms conducting similar lines of business is an ongoing concern, both in terms of competition and with respect to the notion that a break in the weakest link of a chain wreaks havoc upon the chain as a whole.

Nevertheless, federal financial regulators have implemented a complex regime that in many instances includes examinations of institutions' operational, financial, and technological systems. Many financial institutions are regulated and actively supervised at the federal and state levels. The federal financial regulators include the Federal Deposit Insurance Corporation, Federal Reserve System, National Credit Union Administration, Office of the Comptroller of

---

2. Cybersquatting is registering, trafficking in, or using a domain name with bad-faith intent to profit from the goodwill of a trademark belonging to someone else. *See,* the Anti-Cybersquatting Consumer Protection Act.

the Currency, Office of Thrift Supervision, and the Securities and Exchange Commission. In addition, most states have regulatory agencies. Insurance companies are primarily regulated by states as mandated by the McCarran-Ferguson Act of 1945.[3]

Federal regulators either require or expect, depending on the regulation and supervisory guidance, financial institutions to adhere to the following common elements that serve as the foundation for information security programs:

- Secure and maintain senior management's commitment to ensure that organizations have adequate resources and a sound program;

- Assess risks on an ongoing basis, including participation in information sharing and analysis programs;

- Implement appropriate controls (e.g., access controls, authentication, physical security, encryption, employee background checks, and insurance) based on changing risks;

- Manage third-party providers effectively and focus on critical interdependencies with other sectors;

- Establish metrics to measure risks, assess gaps, and measure progress;

- Educate users through training and awareness programs;

- Notify customers in response to data breaches that could result in some level of harm;

- Test systems and methods regularly to ensure that the technology, people, and processes are working effectively at appropriate levels of assumed residual risk;

- Measure progress through independent audits.

Examiners from federal and state regulatory agencies routinely examine all financial institutions and major service providers for compliance with regulatory and supervisory guidance. As part of these examinations, experts in information security assess the adequacy of controls that financial institutions have in place. When deficiencies are detected, examiners mandate changes or impose sanctions on the financial institutions. These examinations are designed to determine the extent to which the institution has identified its financial and nonfinancial risks,

---

3. 15 U.S.C. § 1011 et seq. Congress affirmed the exclusive right of the States to regulate the insurance industry. Except for a few federal laws and regulations, state insurance commissioners generally have regulatory authority over all aspects of a firm's business, including rates and terms of policies, qualifications for licensing, market conduct, and financial structures and practices. There are proposals calling for the creation of an optional federal charter for the insurance industry.

such as information technology infrastructures, and to evaluate the adequacy of controls and applicable risk management practices at the institution.

The most significant laws governing data security in the financial services industry are the Gramm-Leach-Bliley Financial Services Modernization Act of 1999 (GLBA), the Sarbanes-Oxley Act of 2002, and the Fair and Accurate Credit Transactions Act of 2003 (FACTA). In addition, most states have adopted data-breach customer notification laws. Many of these laws are modeled after California's 2003 notification law. The following is a brief overview of these requirements.

10.1.1 Gramm-Leach-Bliley Act of 1999

The Financial Services Modernization Act of 1999, otherwise known as the Gramm-Leach-Bliley Act of 1999 (GLBA), includes security guidelines containing a range of risk management obligations focused on implementing the congressional policy of protecting customer data.[4] A significant component of the GLBA legislation is the affirmative and continuing obligation for financial institutions to respect the privacy of customers. As part of this privacy-related obligation, the GLBA explicitly includes a responsibility to protect certain data—namely the "security and confidentiality of customers' nonpublic personal information."[5] Section 501(b) specifically requires federal banking regulators to develop regulations for safeguarding customer information. In 2001, the federal banking agencies issued "Guidelines Establishing Standards to Safeguard Customer Information." The federal financial regulatory agencies amended portions of the Safeguards rule in 2005 to include customer notification requirements following a data breach.[6] The Safeguards rule affords powerful and prompt enforcement options to the regulators if financial institutions do not establish and maintain adequate information security programs. The regulation marks a continuation of a movement toward emphasizing greater oversight and

---

4. 15 U.S.C.A. § 6801–6809 (1999).

5. 15 U.S.C.A. § 6801.

6. "Interagency Guidance on Response Programs for Unauthorized Access to Customer Information and Customer Notice," *See* 70 Fed. Reg. 15736–15754 (29 March 2005). Office of the Comptroller of the Currency. 12 CFR Part 30; Federal Reserve System. 12 CFR Parts 208 and 225; Federal Deposit Insurance Corporation. 12 CFR 364; Office of Thrift Supervision. 12 CFR Parts 568 and 570. "Interagency Guidance on Response Programs for Unauthorized Access to Customer Information and Customer Notice." The Securities and Exchange Commission did not participate in interagency rule making with the FFIEC agencies and issued a regulation that stated the requirments as outlined in the GLBAct. In 2008, the SEC issued proposed amendments to Regulation S-P, "Privacy of Consumer Financial Information and Safeguarding Personal Information" that were much more consistent with the FFIEC agencies. See http://www.sec.gov/rules/proposed/2008/34-57427fr.pdf.

accountability by a board of directors and senior management, including ongoing assessment of the adequacy of internal risk management processes. In essence, the regulators assess GLBA compliance on an enterprise-wide basis relative to privacy and security management. This approach focuses on enhanced involvement and oversight by the board of directors, as well as senior management engagement including risk management and audit.

10.1.2 The Sarbanes-Oxley Act of 2002

The Sarbanes-Oxley Act of 2002 (SOX) was enacted following several high-profile cases of executive abuse in U.S. corporations coupled with ineffective external audits.[7]

SOX applies to all publicly owned U.S. corporations as well as to their external auditors. The SOX requirement imposed additional requirements on financial institutions that extended beyond requirements included in the Federal Deposit Insurance Corporation Improvement Act of 1991 (FDICIA).[8] It also extends reporting requirements, as well as management assertions and account attestations of internal controls in a more prescriptive fashion. It established a new Public Companies Accounting Oversight Board (PCAOB) as the primary authority over accounting and financial reporting standards for public companies, and it imposes severe penalties on those who violate the law. SOX takes the accountability of the board of directors and senior management oversight to a level beyond previous requirements. For many financial institutions, the SOX requirements resulted in renewed focus on information security controls combined with significant auditing expenses.

10.1.3 The Fair and Accurate Credit Transactions Act of 2003

The Fair and Accurate Credit Transactions Act of 2003 (FACTA) requires financial institutions to develop identity theft "red flags" programs.[9] The Identity Theft Red Flags Rule consists of three parts: risk-based regulation, guidelines, and a supplement. The regulation requires each financial institution and creditor that holds consumer accounts, or any other account for which there is a reasonably foreseeable risk of identity theft, to implement a written identity theft prevention program for new and existing accounts. The program must be

---

7   Pub. L. No. 107-204, 116 Stat.745 (2002).

8. FDICIA mandated that banks develop formal internal controls. Under the annual audit and reporting requirements specified in Section 36 of FDICIA, all insured depository institutions with $500 million or more in total assets are required to submit annual management assessments of their internal control structure, and to obtain attestations of those assessments from their independent external auditor.

9. Pub. L. No. 108-159, 117 Stat. 1952 (2003).

appropriate to the companies' size and complexity and must include reasonable policies and procedures that enable financial institutions or creditors to:

- Identify relevant patterns, practices, and specific forms of activity that are red flags that signal possible identity theft and incorporate those red flags into the program;
- Detect red flags that have been incorporated into the program;
- Respond appropriately to any red flags that are detected in order to prevent and mitigate identity theft;
- Ensure the program is updated periodically to reflect changes in risk.

The rule also describes steps that financial institutions and creditors must take to administer the program, including: obtaining approval of the initial written program by the board of directors or a committee of the board, ensuring oversight of the program, training staff, and overseeing service provider arrangements. The supplement includes twenty-six illustrative red flags in five categories: (1) alerts from a consumer reporting agency; (2) suspicious documents; (3) suspicious personal identifying information; (4) suspicious activity in connection with a covered account; and (5) notice of suspicious activity in connection with a covered account. Financial institutions and creditors may choose to make other red flags part of their program or to modify the enumerated red flags as they wish.

10.1.4 Breach Notification Requirements

In response to public concern over the protection of sensitive information from data breaches and in media reports, California passed a law requiring companies to notify customers in response to the breach of sensitive information about that customer.[10] Other states followed using the California law as the model. As of June 20, 2008, at least 44 states, the District of Columbia, and Puerto Rico have adopted breach notification laws.[11] In March 2005, the federal financial regulatory agencies issued final guidance entitled, "Interagency Guidance on Response

---

10. Cal. Civ. Code § 1798.81.5.

11. *Alaska*, AS § 45.50.900; *Arizona*, A.R.S. § 44-7501; *Arkansas*, A.C.A. § 4-110-105; *California*, Cal.Civ.Code § 1798.82; *Colorado*, C.R.S.A. § 6-1-716; *Connecticut*, C.G.S.A. § 36a-701b; *Delaware*, 6 Del.C. § 12B-102; *District of Columbia*, DC ST § 28-3852; *Florida*, F.S.A. § 817.5681; *Georgia*, Ga. Code Ann., § 10-1-912; *Hawaii*, HRS § 487N-2; *Idaho*, I.C. § 28-51-105; *Illinois*, 815 ILCS 530/10 and /12; *Indiana*, IC 24-4.9-3-1, and IC 4-1-115 and -6; *Iowa*, I.C.A. § 715C.2; *Kansas*, K.S.A. § 50-7a02; *Louisiana*, LSA-R.S. 51:3073; *Maine*, 10 M.R.S.A. § 1348; *Maryland*, MD Code, Commercial Law, § 14-1212.1; *Massachusetts*, M.G.L.A. 93H § 3; *Michigan*, M.C.L.A. 445.72; *Minnesota*, M.S.A. §

Programs for Unauthorized Access to Customer Information and Customer Notice."[12] As of July, 2008, The United States Congress has debated but not passed national standards that could potentially preempt state laws.

Federal preemption may be positive for financial institutions because the majority operate or have customers in multiple states. In the current system, financial institutions are forced to comply with varying state notification laws.[13] Enacting unauthorized access and breach response laws based on customers' permanent residences is problematic for both large, international financial institutions and community-based financial institutions located in a single state. For example, community banks may have locations in only one state, but they almost always have customers who are residents of other states. This forces even community banks to reconcile inconsistent laws and regulations before they begin to notify customers following unauthorized access to sensitive customer information. Proponents of national standards argue that national uniformity, both geographically and across industries, is critical to preserving a fully functioning and efficient national marketplace. Because of the similarities between the current state laws and due to the fear businesses have that a federal law would be too strict, there has not been enough support within Congress for a national bill.[14]

Nevertheless, sensitive customer information is retained by many organizations and government agencies, not just financial institutions. In order to provide meaningful and consistent protection for consumers, all entities that handle sensitive customer information—not just financial institutions—should be subject to similar security and privacy protection standards. This would help to avoid circumstances in which customers of financial institutions may perceive

---

325E.61; *Montana,* MCA 30-14-1704; *Nebraska,* Neb.Rev.St. § 87-803; *Nevada,* N.R.S. 603A.220; *New Hampshire,* N.H. Rev. Stat. § 359-C:20; *New Jersey,* N.J.S.A. 56:8-163; *New York,* McKinney's General Business Law § 899-aa and McKinney's State Technology Law § 208; *North Carolina,* N.C.G.S.A. § 75-65; *North Dakota,* NDCC, 51-30-02; *Ohio,* R.C. § 1347.12 and § 1349.19; *Oklahoma,* 74 Okl.St.Ann. § 3113.1; *Oregon,* O.R.S. § 646A.604; *Pennsylvania,* 73 P.S. § 2303; *Puerto Rico,* 10 L.P.R.A. § 4052; *Rhode Island,* Gen.Laws 1956, § 11-49.2-3; *South Carolina,* Code 1976 § 37-20; *Tennessee,* T. C. A. § 47-18-2107; *Texas,* V.T.C.A., Bus. & C. § 48.103; *Utah,* U.C.A. 1953 § 13-44-202; *Vermont,* 9 V.S.A. § 2435; *Virginia,* Va. Code Ann. § 18.2-186.6; *Washington,* RCWA 42.56.590; *West Virginia,* W. Va. Code, § 46A-2A-102; *Wisconsin,* W.S.A. 895.507; *Wyoming,* W.S.1977 § 40-12-502 [Alabama, Guam, Kentucky, Mississippi, Missouri, New Mexico, South Dakota, and the Virgin Islands either do not have data breach notification laws or the bills are pending].

12. See http://www.occ.treas.gov/fr/fedregister/70fr15736.pdf.

13. Some states even have their own privacy protection and information security offices, like California. *See,* http://www.oispp.ca.gov/consumer_privacy/default.asp.

14. As of March, 2008, there were nine national data breach-notification bills pending before the 110th Congress.

financial institutions as "guilty parties" in a data security breach when a financial institution has no connection to the breach other than to deal with the potential aftermath of issuing new debit or credit cards whose data leakage was caused by another organization's lack of controls.[15] This is a significant risk of damage to a financial institution's reputation, and a vulnerability that is outside the control of the financial institution itself.

In general, current state and federal regulator breach-notification requirements mandate that response programs should contain procedures for:

- Assessing the nature and scope of an incident and identifying what customer information systems and types of customer information have been inappropriately accessed or misused;

- Assessing the risk to the customers of the breach and making a determination whether notification is necessary based on the risk of harm knowing that there are many breaches with a benign or limited outcome;

- Notifying the institution's primary federal regulator as soon as possible when the institution becomes aware of an incident involving unauthorized access to or use of sensitive customer information;

- Filing a timely Suspicious Activity Report (SAR) in situations involving federal criminal violations requiring immediate attention and promptly notifying appropriate law enforcement authorities, such as when a reportable violation is ongoing;

- Taking appropriate steps to contain and control the incident to prevent further unauthorized access to or use of customer information;

- Notifying customers in a clear manner if the financial institution becomes aware of an incident of unauthorized access to the customer's information, and at the conclusion of a reasonable investigation determining that misuse of the information occurred or is reasonably possible to occur.

---

15. According a March 2008 complaint by the Federal Trade Commission against TJX, the FTC stated that TJX "failed to use reasonable and appropriate security measures to prevent unauthorized access to personal information on its computer networks. An intruder exploited these failures and obtained tens of millions of credit and debit payment cards that consumers used at TJX's stores, as well as the personal information of approximately 455,000 consumers who returned merchandise to the stores. Banks have claimed that tens of millions of dollars in fraudulent charges have been made on the cards and millions of cards have been cancelled and reissued." See http://www.ftc.gov/opa/2008/03/datasec.shtm.

10.1.5 Supervisory Guidance

Financial regulators have issued numerous supervisory "guidance" requirements governing information security, authentication, business continuity planning, e-banking, vendor management, and payments. Much of this guidance—on a wide range of risk-based information security requirements and expectations—has been issued through the Federal Financial Institutions Examination Council (FFIEC).[16] For example, the *FFIEC Information Security* booklet serves as a supplement to GLBA regulatory requirements by following the same process-based approach.

10.1.5.1 Authentication

In October 2005, the Federal Deposit Insurance Corporation, Federal Reserve Board, Office of the Comptroller of the Currency, Office of Thrift Supervision, and the National Credit Union Administration jointly issued interagency guidance (under the FFIEC) on authentication for Internet banking. "Authentication in an Internet Banking Environment" replaced the FFIEC's *Authentication in an Electronic Banking Environment,* issued in 2001.[17] Regulators are focusing greater attention on the implementation of stronger authentication requirements for electronic banking transactions that expose nonpublic private information or that allow for third-party funds movement.

10.1.5.2 Vendor Management

An important component of regulatory and supervisory requirements governing data security is the oversight of third-party provider services, or more commonly referred to as outsourcing. Financial institutions increasingly rely on external service providers for a variety of technology-related services. Outsourcing, however, does not reduce the fundamental risks associated with information technology. While federal banking regulators permit financial institutions to outsource many areas of operations, including all or part of any service, process, or system operation, regulators insist that financial institutions have a comprehensive outsourcing risk management process to govern their third-party providers. Regulators require that financial institutions have a process that includes risk assessment, contract review, and ongoing monitoring of service providers. The regulators require that outsourced relationships be subject to the same risk management, security, privacy, and other policies that would be expected if the

---

16. The Federal Financial Institutions Examination Council (FFIEC) is a regulatory consortium comprised of experts from the Federal Reserve Board, The Federal Deposit Insurance Corporation, The Office of the Comptroller of the Currency, The Office of Thrift Supervision, and the National Credit Union Administration. Visit http://www.ffiec.gov/ffiecinfobase/index.html.

17. *See* http://www.ffiec.gov/pdf/pr080801.pdf.

financial institution were conducting the activities in-house. Federal financial regulators have the statutory authority to supervise all of the activities and records of the financial institution whether performed or maintained by the institution, or by a third party on or off of the premises of the financial institution.

Regulators have increased their focus on vendor management, particularly where such vendors process or have access to nonpublic private information. Key indications include vendor management provisions in the Safeguards rule, amendments to the Safeguards rule to address breach-notification requirements, Office of the Comptroller of the Currency (OCC) guidance on domestic and foreign-based sourcing issued in 2001 and 2002, and interagency guidance on business continuity planning and outsourcing.[18] In addition, financial regulators have steadily increased supervisory examinations to assess the vendor management programs of financial institutions. These in-depth vendor management examinations focus on due diligence, security procedures, contract reviews, business continuity plans, and exit strategies. At about this same time, international bodies released guidance on outsourcing.[19] In 2006, U.S. regulators began to increase coordination with foreign-based regulators, which included visits with key service providers in India, a major source of global sourcing for U.S. financial services companies.

10.1.5.3 Security Awareness Training

The regulators have included numerous references to the importance of training staff and educating customers on information security and privacy protection, as well as for business continuity, like flu pandemic planning, in regulation and guidance. Examples include the Identity Theft Red Flags Rule (November 2007) that says: "financial institutions must train staff, as necessary, to effectively implement the Program."[20] The *FFIEC Information Security Booklet* (July 2006) says that financial institutions should educate users regarding their security roles and responsibilities; training should support security awareness and strengthen compliance with security policies, standards, and procedures. In particular, regulators noted that "training should address social engineering and the

---

18. *See* Gramm-Leach-Bliley Act's Info Security Safeguards Rule, OCC Bulletins 2001-47, 2002-16, and 2004-20, Federal Reserve Board/OCC/Securities and Exchange Commission "Sound Practices" paper on business continuity, "Response Programs for Unauthorized Access to Customer Information and Customer Notice," FFIEC booklets on *Supervision of Technology Service Providers* and updated *Information Security* booklet.

19. *See* Joint Forum paper: *Outsourcing in Financial Services* and Bank of International Settlements and IOSCO high level principles for outsourcing.

20. *See* Office of the Comptroller of the Currency—12 C.F.R. pt 41, App. J.

policies and procedures that protect against social engineering attacks."[21] The 2003 *FFIEC E-Banking* booklet and the 2005 *Authentication in an Internet Banking Environment*[22] also included customer awareness requirements. In addition, the federal government, in partnership with the private sector, has initiated customer awareness programs through the work of US-CERT, Cyber Cop Portal, Cyber-Risk Management Programs, Cyber Exercises (e.g., Cyber Storm), and National Outreach Awareness Month.

10.2 Future Focus

Regulators are likely to focus on the following ten aspects of security and privacy protection:

10.2.1 Identity Theft Prevention

Regulators are likely to focus on reducing identity theft and other forms of fraud. The initial focus will be on assessing the identity theft red flags programs in 2008 and 2009. The regulators are likely to look at specific payment channels (e.g., ACH, remote image deposit capture). In addition, nonregulatory government agencies are likely to implement recommendations outlined in government reports aimed at reducing identity theft.[23] Furthermore, nonregulatory government agencies may push for greater restrictions on the use of social security numbers by financial institutions to authenticate or verify customers. There also may be a renewed push for stronger authentication methods and to examine differences in international and examine domestic authentication practices, especially if other regions move to stronger security controls and there are real or perceived security gaps.

10.2.2 Outsourcing and Offshoring

Regulators are likely to continue expanding efforts to ensure effective oversight of third-party providers and increase international coordination with regulators in other countries. Regulators are also likely to look to enhanced assessment tools developed by financial institutions, service providers, and assessment firms

---

21. *See* http://www.ffiec.gov/ffiecinfobase/html_pages/infosec_book_frame.htm.

22. *See* http://www.ffiec.gov/pdf/authentication_guidance.pdf

23. *See* "The President's Identity Theft Task Force Releases Comprehensive Strategic Plan to Combat Identity Theft" (http://www.ftc.gov/opa/2007/04/idtheft.shtm). The first part is a 108-page overview of the identity theft problem and the Administration's strategy to combat it. The second part is an 82-page summary of information ranging from data security laws to guidance for businesses on data breach.

to evaluate the effectiveness of financial institutions' vendor management programs. In response, financial institutions are developing more cost-effective means of managing risks associated with reliance on third-party providers. This includes developing more standardized methods for gathering information on third-party providers and more standardized procedures for evaluating whether adequate controls are in place.[24]

10.2.3 Cross-Border Data Flows

Regulators are likely to focus on ways to address conflicting international laws governing security and privacy protection. The U.S. Commerce Department, U.S. State Department, Federal Trade Commission and private industry are engaged in a pilot program for reciprocal compliance among the United States and 20 other Asia-Pacific countries through the Asia-Pacific Economic Cooperation (APEC) Framework for Cross-border Privacy Enforcement Cooperation. The APEC Framework and corresponding pilot provide a basis for developing mutual recognition of privacy and security compliance mechanisms across participating economies and for independent validation by "accountability agents." The framework and pilot are significant in that they would enable global organizations to voluntarily adopt uniform privacy and security practices on a regional or global basis and provide for accountability agents to certify an organization's entire privacy program or cross-border privacy rules. The pilot also may provide a framework for cross-border cooperation in the enforcement of information privacy and cross-border complaint handling.

10.2.4 Encryption

Regulators are likely to focus on encryption practices given the increase in use by financial institutions. Encryption is increasingly important as a tool for protecting sensitive data, particularly personally identifiable information, from disclosure to unauthorized parties. In particular, regulators may focus on how financial institutions and service providers manage encryption keys. For encryption to be effectively utilized across large enterprises, the encryption keys must be managed carefully for the duration of their entire lifetime to ensure that they are not easily guessed, disclosed or lost, and so that the data they encrypt can be recovered by authorized individuals.

---

24. A consortium of financial institutions, service providers, and assessment firms established a program in 2006 called the Financial Institution Shared Assessments Program," which provides a more cost effective and standardized process for financial institutions to evaluate the security controls of their IT service providers. *See* http://www.bitsinfo.org/FISAP/index.php for an overview the program and two key elements: "Agreed Upon Procedures" and "Standardized Information Gathering Questionnaire."

10.2.5 Online Behavioral Advertising

Regulators are likely to look at the ways financial institutions and others gather and use information about customers for marketing and advertising purpose. In 2008, the Federal Trade Commission sought public input on a proposal to establish privacy principles governing online behavioral advertising that would require greater transparency, consumer controls, reasonable security, limited data retention, consent, and disclosure.

10.2.6 Internet Governance

Regulators and other policy makers are likely to focus greater attention on the role of organizations, like the Internet Corporation for Assigned Names and Numbers (ICANN), concerning the security and stability of the Internet, and oversight of domain name registrars and other key players in the operation of the Internet.

10.2.7 Wireless Security

As the use of mobile financial services becomes more widespread, mobile phones may be targets for hackers and criminals. Consequently, regulators are likely to focus on wireless security concerns as more consumers use Wi-Fi technology and mobile phones to facilitate financial transactions. In 2002 and 2003, some regulatory agencies issued guidance on the risks of Wi-Fi. Regulators are likely to increase coordination with other agencies such as the Federal Communication Commission in new ways. This type of growing regulatory convergence has led to greater coordination with the Federal Trade Commission and other government agencies in recent years.

10.2.8 Capital Requirements for Operational Risk

The United States and international regulators have proposed capital requirements to address operational risks based on the Basel II International Capital Accord. International bank regulatory authorities intend the capital framework to promote enhanced risk management practices and better align minimum regulatory capital requirements with the risk profile of each covered banking institution. The evolving capital requirement could advance risk management of operational risk and internal control systems through a more holistic, enterprisewide risk management framework. The requirements set specific operational risk (which includes IT-related risks), loss data collection, measurement, and modeling requirements. It also requires oversight by senior management and the board of directors.[25]

10.2.9 Security of Web-Based Business Applications

The focus on application security is increasing due to complex applications developed in-house and by partners, the extension of business applications to vulnerable customers, and increasingly organized criminal attacks. Regulators are likely to continue to focus on whether financial institutions have developed adequate strategies for training software developers, automated and manual code reviews, and penetration testing. In 2008, the OCC issued guidance on software application security.[26]

10.2.10 Other Future Focuses in Financial Sector Security

Regulators are likely to develop guidance to address specific concerns based on risks that examiners detect during supervisory processes. For example, in 2008 the OCC issued guidance on bank oversight of payments providers for telemarketers and other merchant clients.[27] In addition, regulators are likely to harmonize security requirements across regulatory agencies. For example, in 2008 the SEC proposed amendments to Regulation S-P that set forth more specific requirements for safeguarding information and responding to information security breaches.[28] The changes to the information security and breach-notification requirements put the SEC more in line with the FFEIC agencies. In addition, regulators are likely to collaborate more. For example, the Federal Reserve Bank of Atlanta established a payments forum that includes OCC and FTC staff. Other areas include:

- Greater integration of information security with risk management and corporate governance;
- Need for data-centric approaches to protecting information;
- Adoption of enterprisewide fraud risks management and integration with Bank Secrecy Act programs.

10.3 Compliance Challenges

Several significant challenges face the financial services industry in compliance with security and privacy requirements. Typically, information security and

---

25. *See* "Reconciliation of Regulatory Overlap for the Management and Supervision of Operational Risk in US Financial Institutions" http://www.bitsinfo.org/downloads/Publications%20Page/regrecoct05.pdf.

26. *See* http://www.occ.treas.gov/ftp/bulletin/2008-16.html.

27. *See* http://www.occ.treas.gov/ftp/bulletin/2008-12.html.

28. *See* http://www.sec.gov/rules/proposed/2008/34-57427.pdf.

compliance efforts are spread throughout an enterprise under separate leaders and separate organizations based on the distinct regulations. For years, compliance has been the primary driver of information security, which has resulted in many organizations adopting the philosophy that compliance equals security. However, this model is not aligned with business objectives and, as the number of requirements increase, the more it is recognized to be inefficient and costly.

Forward-looking, financial institutions are looking to address security and privacy issues in three ways. First, change the philosophy from "become compliant to be secure" to "become secure to be compliant." Second, develop an organizational structure that consolidates disparate compliance efforts throughout the organization. Third, integrate information security into the broader risk management programs.

Specific activities making rapid progress throughout the industry include:

- *Data leakage detection and prevention.* This is constituted of technologies that find patterns in private information traversing through corporate networks in unauthorized patterns. Where patterns can be specifically identified as unauthorized, the data flows can be automatically prevented.
- *Source code vulnerability analysis.* This is a technology that scans software for vulnerabilities that may be exploited by hackers before the software leaves the development environment. This allows the developers to fix the software without unduly affecting production deployment timelines.
- *User anomaly detection.* This is made up of technologies that collect information on typical user-behavior in order to put out alerts on atypical activity. Alerts are typically shared with the user and combined with innovative customer support procedures designed to detect and prevent fraud.

Through these and similar as-yet-unforeseen countermeasures, today's financial institutions hope to maintain a low occurrence rate of identity theft other insidious frauds that accompany privacy violations.

11

Energy

Peter Curtis

There has been a lot of discussion in the security profession on the topic of convergence. Like any loosely bandied about industry jargon, it means different things to different people. But, it centers on the notion that physical and logical security measures overlap to the extent that management of them should be combined on some level. Peter Curtis brings this point home with his description of the energy industry. He makes it crystal clear that in the energy industry, cybersecurity risks have physical consequences and vice versa. Yet, for all that, the situation in the energy industry presents unique and widespread risks. Note that the advice Peter has for his reader is the same basic Security 101 that is taught in every other industry.

My first assignments in information security were in the public switched phone network. The operating systems were mostly based on UNIX, but there would be a piece of equipment here and there that was completely custom and its interfaces would act like nothing we had as yet seen. So, I learned early on that, no matter what type of equipment you have, you have to go back to Security 101 and look for features or compensating controls. What the energy industry seems to be going through is similar to a corporate security auditors' discovery that environmental control systems were placed on the Internet. The systems were designed to have manual operators; controls were not robust enough to be exposed to a network. But, if they were taken off, the data center would be worse off, not better. There is no choice but to attack the issues one device at a time.

—J.L.B.

11.1 Overview of Sector

The nation's exposed energy infrastructure and growing oil dependence present significant risks to the country's security (see Figures 11.1 and 11.2). In fact, inexpensive oil was, until recently, the fundamental building block of our digital society and economy. Oil accounts for over 90% of all the energy for our transportation systems. Electricity, on the other hand, plays a uniquely important role in the operations of all industries and public services. The loss of electricity for any length of time compromises data and communication networks, and virtually all digital electrical loads being deployed for physical and operational

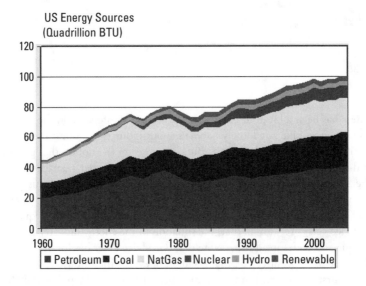

Figure 11.1   Trends in U.S. energy sources.

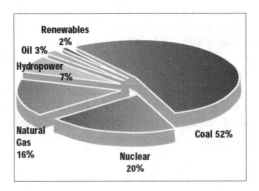

Figure 11.2   Fuel sources for electricity generation in 2000. Electricity is a secondary source of energy generated through the consumption of primary source.

security. Without oil and electricity our economy and security comes to a complete halt ... where life as we know it ceases.

Precisely because it is so critical, a late-2002 White House briefing involving the President's Critical Infrastructure Protection Board specifically noted that the electric power grid now stands "in the cross-hairs of knowledgeable enemies who understand that all other critical-infrastructure components depend on uninterrupted energy for their day-to-day operations." Computer hackers pose a significant threat to our information systems. There have been instances where hackers have gained access to electric power plants, and possibly triggered major power interruptions. These events indicate how vulnerable and fragile our critical infrastructure really is. The electric grid is not the only area we need to be concerned with; the government, military, and business networks are all at risk, and generally, officials are not acting swiftly enough to address these vulnerabilities. Steps need to be taken to improve information security and mitigate the threat of cyber attacks.

The government is a major target for cyber attacks. From 2005 to 2007, the Homeland Security Department, responsible for protecting civilian computer systems, suffered 850 cyber attacks. Recently the threat of cyber attacks has increased, becoming more frequent, targeted, and sophisticated.

Military networks need to be safeguarded as well. Research shows that cyber threats are forming and are searching for ways to remotely disrupt operations. Denial-of-service attacks are a major threat accomplished by bombarding a computer system with automated message traffic, causing it to overload, and its effect could be on the magnitude of a weapon of mass destruction.

Analyses of the vulnerabilities of other critical-infrastructure sectors have reached similar conclusions: The loss of electric power quickly brings down communications and financial networks, cripples the movement of oil, gas, water, and traffic, and it paralyzes emergency response services.[1] The reverse of this can also be true in that, if there was a disruption in the energy sources used to create electricity, it would paralyze the grid.

The stark reality is that a sustained interruption of any energy-delivery system cripples our country. The national electric grid is inherently vulnerable since a small number of large central power plants are linked to millions of locations by hundreds of thousands of miles of exposed cables. Nearly all

---

1. Precisely because it is so critical, a late-2002 White House briefing involving the President's Critical Infrastructure Protection Board specifically noted that the electric power grid now stands "in the cross-hairs of knowledgeable enemies who understand that all other critical-infrastructure components depend on uninterrupted energy for their day-to-day operations." *Computer World,* "Energy: The First Domino in Critical Infrastructure," September 9, 2002, http://www.computerworld.com/governmenttopics/government/policy/story/0,10801,74077,00.html.

high-voltage electric lines run above ground throughout the country with a handful of high-voltage lines serving major metropolitan areas. When one key transmission line fails, the load is spread to other lines which may become overloaded and also fail, causing a domino effect of outages.

Most accidental grid interruptions last less than two seconds, and many "power quality" issues involve problems that persist for only a few cycles. In most areas of the country, electric outages less than a couple of hours occur only a few times per year, and longer outages are even less common.

Unless deliberate, there is a low risk that several high-voltage lines feeding a metropolitan area from several different points could fail simultaneously, and when one high-transmission line does fail, resources are dispatched quickly to isolate the problem and make appropriate repairs and improvements. Deliberate assaults, by contrast, are much more likely to disable multiple points on the network simultaneously. A 2002 National Academy of Sciences report drove this reality home, observing: "A coordinated attack on a selected set of key points in the [electrical] system could result in a long-term, multi-state blackout. While power might be restored in parts of the region within a matter of days or weeks, acute shortages could mandate rolling blackouts for as long as several years." Operations that can afford to simply shut down and wait out short blackouts may not be able to take that approach in response to the mounting threats of longer outages.

The National electric grid is a vast, sprawling, multitiered structure that reaches everywhere, and is used by everyone. The North American grid, along with the Internet are the largest networks on the planet.

Over 70% of the top tier of the grid is typically fueled by coal, uranium, water, or gas, and the remainder by oil and renewables. Each lower tier is typically "fueled" initially by the electric power delivered from the tier above. Power plants in the top tier transport electrical power through miles of high-voltage, long-haul transmission lines, which feed power into substations. The substations dispatch power, in turn, through miles of local distribution wires. At the same time, a few large power plants can provide all the power required by a large city. Many communities are served by just a handful of smaller power plants, or fractional shares of a few larger power plants.

Many different power plants operate in tandem to maintain power flows over regions spanning thousands of miles. In principle, segments of the grid can be cut off when transformers fail or lines go down, so that failures can be isolated before they cascade and disrupt power supplies over much larger regions. The effectiveness of such failure isolation depends on the level of spending on the electric grid, which has been in decline for years as a consequence of electric industry deregulation. Identical strategies of isolation and redundancy are used on private premises to make the supplies of power to critical loads absolutely assured, insulating those loads from problems that may affect the grid.

Switches control the flow of power throughout the grid, from the power plant down to the ultimate load. "Interties" between high-voltage transmission lines in the top tiers allow even the very largest plants to supplement and backup each other. Distributed generation facilities in the middle tiers can power smaller segments of the grid and keep them lit even when power is interrupted in the highest tiers. When power stops flowing through the bottom tiers of the public grid, on premises generators are designed to start up automatically.

In defining priorities and deploying new facilities, collaboration between utilities and critical power customers is becoming increasingly important. Most notably, power is essential for maintaining critical services for first responders; those provided by E911, air traffic control, wireline and wireless carriers, emergency response crews, and hospitals, among others.

11.2 Risks Related to Security and Privacy

The security of all of these networks is the subject of urgent, ongoing assessment. Much of the analysis has been focused on physical and cyber security—protecting the physical structures themselves, or the computers that are used to control them. But, their greatest vulnerability is the power on which every aspect of their control and operation ultimately depends. While the multiple layers of the nation's critical infrastructure are highly interdependent, electric power is, far more often than not, the prime mover—the key enabler of all the others.[2]

However, in the past the energy industry has not typically been focused on information security risks, and even less concerned about privacy. Equipment failures are not anticipated to be due to information security vulnerabilities, and except in an acknowledgement of harm due to data theft, exploiting those vulnerabilities are not foreseen as likely catastrophic events. Though the root cause of the 8/14/03 Canadian event is listed as "Human decisions by various organizations, corporate and industry policy deficiencies, inadequate management,"

---

2. As observed by the Digital Power Group: "The security of all of these networks is the subject of urgent, on-going assessment. Much of the analysis has been focused on physical and cyber security–protecting the physical structures themselves, or the computers that are used to control them. But their greatest vulnerability is the power on which every aspect of their control and operation ultimately depends. While the multiple layers of the nation's critical infrastructure are highly interdependent, electric power is, far more often than not, the prime mover–the key enabler of all the others." Digital Power group white paper "Critical Power: Critical Power," August 2003, http://www.squared.com/us/products/critical_power.nsf/ 2a07e278887999ef8525660b0061eec3/bf7e79498590dae885256f020063b364/$FILE/Digit alPowerGroupWhitePaperAug03v2.pdf.

there is no indication that proper policies backed by strong information security measures is part of the solution.

According to the Federal Energy Regulatory Commission, hackers are now spending considerable time and capital to mapping the technology infrastructures of companies. The network exploitation done to explore a network and map it has to be done whether the intruder is going to steal information, bring the network down, or corrupt it. Information security experts believe that this may be the cause of a few recent major blackouts.

Hackers are like digital spies since they can steal information or disrupt networks remotely. Officials need to be more informative about security breaches, as they are a national security issue. The nation's intellectual capital and industrial secrets are at risk, and holding secrets on the matter only makes the situation worse. The private sector, which owns most U.S. information networks that operate power plants, dams, and other critical infrastructures need to do more to improve security and protect critical data. A cyber attack could disrupt operations and impact customers.

How do power outages relate to the level of reliability your company requires from an energy standpoint? Facilities can be generally classified by tiers, with tier I being the most basic, and tier IV being the most reliable facility. The reason for having different tiers is due in large part to maintainability (i.e., can the facility be maintained without shutting it down). Tiers I and II need to be shutdown; tiers III and IV are deemed "concurrently maintainable." Critical functions will usually require a facility in the tier III to tier IV range to utilize other strategies such as colocation. Although rare, it is possible that critical business functions will be located in a tier II or even a tier I facility configuration, despite the fact that both lack full backup and redundancy support. This is not to be encouraged. Figure 11.3 below identifies types of electric load interruptions associated with recent power outages shown in Figure 11.4.

In fact, the energy industry is just coming of age when it comes to operation technology in itself, without security-specific measures. Some organizations lack even accurate and up-to-date information to provide first responders of grid outages with the intelligence and support necessary to make informed decisions during electric emergencies. Keeping personnel motivated, trained, and ready to respond to emergencies is a challenge, made even greater without an appropriate records retrieval program in place.

Planning rationally for infrequent but grave contingencies is inherently difficult. Organizations that have prepared properly for yesterday's risk profiles may be unprepared for tomorrow's. The risk-of-failure profiles of the past reflect the relatively benign threats of the past—routine equipment failures, lightning strikes on power lines, and such small-scale hazards as squirrels chewing through insulators or cars colliding with utility poles. Now, in addition to concerns about weather-related outages (hurricanes and ice storms in particular), as well

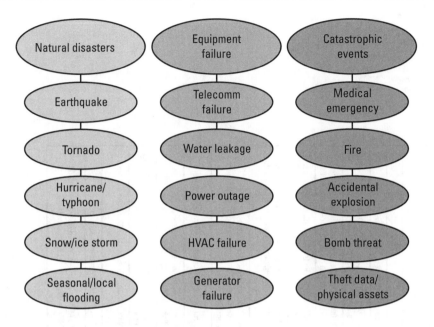

Figure 11.3 Potential causes of load interruption or downtime.

as recent experiences underscoring the possibility of widespread operational outages, there is as well the possibility of deliberate attack on the grid. The latter changes the risk profile fundamentally—that possibility poses the risk of outages that last a long time and that extend over wide areas. The possibility that any parent company of any energy provider may have the ability to link their own network onto those which control the power grid makes this threat increasingly likely to be enacted, perhaps even accidentally. The planning challenge now shifts from issues of power quality or reliability to issues of business sustainability. Planning must now take into account outages that last not for seconds, or for a single hour, but for days due to deliberate actions.

11.3 How Risks Are Addressed

The need to provide continuous operation under all foreseeable risks of failure, such as power outages, equipment breakdown, natural phenomena, and terrorist attacks requires use of many techniques to enhance reliability and resiliency. These techniques include redundant systems and components such as, standby power generation and UPS systems, automatic and static transfer switches, and the use of probability risk analysis modeling software to identify potential weaknesses of critical infrastructure, and develop maintenance programs and upgrade action plans for all major systems.

Recent Power Outages

Location	Cause	Effect
Florida	Significant Equipment Failure (2-26-08)	4,400,000 are left without power.
New England	Lightning storms cause debris to damage power transmission lines (1-14-08)	20,000 people report power loss over the span of a week-long storm
San Francisco	Data Center Backup Power Generators failed (7-24-07)	40,000 customers directly affected. Internet users worldwide couldn't access internet sites.
Los Angeles	Massive Power Outage – Utility Worker wiring error (9-12-05)	Traffic and public transportation problems and fears of a terrorist attack
Gulf Coast (Florida/New Orleans)	2004/05 Hurricanes: Ivan, Charley, Frances, Katrina, etc.	Millions of customers without power, water, food and shelter, government records lost due to flooding
China	20-million kilowatt power shortage – Equivalent to the typical demand in the entire state of New York (Summer 2005)	Multiple sporadic brownouts Government shutdown least energy efficient consumers
Greece	Temperatures near 104°F Mismanagement of electric grid (7-12-04)	Over half of the country left without power
O'Hare Airport	Electrical explosion (7-12-04)	Lost power to two terminals Flight delays over course of a day
Logan Airport	Electrical substation malfunction (7-5-04)	Flight delays and security screening shutdown for 4 hours
Italy	Power line failures Bad Weather (9-29-03)	Nationwide power outage 57 million people effected
London	National grid failure (8-29-03)	Over 250,000 commuters stranded
Northeast, Midwest and Canada	Human decisions by various organizations, corporate & industry policy deficiencies, inadequate management (8-14-03)	50 Million People effected due to the 61,800 MW of capacity not being available

(Source: Google research and Daily Alerts on Power Problems)

Figure 11.4 Causes and effects of recent power outages.

The Customer Average Interruption Duration Index (CAIDI) is a reliability index commonly used by electric power utilities to gauge the average outage duration that any given customer would experience. This index will drive the level of redundancy and business resiliency for an organization as it pertains to the critical infrastructure. As we are all aware, to address human risk factors, standard operating procedures (SOPs), emergency action procedures (EAPs), and alarm response procedures (ARPs) need to be available at a moment's notice so trained personnel can respond with situational awareness.

Many companies use web-based information management systems to address human risk factors. A living document system can produce a "database" of perpetually refreshed knowledge, providing the level of granularity necessary to operate, maintain, and repair mission-critical infrastructure. Keeping the ever-changing documents current and secure can then be easily addressed each time a capital project is completed or an infrastructure change is made. It is important to secure this critical infrastructure knowledge, and also leverage this asset for employees succession planning.

Events such as the terrorist attacks of September 11, the Northeast Blackout of 2003, and the 2006 hurricane season have emphasized our interdependencies with other critical infrastructures—most notably telecommunications. There are numerous national strategies and sector-specific plans such as Basel II, U.S. Patriot Act, SOX, and NFPA 1600, all of which highlight the responsibility of the private sector for "building an increased resiliency and redundancy into business processes and systems." These events have also prompted the revision of laws, regulations, and policies governing reliability and resiliency of the power industry. Some of these measures also delineate controls required of some critical infrastructure sectors to maintain business-critical operations during a critical event.

The unintended consequence of identifying vulnerabilities is the fact that such diligence can actually invite attacks tailored to take advantage of them. In order to avoid this, one must anticipate the vulnerabilities created by responses to earlier ones. New and better technologies for energy supply and efficient end-use will clearly be required if the daunting challenges of the decades ahead are to be adequately addressed.

In late 2000, the Electric Power Research Institute (EPRI) launched a consortium dedicated to improving electric power reliability for the new digital economy. Participants in this endeavor, known as the Consortium for Electric Infrastructure to Support a Digital Society, or CEIDS, include power providers and a broad spectrum of electric reliability stakeholders. Participation in CEIDS is also open to manufacturers of digital equipment—companies whose productivity depends on a highly reliable electricity supply—and industry trade associations.

According to EPRI, CEIDS represents the second phase of a bold, two-phase national effort to improve overall power system reliability. The first phase of the plan, called the Power Delivery Reliability Initiative, launched in early 2000, brought together more than twenty North American electric utilities as well as several trade associations to make immediate and clearly necessary improvements to utility transmission and distribution systems.

In the second phase, CEIDS, addresses more specifically the growing demand for digital-quality electricity.

"Unless the needs of diverse market segments are met through a combination of power delivery and end-use technologies, U.S. productivity growth and prosperity will increasingly be constrained," Stahlkopf said. "It's important that CEIDS study the impact of reliability on a wide spectrum of industries and determine the level of reliability each requires."

Specifically, CEIDS focuses on three reliability goals:

1. Preparing high-voltage transmission networks for the increased capacity and enhanced reliability needed to support a stable wholesale power market.

2. Determining how distribution systems can best integrate low-cost power from the transmission system with an increasing number of distributed generation and storage options.

3. Analyzing ways to provide digital equipment, such as computers and network interfaces, with an appropriate level of built-in protection.

It is only through these wide-reaching efforts to involve all industry constituencies can the industry start raising the bar with respect to protective measures and knowledge sharing.

11.4 Documentation and Its Relation to Information Security

Over the last twenty-four months, there have been critical infrastructure drawings found on unsecure laptop computers, in garbage pails, and blowing around the streets of major cities. These security leaks enable cyber threats to occur, and make our national infrastructure vulnerable to people who want to intentionally disrupt the electrical grid, or specific critical buildings vital to our national and economic security. Examples of these security leaks include a major banking and finance company's laptop computer that was found in India with critical infrastructure drawings on it, transportation drawings found in a trash can outside a major transportation hub, and most recently, the New York City Freedom Tower drawings found by a pedestrian searching through trash containers. The occurrence of these situations can compromise corporate and national safety and security if these documents fall into the wrong hands. Business officials traveling abroad are also a major target for information theft. Spyware installed on electronic devices and laptops can open communications with outside networks, leaving the information on them available to hackers. In the environment we live in today, we need a steadfast plan to secure invaluable information such as critical drawings, procedures, and business processes, such as shown in Figure 11.5. Below are questions and issues you may want to consider when you are evaluating your internal security:

Security Questions:

1. Have you addressed physical security concerns?

2. Have all infrastructures been evaluated for the type of security protection needed (e.g., card control, camera recording, key control)?

3. If remote dial-in or Internet access is provided to any infrastructure system, have you safeguarded against hacking, or do you permit read-only functionality?

4. How frequently do you review and update access permission authorization lists?

5. Are critical locations included in security inspection rounds?

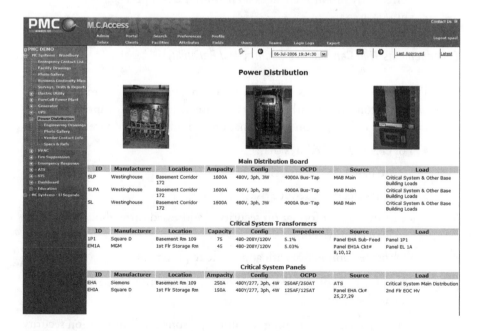

Figure 11.5 Typical screenshot of M.C. Access (courtesy of Power Management Concepts, LLC.)

Network and Access:

1. Do you have a secured network between your facility's IT installations?
2. Do you have an individual on your IT staff responsible for managing the security infrastructure of your data?
3. Do you have an online file repository? If so, how is use of the repository monitored, logged, and audited?
4. How is data retrieved from the repository kept secure once it leave the repository?
5. Is your file repository available through the public Internet?

Techniques for Addressing Information Security:

1. Enforce strong password management for properly identifying and authenticating users.
2. Authorize user access to only permit access needed to perform job functions.
3. Encrypt sensitive data.
4. Effectively monitor changes on mainframe computers.
5. Physically identify and protect computer resources.

Enhancements That Can Improve Security and Reliability:

- Periodic assessments of the risk and magnitude of harm that could result from the unauthorized access, use, disclosure, disruption, modification, or destruction of information and information systems.
- Policies and procedures that:
  - Are based on risk assessments;
  - Cost-effectively reduce risks;
  - Ensure that information security is addressed throughout the life cycle of each system;
  - Ensure compliance with applicable requirements.
- Plans for providing adequate information security for networks, facilities, and systems.
- Security awareness training to inform personnel of information security risks and of their responsibilities in complying with agency policies, procedures, and practices, performed.

- A process for planning, implementing, evaluating, and documenting remedial action to address deficiencies in information security policies, procedures, or practices.
- Plans and procedures to ensure continuity of operations for information systems.

Recommendations for Executive Action:

- Update policies and procedures for configuring mainframe operations to ensure they provide the necessary detail for controlling and logging changes.

- Identify individuals with significant security responsibilities to ensure they receive specialized training.

- Expand scope for testing and evaluating controls to ensure more comprehensive testing.

- Enhance contractor oversight to better ensure that contractors' non-compliance with information security policies is detected.

- Update remedial action plans to ensure that they include what, if any, resources are required to implement corrective actions.

- Identify and prioritize critical business processes as part of contingency planning.

- Test contingency plans at least annually.

11.5 Conclusion

It is important to address the physical and cyber security needs of critical infrastructures including systems, facilities, and assets. Security requirements may include capabilities to prevent and protect against both physical and digital intrusion, hazards, threats, and incidents, and to expeditiously recover and reconstitute critical services. Personnel should be trained and made aware of security risks and consequences, ensuring that sensitive information will not be leaked and lead to a security breach.

A sensible and cost-effective security approach can provide a protection level achieved through design, construction, and operation that mitigates adverse impact to systems, facilities, and assets. This can include vulnerability and risk assessment methodologies which determine prevention, protection, monitoring, detection, and sensor systems to be deployed in the design. Also, less frequent, but greater consequences must be prepared for. No longer are accidents the only risks involved. Deliberate attacks must be accounted for as well.

The increased use of and advances in information technology, coupled with the prevalence of hacking and unauthorized access to electronic networks, requires physical security to be complemented by cyber security considerations. Hacking techniques are becoming more sophisticated, and before enabling remote access for monitoring and/or control of critical infrastructure systems, cyber security protection must be assured. Major damage can be done remotely, and as much as possible should be done to prevent illicit access to critical networks.

Acknowledgments

I would like to recognize and thank the following people for their contribution and efforts in research, document organization, and review of this chapter on energy security. The involvement of these individuals has allowed me to share this vital information to the engineering and IT industries in a more expeditious manner as we evolve into the next generation of energy security: Charles Berry, Thomas Weingarten, P.E, Joseph Cappiello, Michael Recher, Elijan Avdic, Shawn Paul, John Thomas Montana, Kenneth Burke, Richard Reis, P.E., Kristen Quinones, and James Eksi.

Selected Bibliography

Barczak, Sara, and Carroll, Ronald, "Climate Change Implications for Georgia's Water Resources and Energy Future," http://www.cleanenergy.org/documents/ BarczakCarrollWaterPaper8March07.pdf, April 2008.

Brock, J. L., "Critical Infrastructure Protection," *Challenges to Building a Comprehensive Strategy for Information Sharing and Coordination,* July 26, 2006, pp. 9–10.

Curtis, P. M., Lindsey, T., "Bits Financial Services Roundtable," *Bits Guide to Business-Critical Power,* Washington, D.C., Bits, 2006.

Curtis, Peter M., *Maintaining Mission Critical Systems in a 24/7 Environment,* Piscataway, New Jersey, John Wiley & Sons, Inc., 2007.

Curtis, P. M., "The Demand for Power," *Mission Critical,* Volume 1 (Issue 1), 2007, 64 pages.

Davidson, Paul, "New Battery Packs Powerful Punch," http://www.usatoday.com/tech/products/environment/2007-07-04-sodium-battery_N.htm, April 2008.

Digital Power Group, "Critical Power," Washington, D.C.: Mills, M. P., Huber, P., 2003.

Fama, J., "Electric Reliability, Now Comes the Hard Part," *IEEE Power & Energy Magazine,* Nov./Dec. 2004.

Gotfried, S., and McDonald J., APS Announces New Solar Power Plant, Among World's Largest," http://www.businesswire.com/portal/site/google/index.jsp?ndmViewId=news_view&newsId=20080221005237&newsLang=en, April 2008.

Group C Communications, "Unlocking the Value of Your Facilities: Do you have a firm grasp on how your capital and assets are distributed throughout your facilities?" http://www.facilitycity.com/busfac/bf_04_09_services.asp, Sept. 2004.

Harris, Shane. "China's Cyber Militia." *National Journal Magazine,* http://www.nationaljournal.com/njmagazine/cs_20080531_6948.php, May 31, 2008.

Lovins, A. B., and Lovins, L. H., *Brittle Power,* Andover, MA: Brick House Publishing Co., Inc., 1982.

Mufson, S., "Changing the Current; State Environmental Laws Drive Power Producers to Renewable Resources," http://www.washingtonpost.com/wp-dyn/content/article/2008/04/21/AR2008042103004.html, April, 2008.

National Commission on Energy Policy, Ending the Energy Stalemate: A Bipartisan Strategy to Meet America's Energy Challenges. Washington, D.C.: National Commission on Energy Policy, 2004.

National Energy Policy Development Group, "Reliable, Affordable, and Environmentally Sound Energy for America's Future," National Energy Policy, Washington, D.C.: U.S. Government Printing Office, May 2001.

Souder, Elizabeth, "Plans for 8 Texas Coal Plants Formally Canceled," http://www.dallasnews.com/sharedcontent/dws/bus/stories/101607dnbustxucoalplants.172c72818.html, April, 2008.

Stobaugh, R., and Yergin, D., "Conclusion: Toward a Balanced Energy Program," *Energy Future,* R. Stobaugh, and D. Yergin (eds.), New York City, Vintage Books, 1979, pp. 291-308.

The White House, "The National Strategy for The Physical Protection of Critical Infrastructures and Key Assets," February, 2003, pp. 6, 9–10, 21, 28, 58.

12

Transportation Security

Steve Hunt

Transportation—along with other critical industries such as energy, health services, and emergency services—is at the confluence of security, safety, and privacy, where security measures are the means of achieving physical safety for human beings, as well as privacy of sensitive information about them.

Steve Hunt covers the security issues that need to be addressed so as to ensure that physical assets are protected and that terrorists are thwarted in their attempts to destroy human life and critical assets. He provides an interesting overview of the latest technologies in place and in development for detecting and reporting suspicious objects.

While Steve does make mention of the cyber security concerns relative to transportation, it is not a major thrust of the chapter. He alludes to SCADA (supervisory control and data acquisition) systems, which control many physical facilities, particularly in the energy sector, where they are used to manage power plants, dams, electricity distribution systems, oil and gas pipelines, and so on. In transportation SCADA systems are used to manage and control railway and automobile traffic, for facilities management at airports. As these systems increasingly move to the Internet, so the risk of compromise and takeover by terrorists and others with evil intent. The 2007 movie *Live Free or Die Hard* depicts in a fictional, though realistic, manner what the ensuing turmoil might be if criminals were to gain control of such systems.

The privacy aspect of transportation is also becoming significant with personal information being held by government agencies, airline systems, toll systems on highways, and the like. Traffic monitoring and toll-payment systems often know where your vehicle is as it passes by scanners, even if you are not the driver. Such sensitive information can be used merely for the purpose of billing, but it is easy to extrapolate to more insidious uses ranging from the marketing of products and services to the provision of evidence in a lawsuit.

While transportation is not generally considered from the cyber security and privacy aspects, it is easy to see how the sector might be affected by them in addition to the traditional personal safety aspect and the need to protect physical assets.

—C.W.A

12.1 Overview

The average American sees but a small part of the country's massive transportation system, yet its efficient and safe operation is essential to our economy and touches most every aspect of our daily lives. Daily, millions pack onto buses, subways, ferries, and light-rail mass-transit systems, not to mention the constantly growing numbers in highway and air travel. In addition to transporting our selves, billions of tons of freight and supplies critical to the national economy are crossing the land each day via truck, rail car and a huge number of cargo containers. Whether hauling people or products, transportation systems provide the backbone to the economy of the United States, making it an attractive target for terrorists with catastrophic potential.

The vital role of our expansive transportation infrastructure provides inviting opportunity for terrorists to extract both human and economic damage. In recent years, terrorists have killed hundreds during attacks on transportation facilities in London, Moscow, Madrid, and Mumbai. Reports indicate that between 1995 and July 2005 over 250 terrorist attacks worldwide were launched against rail systems, resulting in more than 900 deaths and over 6,000 injuries. Here at home, several specific plots have been reported recently against the New York mass-transit system alone. The Department of Homeland Security (DHS) continues to warn transit operators of "continued terrorist interest in mass-transit systems as targets," and has issued statements that "Trains and rail stations remain potential targets for terrorist groups...." In addition, the DHS cautions that terrorists might use trucks as weapons, in part because improved airport security is making aviation targets less attractive.

With the thought that ground assets such as trucks or rail tankers filled with hazardous materials can be so easily transformed into a weapon of catastrophic proportion, transportation security of surface transportation weighs in with the same importance today as air travel. In the wake of the tragic events of the 9/11 attacks on the World Trade Center Towers, the importance of more—and more comprehensive—plans for transportation security has come clearly into view.

Post 9/11, the transportation industry has focused on improving security on many fronts, including joint efforts, like U.S. Department of Transportation and U.S. Customs Service's Operation Safe Commerce, that seeks to address security concerns of shipping load centers, testing end-to-end solutions through the international supply chains that serve American consumers and businesses; and summits, like G8 and APEC, that foster collaborations across national borders and shed light on the inherent gaps in the security of diverse transportation systems and methods of operation.

Other organizational initiatives are bearing fruit for ports and transportation operations who are aggressively pursuing more elaborate and efficient corporate documentation and identity management; consolidating contact information repositories for human resources, which include data on employees, contractors, vendors, and job shoppers; building more robust IT infrastructures with redundant networks and redesigned operating architectures; introducing layered security architectures and paying more attention to available third-party solutions with a view towards outsourcing where significant advantages can be had.

In addition to the obvious need for increased security and surveillance at the nation's air transportation hubs, agencies and transportation authorities are becoming more attuned to vulnerabilities of ground security and transportation routes, but much more needs to be done and technology is playing a key role.

12.2 Technology's Role in Transportation Security

Just as action and coordination of government agencies, port authorities, and business entities are coming together, so demands on technology for transportation security are increasing. Computer-based data collection and monitoring systems, along with the networks that transport data to central locations where it can be analyzed and stored, are key components in the transportation security picture. While much new technology is available, it is commonly agreed that to be successful, technology solutions designed for this fast-paced and diverse industry must integrate well, be scalable, robust, and cost effective.

Technological components for transportation industry security include:

- Intelligent video surveillance systems, including integrated sensors, wireless transmission, and IP networking;
- Analytical and data management software;

- CBRNE (chemical, biological, radiological, nuclear, explosive) detection equipment;

- Global positioning systems (GPS) and radio frequency identification (RFID);

- Access and identity control;

- Systems integration for networks and information.

Intelligent video surveillance—The deployment of video surveillance has been wide spread in the wake of 9/11, much of this growth has been the result of the replacement of traditional analog systems and cumbersome video tape recording devices with inexpensive and easily scalable IP-based systems. In addition to expense, advances in thermal and infrared (IR) technology that allow cameras to see record in low-light and no-light environments. On-board camera features, like motion detection, have made video surveillance more attractive for transportation security. The development of advanced software delivers features like behavior detection, which can recognize that someone has left a suitcase unattended and can prompt an "unattended baggage alert" sending video of the scene. Such technologies not only create substantial security and loss-control benefits, but also a serious ROI for security operations, who no longer need to have human beings reviewing a never-ending stream of video surveillance feeds.

The practical application of scalable networking allows video captured in digital format to be networked using the Internet or company intranets, allowing multisite command and control. Digital networking also allows the integration of other sensors, such as chemical or explosive detectors, giving systems greater coverage and potential. Video surveillance can coexist and correlate with other applications, such as fire detection, as data is centralized and protected on strategically placed file servers.

Analytical and data management software—Once recorded and transmitted across the network, digital images provide a variety of safety options for transportation industry, in and around ports and on the road. For example, the powerful combination of physical security information management (PSIM) technology and video analytics enables powerful surveillance solutions from large amounts of information from a wide range of devices, data sources, and networks. By aggregating and coordinating related data, PSIM provides a means to quickly distill the most important intelligence from the collected data using advanced software techniques. PSIM can be used to integrate and analyze multiple data feeds on a centralized platform, thus enabling decision-makers to conduct faster and more accurate assessment of unfolding situations and direct faster and more effective responses.

While video surveillance has many applications outside the transportation industry, CBRNE detection equipment is particularly well suited for use with freight, baggage, and passenger inspection.

Most CBRNE sensors for transportation security systems, other than the nuclear detection, are focused on the detection of explosives. Many of the technologies developed and in use for aviation security are currently being studied for application in ground transportation systems.

- *Metal detectors* that use magnetic fields to detect guns, knives or other metal objects.

- *X-ray machines* employing electromagnetic waves to penetrate bags and create two-dimensional images screeners review to look for guns or other contraband.

- *Explosive detection systems (EDS)* currently inspect checked bags at airports. Using X-rays, they employ computed tomography (CT or CAT scan) to create more complex three-dimensional (3D) images that can compare the density of objects in bags with the density of known hazardous material, such as explosives. Used in concert with analytical software these systems can produce automatic alerts when potential threats are identified. Current EDS units can be as large as a car and cost in the million dollar range. Highly automated and capable of being networked, they can scan hundreds of bags an hour, but can have high false positive rates when they detect common objects that possess similar densities as explosives.

- *Explosive trace detection systems (ETD)* are also used in airports. About the size of a laser printer, they can cost less than $1,000. They detect tiny traces of explosives on a bag's surface that may have been produced by a bomb placed inside or by someone who touched the bag after handling explosives. While ETD machines have lower false positive rates than EDS systems, current versions are slow and labor intensive. An operator has to "swab" the bag and then analyze the swab with the ETD machine. ETD has recently been built into much more expensive new systems such as "puffer" portals through which passengers walk, devices that check the tickets or other travel documents for traces of explosives, and systems to automate ETD of bags. This technology is also used in portable "sniffers" and other devices.

- *Concealed object imaging systems* can "see through" clothing to reveal hidden items such as suicide bombs—a key transportation security requirement. Systems can be "active," meaning they emit energy to "illuminate" a subject such as X-rays, or "passive," meaning they work using waves naturally emitted by passengers. Active systems, like backscatter X-ray machines, create a highly revealing, controversial (and, so, problematic) image of the scanned subject, while passive IR thermography, or thermal imaging detects concealed items by using the heat naturally emitted by our bodies. Passive millimeter wave (MMW) technology uses complex technology to track waves generated and/or reflected from a passenger. Of particular interest for passenger and personnel screening, MMW can detect concealed objects at a distance, giving security officials a highly desirable "stand off" capability. New, active MMW machines can surround the subjects with MMW energy to create reflections from their body, but such active systems have raised concerns about health issues and the privacy of passengers. Similar to MMW, systems based on Terahertz (THz) technology rely on electromagnetic energy naturally emitted by humans.

- *Cybersecurity software products* provide a layer of security for transportation IT systems to protect them from hackers. Supervisory control and data acquisition, or SCADA, systems use IT to control physical systems need to by closely protected from virus attacks that could seriously impair or completely shut down systems. Analytical and information sharing software allow operators to closely track operations, uncover trends, and enhance IT security.

- *Tracking technologies* such as cargo information systems, electronic seals (eSeals), global positioning system (GPS), and radio frequency identification (RFID) enable operators to monitor key assets and inventory while stored, staged, and en route. For example, a hijacked truck with a working GPS unit could be tracked across the nation. RFID tags, on goods or tickets, can provide information to electronic readers, for the purpose of tracking or sending alerts. Electronic seals help guarantee that containers are not tampered with or cargo altered during shipment.

- *Access control,* from smart credentialing to technology for perimeter security, can prevent unauthorized personnel from entering controlled spaces in and around ports or transportation facilities. Access control can require entrants to provide biometric information, such as fingerprints or iris scans. A high level of systems integration and design is required to pull together complex transportation security systems, especially those involving networked sensors, command and control, intrusion detection and access control.

- *Target hardening and better communications* can reduce many vulnerabilities of transportation facilities and support information flow to officials, responders, and passengers. To compliment advanced data networks for surveillance, threat detection, and monitoring, programs such as Crime Prevention Through Environmental Design (CPTED) are removing regular trash cans, installing resistant glass, and eliminating dead space where bombs might be hidden. Such considerations have also created demand for products such as ballistic resistant trash receptacles and other innovative safety products. On a much larger scale, transit officials are taking steps to improve terminal security and safety with agencies focusing on improving passenger information systems to increase awareness and improve emergency response.

12.3 Security in Transit

The application of new technology to the unique challenges of transportation security can most easily be reviewed by addressing the different sectors of the industry: Ports (air and sea), the shipping load centers linked though international supply chains to the ports of origin for containers and cargo in demand by American consumers and business; terminals, where large numbers of travelers or commuters embark daily; and ground transportation, including roadway and rail systems.

At the nation's largest ports, including NY/NJ, Seattle/Tacoma, and Los Angeles/Long Beach, sea port hardening grants and operations like the U.S. Department of Transportation and U.S. Customs Service's Operation Safe Commerce (OSC) are steering programs and providing funding to aid in the application of new computer-based technology, information handling, and networked architectures to develop a supply chain security architecture as a basis for global standard for ports and shippers. It is hoped that these efforts will yield a scalable and repeatable architecture that will prevent unmanifested cargo from being introduced into the supply chain. OSC is about finding new ways to integrate technology to address traditional areas of concern for shippers, including better abilities to:

- *Validate security at the point of origin.* Ensuring that containers do not have security risks loaded into them in the first place is perhaps the single most important element of a secure supply chain. Without that, any subsequent application of technology can only monitor or secure an assumption of security, not the fact of security.

- *Secure the supply chains.* Preventing unmanifested and dangerous cargo from entering the supply chain by following a well-understood supply chain model and the use of technology such as electronic seals and RFID to provide added security through container tracking and transmitting tamper evidence.

- *Enhance the accuracy and communication of cargo information.* Developing systems for better cargo documentation requirements and better data availability and handling.
- *Monitor the movement and integrity of cargo in transit.* Exploring the use of new technology, like GPS tracking, to provide real-time tracking of containers.

The U.S. air transportation system is an attractive target for terrorists because of the potential that attacks on it will cause immediate harm and anxiety to large numbers of people, as well as cause massive economic disruption to the nation. The Transportation Security Administration (TSA), charged with responsibility for the implementation of technology for countering such threats, has invested extensively in the development and deployment of technological and procedural systems designed to protect the traveling public and the nation.

Airports, like mass-transit stations, are particularly vulnerable owing to commercial airlines' mission to provide a transportation service with a minimum of intrusion on privacy and with minimal disruption of access. The detection and mitigation of attacks on the system are made more difficult by the transient nature of the passengers' movement through airports and the fact that it is common for passengers to be carrying several bags, making it relatively easy to conceal hazardous materials.

While future attacks might involve the use of toxic chemicals, chemical and biological warfare agents (even radiological and nuclear materials), terrorist attacks to date have involved the hijacking and bombing of aircraft, so current technology concentrates on detecting weapons or explosives. Airports have been the prime proving ground for the use of metal detectors and explosive detection systems for baggage and passenger inspection. Explosive trace systems are in wide use today and, as threats of other hazards increase, more chemical, biological, radiological, and nuclear detection could play a role in regular passenger security checks.

The complex U.S. ground transportation system, including rail and trucking systems, affects every American every day. Some 14 million Americans each weekday on buses, subways, ferries, and light rail, which far exceeding the number of passengers on airplanes. At the same time huge quantities of supplies critical to the national economy are crossing the land. Rail and trucking systems present unique security issues as they transport cargo, as harmless as children's toys or as potentially deadly as hazardous chemicals, to and from nations' ports and terminals.

The TSA has identified 46 high threat urban areas (HTUA) to allow carriers to find alternate routes for hazardous shipments and has established ground-level safety inspection regulations to check for the introduction of improvised explosive devices. With more than 1.7-million rail shipments of hazardous materials annually, and because of their potential use by terrorists, protection of hazardous chemicals or radioactive materials during transport has represented a strong area of concern for the application of tracking technology like GPS and security devices like electronic seals.

Unfortunately, both GPS and electronic seals have drawbacks when applied to ground transportation, as GPS units can be moved between containers and electronic seals have fallen short of being endorsed by transportation authorities. Dan Murray, of the American Transportation Research Institute, recognizes the complex nature of the trucking industry as relates to national security. "We will never have a one-size-fits-all security solution," says Murray, who identifies recommendations for a suite of layered security solutions ranging from the overt to covert, with some balance between deterrence and monitoring. He sites reports that recognize that "a certain amount of risk acceptance in the Surface Transportation System." Adding to the complexities of trucking are issues of cost for new technologies and the custody and jurisdiction issues that arise as truckers and rail services move containers between port parameters and open road or rail.

12.4 Best Practices Applied

Michael Frank, assistant director of the Technology Services Department of the NY/NJ Port Authority Technology Center at the time of the 9/11 attacks, deployed many successful technologies including IP-based cameras, communications and tracking systems, and integrated data networks for the Port Authority. According to Frank, "It should be as easy to do things securely as it is without security." He sites the following IT management best practices he has applied to his divergent and successful security solutions:

- Have a balanced approach;
- Work with a dedicated staff;
- Learn from experience;
- Focus on standards;
- Look for efficiencies;
- Provide solutions that add value while being cost effective;
- Understand that you can't be masters at everything, so have strategies to maintain all employed technology.

13

Academia

Markus Jakobsson

As the author states, academia has some very different characteristics from industry and government. First the demographics in academia are biased towards younger, more inquisitive, less risk adverse users, users who are more likely to try new things and take chances. Second, the student is a customer rather than an employee of the school and therefore harder to control and discipline. Third, there is greater turnover; every year some existing students leave and new students join the school and the network. Finally, controls are more lax in an academic environment. As a result there is greater risk and less control. Unfortunately, since everything is interconnected, this situation can impact other sites. If academic networks and student machines get attacked and compromised, they can be used to launch cyber attacks. Corrupted computers in academia can be used as proxies and bots. Markus Jakobsson help us collectively to understand these issues, as well as their implications for a broader society.

At a first glance, one might ask why security and privacy in academia would be any different from security and privacy elsewhere. Nothing could be less true. There is a tremendous difference between corporate networks, governmental networks, and academic network. This chapter aims to describe what these differences are, and how the—often weaker—security in academia can impact security elsewhere.

—D.S.

13.1 Overview

13.1.1 Age and Demographics

To begin with, we need to recognize the demographic differences. Academic institutions, needless to say, are dominated in terms of numbers by students. The average age of users within academic institutions is much lower than many other institutions. There are indications suggesting that people become more risk averse as they grow older, which means that colleges and universities may be exposed to greater risks. At the same time, teenagers and twentysomes are often much earlier adopters as it comes to technology than older generations. This increases the threat they are exposed to in at least two ways: First, they are more likely to use applications such as social networking applications. This increases their exposure to targeted attacks, as we will describe in a case study below. Second, they are more likely to agree to try new applications—and not all applications are what they claim to be! Furthermore, in academia, everybody has network access. In other organizations, not everybody does, at least not as representatives of the organization.

13.1.2 You Cannot Fire Me

If a bank employee acts negligently, he or she can face serious consequences—whether lack of promotion, suspension, or even loss of his or her job. The same goes for employees of corporations, and to some extent government employees as well. This is well understood by the employees. In contrast, the worst that could possibly happen to a negligent student is the potential loss of network access, and even that is rather unlikely. This, too, is well understood. As a result, there is a much lesser feeling of responsibility in academia than elsewhere, at least as far as the role of the individual when it comes to protecting the security of the organization. Moreover, it may be less clear to many why the resources in colleges and universities must be protected. It is evident within most other organizations. For many attacks, though, there is no difference: For example, a botnet with a large number of nodes in universities is equally powerful as one with many nodes in corporations.

13.1.3 Hard to Educate Users

Ironically, it may be harder to educate academic computer users than users within corporations and government institutions. This is not to say that students (and professors) are less receptive to education than others. Rather, it is due to the much larger turnover within academia than many other institutions. The undergraduate student population is largely replaced every four years, and the population of masters students every year and a half. Those who have been educated to avoid risks will soon be elsewhere, and replaced by users without any exposure to previous security campaigns. Of course, this only means that the educational effort must be continuous and tireless.

13.1.4 Lax Controls

In corporations and government institutions, most users of the network connect using machines owned by and maintained by their employer. This is not the situation in academia, and this frustrates efforts to control the applications run by system users. Students often connect from home, and often own their own access points. As we will describe later, these often constitute a security problem. To further aggravate the problem, students are much more involved in exchange of files and applications than many other users—partly because their computers are also used for recreational purposes to a larger extent, but also due to demographic reasons. Students are more inclined to engage in piracy—which means that they are also more susceptible to attacks involving corrupted applications.

13.1.5 How Everything Is Connected

We have argued that academic institutions are at a greater risk for attacks than many other institutions. In turn, that might make these places more dangerous to others: It is important to understand that the security of two independent organizations depends on each other. A possible analogy is that of flu epidemics: if a large enough number of people have been vaccinated, then the population as such is less prone to epidemics, as the number of carriers is reduced. In particular, corrupted computers can be used as proxies (to anonymize traffic between the attacker and the victim in another attack), and as bots in a botnet (to use the corrupted computer as part of a coordinated attack). The latter are traditionally used for distribution of spam and phishing emails, but can also be used to host crimeware distribution centers and webpages impersonating legitimate service providers. If a very large number of computers are used to host content of these types, this severely hampers countermeasures based on take-down (by the blocking of offending computers). It also complicates blacklisting attempts—since blacklisting is a cornerstone in the defense against spam and phishing, this is a concern.

13.2 Case Studies

Although the following case studies included subjects that were not limited to academia, they provide good examples of the type of threats faced in the open academic culture described above.

13.2.1 Case Study: Social Networking and Crimeware

People are drawn in by websites containing fun content or something humor-ous, and they generally want to share it with their friends. In turn, these peoples' friends generally enjoy the site and will often share it with their friends too. This is considered social transmission: referral to a location based on recommenda-tion of peers. Often referred to as "viral advertising," this type of distribution of content has applications outside advertising. In particular, it can very easily be used to distribute crimeware—with the blessing of the people whose computers are infected! We will now review an experiment performed by Stamm, Jakobsson, and Gandhi [1] in mid-2007. The experiment was based on the cloning of an existing web-based executable, along with minor modifications to mimic the effects of the introduction of a Trojan. The goal of the experiment was to determine the extent to which people would agree to run an executable recommended by a friend of theirs.

Many web sites, including Carlton Beer's "Big Ad" commercial aired in 2007 from www.bigad.com.au, use Java Applets (Java programs embedded in web pages) to display content. A trusted applet is given more access on the visi-tor's computer in order to display full-screen video or make network connec-tions. People's willingness to trust their friends (and general lack of understanding about signed applets) lead to a possibility that the signed applets are installing viruses or other malware on visitors' computers. Trusted applets essentially have no restrictions. An applet is considered trusted when the following conditions are met:

1. The code (usually a JAR file: a java archive containing the code) has been signed by the author);

2. The browser has verified the signature against a certificate provided by the applet's author;

3. The client's browser accepts the certificate as trusted: it is issued by a trusted authority such as Thawte or Verisign and accepted by the user, or the user (who is prompted) chooses to accept an untrusted certificate. The most common untrusted certificate is not signed by an authority at all, but self-signed: the person who created the appli-cation also signs the certificate to say the applet should be trusted.

Before an applet is loaded, it is verified using the provided certificate and then the browser displays a "do you wish to run this applet" prompt to the user (see sidebar). If the user clicks "Yes," then the applet is trusted and given height-ened access to the visitor's computer. Many people simply click through the prompts presented by a browser, even if those prompts warn that an applet should not be trusted. One reason is laziness, and a desire to complete the task the user set out to do. Another is a failure to understand the consequences of not being cautious. In this particular example, yet another reason might be a matter of confused trust: the user trusts his friend's taste (and general benevolence), and confuses this with the trust that the software is secure.

Stamm, Jakobsson, and Gandhi found that people will quickly grant applets unrestricted access to their computers when they think a web site should be trusted for one of many reasons including: friends recommending the web site or the site appears (though is not proven) to be authored by a socially accepted group or company. An attacker can masquerade as this group or peoples' friends in order to get visitors to allow malicious code to be installed onto their machine.

Once its applet in their study was authorized, the Carlton Beer site downloads and installs the Vividas media player onto a visitor's computer. This application is then run to provide access to streaming media that is presented in full screen. The result is a video that starts to play immediately. An attacker could do the same thing, but with the exception that the downloaded code could also contain malicious segments that cause an infection of the user computer. (Even if that is not possible, one could consider the computer corrupted for the duration of the execution. That means that even if the program runs in a sandbox, it would have the ability to send information to other networked computers.)

The ability to download and install arbitrary executables onto a computer would allow an evil person to install crimeware instead of a media player. An even more malicious person could do both, thus making it seem like all that was run was a media player when in fact other software was installed in the background. A clever attacker could mirror the site and draw people to his site instead. He would erect a site that appears exactly the same but the applets would be re-packaged and re-signed to contain the crimeware too.

In an attempt to assess how successful such a mirror attack could be (where existing applets were injected with malware), Stamm et al. erected an exact copy of the Carlton Beer site at http://www.verybigad.com by downloading all the files from their server and placing them on theirs. To simulate an attacker's site, they then deleted the certificates and removed signatures from the applets and created their own self-signed certificates. They did not change the code in the applets to include malware, but they could have done that. Next, they modified the web site to record each visitor's access when (1) they initially loaded the site, (2) when they loaded the quicktime copy of the video that was not deployed by a signed applet, and (3) when the visitor finished loading the signed applet. This allowed them to gauge what percentage of visitors clicked "yes" to run the possibly malicious self-signed applet.

They found that roughly 70% of the visitors to the site loaded the self-signed applet. This is likely to be a low estimate, due to the fact that an early version of their code did not work on some versions of Internet Explorer. Thus, clients such versions were not properly delivered the applet, so they could not run it. This added to the number of hits to the site that did not load the applet (though perhaps they wanted to), and reduced the number of people who would be prompted by a friend of theirs to take a look at the video.

13.2.2 Case Study: Social Phishing

In a second case study, we will elaborate on the effects on security of social networks. In the corresponding experiment, Jagatic et al., simply harvested freely available acquaintance data by crawling a prominent social networking web site. That way, they quickly and easily built a database with tens of thousands of relationships. This could be done using off-the-shelf crawling and parsing tools such as the Perl LWP library, accessible to anyone with introductory-level familiarity with web scripting.

The phishing experiment was performed in April 2005. The researchers launched an actual (but harmless) phishing attack targeting college students aged 18- to 24-years old. Targets were selected based upon the amount and quality of publicly available information disclosed about themselves; they were sampled to represent typical phishing victims rather than typical students. The intent in performing such an experiment was to quantify, in an ethical manner, how reliable social context would increase the success of a phishing attack. A large number of subjects received emails that were spoofed, and which appeared to be sent by a friend of theirs, asking them to visit a web site indicated in the e-mail. A subject was considered phished if he or she entered his or her university credentials on this site. If this had been a real attack, they the phisher would have gained access to their account, and could have used this to install keyloggers, spam engines, or other crimeware. Of course, in the experiment, none of these actions were carried out.

It was found that over 70% of the selected victims fell for the simulated attack; this is at least an order of magnitude greater than the yield of typical phishing attacks that do not use any targeting. A detailed account of the study can be found in [2], and a description of the ethical aspects of the experiment in [3, 4].

13.2.3 Case Study: Infected Access Points

A very large number of people use a wireless network at home and in public hotspots, such as cafes and bookstores, and students are well represented among those who do. When they type www.mybank.com into their browser's address bar and press "go" their computer asks another computer, called a domain name server or DNS, "What is the address of www.mybank.com?" The DNS responds with a number, say 192.168.2.68, and your web browser begins a session using this address. The current infrastructure does not have safeguards to prevent incorrect or malicious responses from DNS.

Pharming or DNS spoofing exploits this weakness. A user's computer asks the DNS for www.mybank.com's address, and the DNS returns the address of a spoofed www.mybank.com, where the user eventually enters his or her username and password. It is both common and reasonable to trust DNS lookups.

The DNS on a wireless router is controlled by a small internal computer, called an *embedded system*, running specialized software or *firmware*. On some routers, it is possible to replace this software and to program arbitrary behavior. Misrouting DNS lookup is among the easiest ways to defy trust in a router. Worse, there is no physical evidence of these changes, and no virus scanners can detect these changes.

In an early paper, Tsow [5] showed how consumer routers are vulnerable to this type of attack. He argued that a scammer with $50,000 startup money can buy 500 routers and compromise them all over a weekend, later selling them at a discount or giving them away. The 2006 Identity Fraud Survey Report by the Javelin Strategy and Research shows that the average identity fraud amount is about $6,300 per instance. Assuming Bob can commit identity fraud against 3 people per router on average, his gross income from this seed money is about $9,450,000. At this rate, there is plenty incentive to distribute maliciously con-figured routers that steal private information.

In a follow-up, Tsow and three collaborators showed [6] that the attacker would not have to have physical access to the routers to be attacked, but that it would be enough for him to be within wireless range. They quantified this vul-nerability, showing that more than half of all deployed consumer routers are vul-nerable. Later, it was shown by Stamm, Ramzan, and Jakobsson [7] that this type of attack can also be perpetrated remotely, and simply by tricking a user to visit an infected webpage. This takes us back to the previously described case studies—what if an attacker somehow causes a large number of users to visit a bad webpage? These might be propagated using a recommendation by a friend or be due to a believed recommendation by a friend (that in reality was spoofed and generated by an attacker).

13.3 Protection

Of course, system administrators in academia recognize the extent of the threats to the user community as well as university data. They do their best to enforce controls at the operating system level (e.g., requiring strong passwords). They install antimalware software on university-operated computers and make that software available to their user communities. However, these efforts address only symptoms of the underlying security issues, not root causes. A comprehensive approach to securing academia is as yet an elusive research goal.

References

[1]   Stamm, Sid, Jakobsson, Markus, Gandhi, Mona, "verybigad.com: A study in socially transmitted malware," http://www.indiana.edu/~phishing/verybigad/

[2]   Jagatic, Tom, et al., , "Social Phishing," *Communications of the ACM*, October, 2007.

[3]   Jakobsson, Markus, Johnson, Nate, Finn, Peter, "Why and How to Perform Fraud Experiments," *IEEE Security and Privacy*, March/April 2008 (Vol. 6, No. 2) pp. 66–68.

[4]   Finn, Peter, and Jakobsson, Markus, "Designing and Conducting Phishing Experiments." *IEEE Technology and Society Magazine*, Special Issue on Usability and Security, *Communications of the ACM*, October 2007 (Vol. 50, Issue 10), pp. 94–100.

[5]   Tsow, Alex, "Phishing with Consumer Electronics—Malicious Home Routers," In *Models of Trust for the Web*, a workshop at the 15th International World Wide Web Conference (WWW2006), May 22–26, 2006, Edinburgh, Scotland.

[6]   Tsow, Alex, et al., "Warkitting: the Drive-by Subversion of Wireless Home Routers," In *Journal of Digital Forensic Practice*, 1(3):179–192, September 2006.

[7]   Stamm, Sid, Ramzan, Zulfikar, and Jakobsson, Markus, "Drive-by Pharming,"In *Proceedings Lecture Notes in Computer Science*, 4861, Springer 2008, ISBN 978-3-540-77047-3, pp. 495–506.

Appendix A
Key Information Security Law References

A.1   Federal Statutes

1. COPPA: Children's Online Privacy Protection Act of 1998, 15 U.S.C. 6501 et seq.

2. E-SIGN: Electronic Signatures in Global and National Commerce Act, 15 U.S.C. § 7001(d).

3. FCRA/FACTA: Fair Credit Reporting Act,

4. FISMA: Federal Information Security Management Act of 2002, 44 U.S.C. Sections 3541-3549.

5. FTC Act Section 5: Federal Trade Commission Act, 15 U.S.C. § 45(a)(1).

6. GLB Act: Gramm-Leach-Bliley Act, Public L. 106-102, Sections 501 and 505(b), 15 U.S.C. Sections 6801, 6805.

7. HIPAA: Health Insurance Portability and Accountability Act, 42 U.S.C. 1320d-2 and 1320d-4.

8. Homeland Security Act of 2002: 44 U.S.C. Section 3532(b)(1).

9. Privacy Act of 1974: 5 U.S.C. Section 552a

10. Sarbanes-Oxley Act: Pub. L. 107-204, Sections 302 and 404, 15 U.S.C. Sections 7241 and 7262.

11. Federal Rules of Evidence 901(a): see American Express v. Vinhnee, 2005 Bankr. LEXIS 2602 (9th Cir. Bk. App. Panel, 2005), and

Lorraine v. Markel, 2007 U.S. Dist. LEXIS 33020 (D. Md. May 4, 2007).

A.2   State Statutes

1. UETA: Uniform Electronic Transaction Act, Section 12 (now enacted in 46 states).

2. Law Imposing Obligations to Provide Security for Personal Information:

Arkansas	Ark. Code Ann. § 4-110-104(b)
California	Cal. Civ. Code § 1798.81.5(b)
Maryland	Md. Commercial Law Code Ann. § 14-3503
Massachusetts	Mass. Gen. Laws. Ch. 93H, § 2(a); 2007 H.B. 4144
Nevada	Nev. Rev. Stat. 603A.210
Rhode Island	R.I. Stat. 11-49.2-2(2) and (3)
Oregon	2007 S.B. 583, Section 12
Texas	Tex. Bus. & Com. Code Ann. § 48.102(a)
Utah	Utah Code Ann. § 13-44-20

3. Law Imposing Obligations to Provide Security for Credit Card Information:

Minnesota	Minn. Stat. Chapter 325E.64

4. Data Disposal/Destruction Laws:

Arkansas	Ark. Code Ann. § 4-110-104(a)
California	Cal. Civil Code § 1798.81.
Georgia	Ga. Stat § 10-15-2
Hawaii	Haw. Stat Section § 487R-2
Illinois	815 ILCS 530/30 (state agencies only)
Indiana	Ind. Code § 24-4-14
Kentucky	Ken. Rev. Stat. § 365.720
Maryland	Md. Code, § 14-3502; Md. HB 208 & SB 194
Massachusetts	Mass. Gen. laws. Ch. 93I
Michigan	MCL § 445.72a
Montana	Mont. Stat. § 30-14-1703
Nevada	Nev. Rev. Stat. 603A.200

New Jersey	N.J. Stat. 56:8-162
North Carolina	N.C. Gen. Stat § 75-64
Oregon	2007 S.B. 583, Section 12
Texas	Tex. Bus. & Com. Code Ann. § 48.102(b)
Utah	Utah Code Ann. § 13-42-201
Vermont	Vt. Stat. Tit. 9 § 2445 et seq.
Washington	RCWA 19.215.020

5. Security Breach Notification Laws

Alaska	Ala. Stat. §§ 45.48.010—45.48.90
Arizona	Ariz. Rev. Stat. § 44-7501
Arkansas	Ark. Code § 4-110-101 et seq.
California	Cal. Civ. Code § 1798.82
Colorado	Col. Rev. Stat. § 6-1-716
Connecticut	Conn. Gen Stat. 36A-701(b)
Delaware	De. Code tit. 6, § 12B-101 et seq.
District of Columbia	DC Official Code § 28-3851 et seq.
Florida	Fla. Stat. § 817.5681
Georgia	Ga. Code § 10-1-910 et seq.[1]
Hawaii	Hawaii Rev. Stat. § 487N-2
Idaho	Id. Code §§ 28-51-104 to 28-51-107
Illinois	815 Ill. Comp. Stat. 530/1 et seq.
Indiana	Ind. Code § 24-4.9
Iowa	2008 Iowa S.F. 2308
Kansas	Kansas Stat. 50-7a01, 50-7a02 (2006 S.B. 196, Chapter 149)
Louisiana	La. Rev. Stat. § 51:3071 et seq.
Maine	Me. Rev. Stat. tit. 10 §§ 1347 et seq.
Maryland	Md. Code, §§ 14-3501 thru 14-3508; Md. HB 208 & SB 194
Massachusetts	Mass. Gen. Laws. Ch. 93H; 2007 H.B. 4144
Michigan	MCL 445.63, Sections 12, 12a, & 12b; 2006 S.B. 309

---

1. Applies to information brokers only.

Minnesota	Minn. Stat. § 325E.61, § 609.891
Montana	Mont. Code § 30-14-1701 et seq.
Nebraska	Neb. Rev Stat 87-801 et. seq.
Nevada	Nev. Rev. Stat. 603A.010 et seq.
New Hampshire	N.H. RS 359-C:19 et seq.
New Jersey	N.J. Stat. 56:8-163
New York	N.Y. Bus. Law § 899-aa
North Carolina	N.C. Gen. Stat § 75-65
North Dakota	N.D. Cent. Code § 51-30-01 et seq.
Ohio	Ohio Rev. Code § 1349.19, §1347 et seq.
Oklahoma	Okla. Stat. § 74-3113.1[2]
Oregon	2007 S.B. 583
Pennsylvania	73 Pa. Cons. Stat. § 2303
Puerto Rico	2005 H.B. 1184
Rhode Island	R.I. Gen. Laws § 11-49.2-1 et seq.
South Carolina	S.C. Code § 39-1-90
Tennessee	Tenn. Code § 47-18-2107
Texas	Tex. Bus. & Com. Code § 48.001 et seq. and § 35.58
Utah	Utah Code § 13-44-101 et seq.
Vermont	Vt. Stat. Tit. 9 § 2430 et seq.
Virgin Islands (US)	14 V.I.C. § 2209 (2007) [§ 2208 for Govt. Agencies]
Virginia	Va. Code. 18.2-186.6
Washington	Wash. Rev. Code § 19.255.010
West Virginia	W. Va. Code §§46A-2A-101—46A-2A-105
Wisconsin	Wis. Stat. § 895.507
Wyoming	Wyo. Stat. §§ 40-12-501—40-12-502

6. State SSN Laws

Arizona	Ariz. Rev. Stat. § 44-1373
Arkansas	Ark. Code Ann. § 4-86-107; § 6-18-208
California	Cal. Civ. Code § 1798.85; Fam. Code § 2024.5

---

2. Applies to state agencies only.

Colorado	Colo. Rev. Stat. § 6-1-715; § 23-5-127;
Connecticut	Conn. Gen. Stat. § 8-64b; § 42-470
Delaware	Del. Code Ann., tit. 7 § 503
Florida	Fla. Stat. Ch. 97.05851
Georgia	Ga. Code Ann. § 10-1-393.8; § 50-18-72
Hawaii	Haw. Rev. Stat. § 12-32; §§ 487J-2 to 487J-3
Illinois	815 Ill. Comp. Stat. 505/2QQ3 and 505/2RR
Indiana	Ind. Code § 4-1-10-1 et seq.; § 9-24-6-2; § 9-24-9-2;§ 9-24-11-5; § 9-24-16-3; §§ 24-4-14-1 to 24-4-14-8
Kansas	Kan. Stat. Ann § 75-3520
Louisiana	La. Rev. Stat. Ann. 9:5141; 35:17
Maine	Me. Rev. Stat. Ann tit. 10 § 1272-B
Maryland	Md. Code Ann., Com. Law § 14-3401 et seq.
Massachusetts	Mass. Gen. Laws Ch. 167B, § 14 & § 22
Michigan	Mich. Comp. Laws § 445.81 et seq.
Minnesota	Minn. Stat. § 325E.59
Missouri	Mo. Rev. Stat. § 407.1355
Montana	Mont. Code Ann. § 30-14-1702, § 30-14-1703
Nebraska	Neb. Rev. Stat. § 48-237
Nevada	Nev. Rev. Stat. Chapter 239; Chapter 239B; Chapter 603
New Jersey	N.J. Stat. Ann. § 47:1-16
New Mexico	N.M. Stat. Ann. § 57-12B-1 et seq.
New York	N.Y. Gen. Bus. Law § 399-dd (2007)
North Carolina	N.C. Gen. Stat. §§ 75-62
North Dakota	N.D. Cent. Code § 39-06-14
Oklahoma	Okla. Stat. tit. 40, § 173.1
Oregon	Ore. Als. 759
Pennsylvania	74 Pa. Stat. Ann. §§ 201 to 204
Rhode Island	R.I. Gen. Laws § 6-13-19
South Carolina	S.C. Code Ann. § 7-5-170
South Dakota	S.D. Codified Laws § 32-12-17.10; § 32-12-17.13
Texas	Tex. Bus. & Com. Code Ann. 35.48

Texas	Tex. Bus. & Com. Code Ann. 35.58; Elec. Code Ann. § 13.004
Utah	Utah Code Ann. § 31A-21-110
Vermont	9 Ver. Stat. Ann §§ 2030, 2440
Virginia	Va. Code Ann. § 59.1-443.2
Wisconsin	Wis. Stat. § 36.32
West Virginia	W. Va. Code § 17E-1-11

A.3   Federal Regulations

1. Regulations Imposing Obligation to Provide Security

COPPA Regulations: 16 C.F.R. 312.8.

DHS Regulations: Electronic Signature and Storage of Form I-9, Employment Eligibility Verification, 8 C.F.R. Part 274a (e), (f), (g), and (h).

FCC Order Regarding Pretexting: April 2, 2007—In the Matter of Implementation of the Telecommunications Act of 1996: Telecommunications Carriers' Use of Customer Proprietary Network Information and Other Customer Information IP-Enabled Services, CC Docket No. 96-115, WC Docket No. 04-36, April 2, 2007, at Paragraphs 33-36; available at http://hraunfoss.fcc.gov/edocs_public/attachmatch/FCC-07-22A1.pdf.

FDA Regulations: 21 C.F.R. Part 11.

FFIEC Guidance: Authentication in an Internet Banking Environment, October 12, 2005, available at http://www.ffiec.gov/pdf/authentication_guidance.pdf. See also "Frequently Asked Questions on FFIEC Guidance on Authentication in an Internet Banking Environment," August 8, 2006 at p. 5, available at http://www.ncua.gov/letters/2006/CU/06-CU-13_encl.pdf.

GLB Security Regulations: Interagency Guidelines Establishing Standards for Safeguarding Consumer Information (to implement §§ 501 and 505(b) of the Gramm-Leach-Bliley Act), 12 C.F.R. Part 30, Appendix B (OCC), 12 C.F.R. Part 208, Appendix D (Federal Reserve System), 12 C.F.R. Part 364, Appendix B (FDIC), 12 C.F.R. Part 568 (Office of Thrift Supervision), and 16 C.F.R. Part 314 (FTC).

GLB Security Regulations (FTC): FTC Safeguards Rule (to implement §§ 501 and 505(b) of the Gramm-Leach-Bliley Act), 16 C.F.R. Part 314 (FTC).

HIPAA Security Regulations: Final HIPAA Security Regulations, 45 C.F.R. Part 164.

IRS Regulations: Rev. Proc. 97-22, 1997-1 C.B. 652, 1997-13 I.R.B. 9, and Rev. Proc. 98-25.

IRS Regulations: IRS Announcement 98-27, 1998-15 I.R.B. 30, and Tax Regs. 26 C.F.R. § 1.1441-1(e)(4)(iv).

OFHEO Safety and Soundness Regulation: 12 C.F.R. Part 1720, Appendix C—Policy Guidance; Safety and Soundness Standards for Information, available at www.ofheo.gov/Media/Archive/docs/regs/finalssr.pdf.

OFHEO Record Retention Regulation: 12 C.F.R. Part 1732 (at Section 1732.6), available at www.ofheo.gov/media/pdf/RecordRetentionfinalreg102706.pdf.

SEC Regulations: 17 C.F.R. 240.17a-4, and 17 C.F.R. 257.1(e)(3).

SEC Regulations: 17 C.F.R. § 248.30 Procedures to safeguard customer records and information; disposal of consumer report information (applies to any broker, dealer, and investment company, and every investment adviser registered with the SEC).

2. Regulations Imposing Authentication Requirements

ACH Operating Rules: Section 2.10.2.2 ("Verification of Receiver's Identity").

FCC Order re Pretexting: April 2, 2007—In the Matter of Implementation of the Telecommunications Act of 1996: Telecommunications Carriers' Use of Customer Proprietary Network Information and Other Customer Information IP-Enabled Services, CC Docket No. 96-115, WC Docket No. 04-36, April 2, 2007, at Paragraphs 13-25; available at http://hraunfoss.fcc.gov/edocs_public/attachmatch/FCC-07-22A1.pdf

FFIEC Guidance: Authentication in an Internet Banking Environment, October 12, 2005, available at http://www.ffiec.gov/pdf/authentication_guidance.pdf.

(a) USA PATRIOT Act

31 U.S.C. 5318—Section 326—"Verification of Identification"

Know your customer rules.

(b) UN Convention on the Use of Electronic Communications in International Contracts—Article 9.

3. Data Disposal/Destruction Regulations

(a) *FCRA Data Disposal Rules:* 12 C.F.R. Parts 334, 364.

(b) *SEC Regulations:* 17 C.F.R. § 248.30 Procedures to safeguard customer records and information; disposal of consumer report information (applies to any broker, dealer, and investment company, and every investment adviser registered with the SEC).

4. Security Breach Notification Regulations

(a) *FCC Order re Pretexting:* April 2, 2007—In the Matter of Implementation of the Telecommunications Act of 1996: Telecommunications Carriers' Use of Customer Proprietary Network Information and Other Customer Information IP-Enabled Services, CC Docket No. 96-115, WC Docket No. 04-36, April 2, 2007, at paragraphs 26-32; available at http://hraunfoss.fcc.gov/edocs_public/attachmatch/FCC-07-22A1.pdf

(b) *GLB Security Breach Notification Rule:* Interagency Guidance on Response Programs for Unauthorized Access to Customer Information and Customer Notice, 12 C.F.R. Part 30 (OCC), 12 C.F.R. Part 208 (Federal Reserve System), 12 C.F.R. Part 364 (FDIC), and 12 C.F.R. Part 568 (Office of Thrift Supervision), available at www.occ.treas.gov/consumer/Customernoticeguidance.pdf.

(c) *IRS Regulations:* Rev. Proc. 97-22, 1997-1 C.B. 652, 1997-13 I.R.B. 9, and Rev. Proc. 98-25.

A.4   State Regulations

1. Insurance—NAIC Model Regulations:

National Association of Insurance Commissioners, Standards for Safeguarding Consumer Information, Model Regulation.

2. Attorneys:

New Jersey Advisory Committee on Professional Ethics, Opinion 701 (2006) available at http://www.judiciary.state.nj.us/notices/ethics/ACPE_Opinion701_ElectronicStorage_12022005.pdf.

A.5   Court Decisions

1. In Re TJX Companies Retail Security Breach Litigation, 2007 U.S. Dist. Lexis 77236 (D. Mass. October 12, 2007) (rejecting a negligence claim due to the economic loss doctrine, but allowing a negligent misrepresentation claim to proceed).

2. Wolfe v. MBNA America Bank, 485 F.Supp.2d 874, 882 (W.D. Tenn. 2007).

3. Lorraine v. Markel, 2007 U.S. Dist. LEXIS 33020 (D. Md. May 4, 2007).

4. Guin v. Brazos Higher Education Service, 2006 U.S. Dist. LEXIS 4846 (D. Minn. Feb. 7, 2006).

5. American Express v. Vinhnee, 336 B.R. 437; 2005 Bankr. LEXIS 2602 (9th Cir. December 16, 2005).

6. Bell v. Michigan Council 25, No. 246684, 2005 Mich. App. LEXIS 353 (Mich. App. Feb. 15, 2005) (Unpublished opinion).

7. Inquiry Regarding the Entry of Verizon-Maine Into The InterLATA Telephone Market Pursuant To Section 271 of Telecommunication Act of 1996, Docket No. 2000-849, Maine Public Utilities Commission, 2003 Me. PUC LEXIS 181, April 30, 2003; available at www.maine.gov/mpuc/orders/2000/2000-849o.htm.

A.6 FTC Decisions and Consent Decrees

1. In The Matter of The TJX Companies, Inc., FTC File No. 072-3055 (Agreement Containing Consent Order, March 27, 2008), available at www.ftc.gov/os/caselist/0723055.

2. In the Matter of Reed Elsevier Inc. and Seisint, Inc., FTC File No. 052-3094 (Agreement Containing Consent Order, March 27, 2008), available at www.ftc.gov/os/caselist/0523094.

3. U.S. v. ValueClick, Inc., Case No. CV08-01711 MMM (RZx), FTC File Nos. 072-3111 and 072-3158 (Stipulated Final Judgment, C.D. Cal. Mar. 17, 2008), available at www.ftc.gov/os/caselist/0723111.

4. In the Matter of Goal Financial LLC (Agreement Containing Consent Order, FTC File No. 072 3013, March 4, 2008), available at www.ftc.gov/os/caselist/0723013 (for alleged failure to provide "reasonable and appropriate security" for consumers' personal information in violation of the FTC's Standards for Safeguarding Customer Information Rule and its Privacy of Customer Financial Information Rule [both of which implement provisions of the Gramm-Leach-Bliley Act]).

5. In the Matter of Life is good, Inc. (Agreement Containing Consent Order, FTC File No. 072 3046, January 17, 2008), available at www.ftc.gov/os/caselist/0723046.

6. In the Matter of Guidance Software (Agreement Containing Consent Order, FTC File No. 062 3057, November 16, 2006), available at www.ftc.gov/opa/2006/11/guidance.htm.

7. In the Matter of CardSystems Solutions, Inc., (Agreement Containing Consent Order, FTC File No. 052 3148, February 23, 2006), available at www.ftc.gov/opa/2006/02/cardsystems_r.htm.

8. United States v. ChoicePoint, Inc. (Stipulated Final Judgment, FTC File No. 052 3069, N.D. Ga. Jan. 26, 2006), available at www.ftc.gov/os/caselist/choicepoint/choicepoint.htm.

9. In the Matter of DSW Inc., (Agreement containing Consent Order, FTC File No. 052 3096, Dec. 1, 2005), available at www.ftc.gov/opa/2005/12/dsw.htm.

10. In the Matter of BJ's Wholesale Club, Inc. (Agreement containing Consent Order, FTC File No. 042 3160, June 16, 2005), available at www.ftc.gov/opa/2005/06/bjswholesale.htm.

11. In the Matter of Sunbelt Lending Services, Inc. (Agreement containing Consent Order, FTC File No. 042 3153, Nov. 16, 2004), available at www.ftc.gov/os/caselist/0423153/04231513.htm.

12. In the Matter of Petco Animal Supplies, Inc. (Agreement containing Consent Order, FTC File No. 042 3153, Nov. 7, 2004), available at www.ftc.gov/os/caselist/0323221/0323221.htm.

13. In the Matter of MTS, Inc., d/b/a Tower records/Books/Video (Agreement containing Consent Order, FTC File No. 032-3209, Apr. 21, 2004), available at www.ftc.gov/os/caselist/0323209/040421agree 0323209.pdf.

14. In the matter of Guess?, Inc. (Agreement containing Consent Order, FTC File No. 022 3260, June 18, 2003), available at www.ftc.gov/os/2003/06/guessagree.htm.

15. FTC V. Microsoft (Consent Decree, Aug. 7, 2002), available at www.ftc.gov/os/2002/08/microsoftagree.pdf.

16. In the Matter of Eli Lilly and Company (Decision and Order, FTC Docket No. C-4047, May 8, 2002), available at www.ftc.gov/os/2002/05/elilillydo.htm.

A.7 State Attorneys General Consent Decrees

1. In the Matter of Providence Health System-Oregon (Attorney General of Oregon, Assurance of Discontinuance), September 26, 2006, available at www.doj.state.or.us/media/pdf/finfraud_providence_avc.pdf.

2. In the Matter of Barnes & Noble.com, LLC (Attorney General of New York, Assurance of Discontinuance, Apr. 20, 2004), available at www.bakerinfo.com/ecommerce/barnes-noble.pdf.

3. In the Matter of Ziff Davis Media Inc. (Attorneys General of California, New York, and Vermont), Assurance of Discontinuance, August 28, 2002), available at www.oag.state.ny.us/press/2002/aug/aug28a_02_attach.pdf.

A.8 European Union—Directives

See http://ec.europa.eu/justice_home/fsj/privacy/law/implementation_en.htm.

1. *EU Data Protection Directive:* European Union Directive 95/46/EC of February 20, 1995, on the protection of individuals with regard to the processing of personal data and on the free movement of such data (Data Protection Directive), Article 17, available at http://eur-lex.europa.eu/LexUriServ/LexUriServ.do?uri=CELEX:319 95L0046:EN:HTML.

2. *EU Data Protection Directive:* European Union Directive 2006/24/EC of March 15, 2006, on the retention of data generated or processed in connection with the provision of publicly available electronic communications services or of public communications networks and amending Directive 2002/58/EC, available at http://eurocrim.jura.uni-tuebingen.de/cms/en/doc/745.pdf.

A.9 European Union—Security Provisions in Country Implementations of Data Protection Directive

See http://ec.europa.eu/justice_home/fsj/privacy/law/implementation_en.htm

Belgium—Belgian Law of 8 December 1992 on Privacy Protection in relation to the Processing of Personal Data, as modified by the law of 11 December 1998 Implementing Directive 95/46/EC, and the law of 26 February 2003; available at www.law.kuleuven.ac.be/icri/publications/499Consolidated_Belgian_Privacylaw_v200310.pdf. See Chapter IV, Article 16 (Confidentiality and security of processing). See also, 13 February 2001—Royal Decree Implementing the Act of December 8, 1992 on Privacy Protection in relation to the Processing of Personal Data.

Czech Republic—Consolidated version of the Personal Data Protection Act, Act 101 of April 4, 2000 on the Protection of Personal Data and on Amendment to Some Acts; available at http://ec.europa.eu/justice_home/fsj/privacy/docs/implementation/czech_republic_act_101_en.pdf See Articles 15, 27, 44, and 45.

Cyprus—Law of 2001, amended 2003; Available at www.dataprotection.gov.cy/dataprotection/dataprotection.nsf/697e70c0046f7759c2256e8c00

4a0a49/f8e24ef90a27f34fc2256eb4002854e7/$FILE/138(I)-2001_en.pd
f. See Article 10(3).

Denmark—Act on Processing of Personal Data,; Act No. 429 of 31 May
2000, (unofficial English translation); available at
www.datatilsynet.dk/include/show.arti-
cle.asp?art_id=443&sub_url=/lovgivning/indhold.asp&nodate=1. See Title IV, Part 11, Sections 41 and 42 (Security of processing).

Estonia—Personal Data Protection Act; Passed 12 February 2003 (RT1 I
2003, 26, 158), entered into force 1 October 2003; available at
www.legaltext.ee/text/en/X70030.htm. See Chapter 3, Sections 18-20
(Personal Data Processing Requirements and Security Measures to Protect
Personal Data).

Finland—The Finnish Personal Data Act (523/1999), given on
22.4.1999; available at www.tietosuoja.fi/uploads/hopxtvf.htm. See
Chapter 7, Sections 32-35 (Data security and storage of personal data).

France—ACT 78-17 of January 6th, 1978 on Data Processing, Data Files
and Individual Liberties; Amended by the Act of 6 August 2004 relating
to the protection of individuals with regard to the processing of personal
data); available at http://www.cnil.fr/fileadmin/docu-
ments/uk/78-17VA.pdf. See Articles 34 and 35.

Germany—Federal Data Protection Act as of 1 January 2003; available at
www.bfd.bund.de/information/bdsg_eng.pdf. See Section 9 (Technical
and organisational measures), Section 9a (Data protection audit), and Annex (to the first sentence of Section 9 of this Act).

Greece—Law 2472/1997 on the Protection of Individuals with regard to
the Processing of Personal Data (as amended by Laws 2819/2000[3] and
2915/2001[4]); available at www.dpa.gr/Docu-
ments/Eng/2472engl_all2.doc. See Article 10 (Confidentiality and security of processing).

Hungary—Act LXIII of 1992 on the Protection of Personal Data and
Public Access to Data of Public Interest; available at
http://abiweb.obh.hu/dpc/legislation/1992_LXIIIa.htm. See Article 10
(Data Security).

Ireland—Data Protection Act of 1988; available at
www.dataprivacy.ie/6ai.htm; Data Protection (Amendment) Act 2003;
available at www.dataprivacy.ie/images/;Act2003.pdf. See Section 2-(1),
Security measures 2C, and First Schedule Article 7 (Data Security).

---

3. Official Gazette 84 A 15.03.2000.
4. Official Gazette 109 A 19.05.2001.

Italy—Personal Data Protection Code, Legislative Decree No. 196 of 30 June 2003; available at www.garanteprivacy.it/garante/document?ID=311066. See Chapter II (Minimum Security Measures) at Sections 33 (Minimum Security Measures), Section 34 (Processing by Electronic Means), Section 35 (Processing without Electronic Means), Section 36 (Upgrading), and Annex B (Technical Specifications Concerning Minimum Security Measures).

Latvia—Personal Data Protection Law, amended by Law of 24 October 2002; available at www.dvi.gov.lv/eng/legislation/pdp. See Section 26.

Lithuania—Law on Legal Protection of Personal Data, 21 January 2003, No. IX-1296, Official translation, with amendments 13 April 2004; available at www.ada.lt/en/docs/Official%20translation.doc. See Chapter 4, Article 24 (Security of Data).

Luxembourg—DPL approved on 2 August 2002 and published in Memorial A 91 of 13 August 2002. (English version not available.)

Malta—Data Protection Act of December 14 2001 (Act XXVI of 2001), as amended by Act XXXI of 2002, Full entry into force July 15, 2003, available at http://ec.europa.eu/justice_home/fsj/privacy/docs/implementation/malta_en.pdf. See Articles 26 and 27.

Netherlands—25 892 - Rules for the protection of personal data (Personal Data Protection Act) (Unofficial translation); available at www.cbpweb.nl/en/structuur/en_pag_wetten.htm. See Articles 13-15.

Poland—Act of August 29, 1997 on the Protection of Personal Data, amended January 1, 2004, March 1, 2004, May 1, 2004; available at http://ec.europa.eu/justice_home/fsj/privacy/docs/implementation/poland_en.pdf. See Articles 7, 31, 36, and 39a. See also, Ordinance of the Minister for Internal Affairs and Administration of 29 April 2004; documentation of processing of personal data and technical and organizational requirements which should be fulfilled by equipment and computer systems used for processing personal data (Journal of Laws of 1 May 2004).

Portugal—Act on the Protection of Personal Data (transposing into the Portuguese legal system Directive 95/46/EC of the European Parliament and of the Council of 24 October 1995 on the protection of individuals with regard to the processing of personal data and on the free movement of such data); available at www.cnpd.pt/Leis/lei_6798en.htm. See Chapter II, Section III (Security and confidentiality of processing), at Article 14 (Security of processing), Article 15 (Special security measures), Article 16 (Processing by a processor), and Article 17 (Professional secrecy).

Slovakia—Act No 428 of 3 July 2002 on personal data protection; available at www.dataprotection.gov.sk/buxus/docs/act_no_428.pdf. See

Chapter Two (Security of personal data), at Section 15 (Responsibility for personal data security), Section 16 (The security project), Section 17 (Instruction), Section 18 (Confidentiality obligation), and Section 19 (Personal data protection supervision).

Slovenia—Personal Data Protection Act, available at http://ec.europa.eu/justice_home/fsj/privacy/docs/implementation/personal_data_protection_act_rs_2004.pdf. See Chapter 3, Articles 24 (Security of Personal Data), and Article 25 (Duty to Secure).

Spain—Organic Law 15/1999 of 13 December on the Protection of Personal Data; available at http://europa.eu.int/comm/internal_market/privacy/docs/organic-law-99.pdf. See Article 9 (Data security), Article 10 (Duty of secrecy), and Royal Decree 994/1999, on Security Measures of Automated Databases Containing Personal Data.

Sweden—Personal Data Act (1998:204); issued 29 April 1998; available at www.datainspektionen.se/pdf/ovrigt/pul-eng.pdf. See Security in processing at Section 30 (Persons who process personal data), Section 31 (Security measures), and Section 32 (The supervisory authority may decide on security measures). See also Personal Data Ordinance (1998:1191); issued 3 September 1998, available at www.sweden.gov.se/content/1/c6/02/56/33/ed5aaf53.pdf.

United Kingdom—Data Protection Act 1998; available at www.hmso.gov.uk/acts/ acts1998/19980029.htm. See Article 7 and The Seventh Principle.

A.10   Other Countries

Argentina—Act 25,326, Personal Data Protection Act (October 4, 2000), § 9; Security Measures for the Treatment and Maintenance of the Personal Data Contained in Files, Records, Databanks and Databases, either non state Public and Private (November 2006).

Australia—Privacy Act 1988, Act No. 119 of 1988 as amended taking into account amendments up to Act No. 86 of 2006, Schedule 3, Clause 4.

Canada—Personal Information Protection and Electronic Documents Act (2000, c. 5), Schedule 1, § 4.7.

Hong Kong—Personal Data (Privacy) Ordinance, December 1996, Schedule 1, Principle 4.

Japan—Act on the Protection of Personal Information, Law No.57, 2003, Articles 20, 21, 22, and 43.

South Korea—The Act on Promotion of Information and Communications Network Utilization and Information Protection, Etc., Amended by Act No. 7812, December 30, 2005, Articles 28, 29.

About the Authors

Julia H. Allen is a senior member of the technical staff within the CERT Program at the Software Engineering Institute (SEI), a unit of Carnegie Mellon University in Pittsburgh, PA. Allen is engaged in developing and transitioning executive outreach programs in enterprise security and governance as well as conducting research in software security and assurance. Prior to this technical assignment, Allen served as acting director of the SEI for an interim period of 6 months as well as deputy director/chief operating officer for 3 years. Before joining the SEI, she was a vice president in embedded systems software development for Science Applications International Corporation and managed large software development programs for TRW (now Northrop Grumman). In addition to her work in security governance, Ms. Allen is the author of *The CERT Guide to System and Network Security Practices* (Addison-Wesley, June 2001) and the CERT podcast series: *Security for Business Leaders* (2006-2008). She is a coauthor of *Software Security Engineering: A Guide for Project Managers* (Addison-Wesley, May 2008). Ms. Allen's degrees include a bachelor of science in computer science from the University of Michigan, an M.S. in electrical engineering from the University of Southern California, and an executive business certificate from the University of California–Los Angeles.

    Edward G. Amoroso serves as senior vice president and chief security officer for AT&T Services, Inc. His responsibilities include real-time protection of AT&T's vast network and computing infrastructure, security policy, planning, and architecture for AT&T's enterprise, digital rights management (DRM) and security support for AT&T's IPTV and entertainment initiatives, and lead design, development, and operations support for AT&T's managed and network-based security services. Ed's career at AT&T began at Bell Laboratories, where he worked on securing the Unix operating system, as well as numerous federal government security initiatives. Ed has authored research papers and four books on information security including *Cyber Security* (Silicon Press, 2007), which is written for mainstream readers. Ed holds M.S. and Ph.D. degrees in computer science from the Stevens Institute of Technology and is a graduate of the Senior Executive Program at the Columbia Business School. He has served as an adjunct professor in the Computer Science Department at Stevens for the past eighteen years, and his work has been featured in many publications such as the *Wall Street Journal.*

C. Warren Axelrod is the research director for financial services for the U.S. Cyber Consequences Unit (US-CCU) and an executive adviser to the Financial Services Technology Consortium (FSTC). He was the chief privacy officer and business information security officer for U.S. Trust. Warren has represented financial services information security interests in several nationwide forums. He was honored with the prestigious Information Security Executive (ISE) Luminary Leadership Award 2007. He also received a *Computerworld* Premier 100 IT Leaders Award in 2003 and his department's implementation of an intrusion detection system was given a Best in Class award. He is on the editorial advisory board of the *ISSA Journal.* Warren has participated in many professional and industry conferences in the United States, Europe, and Asia. He has published two books on computer management, one on outsourcing security, and numerous articles on a variety of information technology and information security topics, including computer and network security, contingency planning, and computer-related risks. Warren holds a Ph.D. in managerial economics from the Johnson Graduate School of Management at Cornell University and honors bachelors and masters degrees in electrical engineering, economics, and statistics from the University of Glasgow, Scotland. He is certified as a CISSP and CISM and acquired NASD Series 7 and Series 24 licenses. Warren can be reached at warren.axelrod@usccu.us.

Jennifer Bayuk is an independent consultant on topics including information security policy, process, management, and metrics. Her industry experience includes being a chief information security officer, a manager of information systems internal audit, a Big 4 Security principal consultant and auditor, and security software engineer at AT&T Bell Laboratories. Jennifer frequently publishes on information security and audit topics ranging from security process management to client/server application controls. Her publications include two textbooks for the Information Systems Audit and Control Association (*Stepping Through the IS Audit* and *Stepping Through the InfoSec Program*). While in financial services, Jennifer chaired the Securities Industry and Financial Markets Association Information Security Subcommittee and the Financial Services Sector Coordinating Council Technology R&D committee. Jennifer has lectured for organizations that include ISACA, NIST, CSI, and Columbia University.

She is certified in information systems audit (CISA), information security management (CISM), information system security professionalism (CISSP), and IT governance (CGEIT). She has masters degrees in computer science and philosophy. Jennifer can be reached at www.bayuk.com.

Kenneth F. Belva currently manages an information technology risk management program for a bank whose assets are billions of dollars. He reports directly to the senior vice president and deputy general manager (CFO). ITsecurity.com recognized him as one of the top information security influencers in 2007. He is active in the New York Metro Chapter of the Information Systems Security Association (ISSA) and other information security related professional organizations. He has spoken and moderated at the United Nations as well as presented on AT&T's Internet Security News Network (ISNN) on discovering unknown web application vulnerabilities as well as being interviewed on security enablement. He taught as an adjunct professor in the business computer systems department at the State University of New York at Farmingdale. Mr. Belva is credited by Microsoft and IBM for discovering vulnerabilities in their software. He is the author of a variety of information security-related topics. He is the publisher and editor-in-chief of bloginfosec.com. He frequently presents at information security conferences. Mr. Belva holds the certified information systems security professional (CISSP), certified ethical hacker (CEH) certifications and has passed the certified information security manager (CISM) exam. He sits on the board of directors for Franklin and Marshall College's Regional Alumni Council for the New York Metro area.

Scott Borg is the director and chief economist of the U.S. Cyber Consequences Unit (US-CCU), an independent, nonprofit research institute that investigates the strategic and economic consequences of possible cyber attacks. He is responsible for many of the concepts that are currently being used to understand the implications of cyber attacks in business contexts. In collaboration with John Bumgarner, he is the author of the *US-CCU Cyber-Security Check List*, the most comprehensive survey to date of cyber vulnerabilities. He regularly advises a number of different U.S. government departments and industry associations. Before being asked by government officials to tackle cyber-security issues, Scott Borg was one of the principal developers of Value Creation Analysis, a set of business strategy models for understanding how much value can be created by various types and components of value chains. He has been a guest lecturer at Harvard, Yale, the University of Massachusetts, Columbia, and other leading universities. He is currently a senior research fellow in international security studies at the Fletcher School of Law and Diplomacy of Tufts University.

Glenn Brunette is a global systems engineering director and chief security architect at Sun Microsystems where he leads a global team focused on information security and assurance. For his achievements and contributions to information security, Glenn was named a Sun Distinguished Engineer, an honor granted to less than 100 people in the company. For over 15 years, Glenn has architected, developed, and delivered security solutions for a wide range of customers and industries. Currently, Glenn works in the Chief Architect's Office where he defines Sun's global security strategy and architecture and works to improve the security of products and services delivered to Sun's customers.

John Carlson is senior vice president of BITS/Financial Services Roundtable where he manages the BITS regulatory affairs program. From 2002 to 2007, Carlson managed the BITS security program. Prior to joining BITS in 2002, Carlson served in a variety of leadership and technical roles at the Office of the Comptroller of the Currency and was involved in developing regulations and guidance on information security and technology risk management. Carlson earned a masters in public policy from Harvard University's Kennedy School of Government and a B.A. from the University of Maryland.

Peter M. Curtis is the founder of Power Management Concepts, LLC. He has built a multifaceted business focused on reliability, business resiliency, and clean/secure energy solutions. He is a graduate of New York Institute of Technology with both a bachelors degree in electro-mechanical computer technology, and a master of science degree in energy management. Mr. Curtis has over twenty-five years of experience within the mission critical facilities engineering industry, specifically, the areas of banking and finance, defense, electric and water utilities, energy management, and education. Former positions held include vice president of critical systems at Bankers Trust Company, senior engineer at SIAC, and superintendent of electrical construction at SCWA. He has been an associate professor at New York Institute of Technology since 1994 and an adjunct professor at New York University since 2001. Peter's publications include an IEEE online book entitled *An Introduction to Mission Critical Facilities Operations,* a Wiley/IEEE book, *Maintaining Mission Critical Systems in a 24/7 Environment,* a bimonthly column for *Mission Critical Magazine,* and over twenty whitepapers and articles concerning critical power and business resiliency for data centers and critical infrastructures. He holds numerous advisory board positions including: Alternative Energy at New York Institute of Technology, *Mission Critical Magazine,* Association of Facilities Engineers, and chairman of Long Island Forum for Technology Center of Excellence for Homeland Security. He is a member of 7 x 24 Exchange, Association for Facilities Engineers, Institute of Electrical and Electronic Engineers, International Electrical and Testing Association, International Facility Management Association, and Association of Energy Engineers.

Sam DeKay, who is at the Bank of New York Mellon Corporation, is responsible for the development of policies and standards related to information security. Prior to BNYM, he served as manager of information security for

Empire Blue Cross/Blue Shield; before this he worked at ABN Bank, also as manager of information security. His areas of expertise include security risk assessment, policy development, information security and law, and business/corporate communications. He is certified as an information security manager (CISM). Dr. DeKay has received Ph.D. degrees from Fordham University and Columbia University.

Michelle Dennedy is chief privacy officer for Sun Microsystems, Inc. Michelle is responsible for the continued development and implementation of Sun's data privacy policies and practices, working across Sun's business groups to drive the company's continued data privacy excellence. Data privacy is a cornerstone of Sun's approach to compliance with complex, demanding regulations including Sarbanes-Oxley, the EU Directive, California state senate bills, as well as escalating policy and process-oriented requirements being imposed globally. Michelle also works with Sun's product development teams and partners to deliver best-practice privacy enabling products and services. Michelle is a sought-after and provocative public speaker, evangelizing new approaches and business justifications for soundly defined, transparent privacy policies and systems that protect healthy, safe global businesses. Michelle has a J.D. from Fordham University School of Law and a B.S. degree with university honors from Ohio State University.

Mahi Dontamsetti has over 15 years of experience in information security. He has worked on projects for the government including Department of Homeland Security (DHS), the Pentagon, and the Transportation Security Agency (TSA), as well as large Fortune 100 firms in the financial, telecommunications, healthcare, and transportation sectors. He has served as chief technologist, CIO, vice president of professional services, and managing principal in various firms. His team is credited with building the world's first wireless switch and radio controller for GSM networks. His volunteer works involves serving on the board of OWASP (Open Web Application Security Project) a worldwide community based effort to provide research, education, and tools for application security. He is also involved with ISM3, which is an effort to bring maturity levels to information security (www.ism3.com). He is the author of two books: *Wireless PCS* and *Technology Wireless*. He has also contributed a chapter to the book *Social and Human Elements of Information Security: Emerging Trends & Countermeasures*. He has a M.S. in computer science from the University of Missouri-Kansas City and is a CISSP. Currently Mr. Dontamsetti is head of application security at Barclays Capital.

Steve Hunt was named one of the 25 most influential people in the security industry by *Security Magazine* and *CSO Magazine* named him "Industry Visionary" Compass Award Winner in 2006. Steve is an industry advisor, investor, futurist, and consultant. From 1998 to 2005 he ran security think tanks at Giga Information Group and Forrester Research. Steve founded Hunt Business

Intelligence to support best practices, investments, and technological innovations related to security. His analysis appears in newspapers like the *Wall Street Journal* and many trade magazines, and he has appeared as a security analyst on MSNBC, CNN, and Fox. Steve authors the popular blog SecurityDreamer.com.

Markus Jakobsson is a Principal Scientist at Palo Alto Research Center, and a cofounder of RavenWhite Inc. and Extricatus LLC. He has previously been a principal research scientist at RSA Laboratories, a member of the technical staff at Bell Labs, an associate professor at Indiana University, and an adjunct associate professor at New York University. He holds a Ph.D. in computer science from the University of California at San Diego. He is a member of the team behind SecurityCartoon, and of the PARC security group.

Gene Kim is the CTO and cofounder of *Tripwire, Inc.* In 1992, he coauthored *Tripwire* while at Purdue University with Dr. Gene Spafford. Since 1999, he has been studying high performing IT operations and security organizations. In 2004, he cowrote *The Visible Ops Handbook*, codifying how to successfully transform IT organizations from "good to great." In 2008, he coauthored *Security Visible Ops Handbook*, a handbook describing how to link IT security and operational objectives in four practical steps by integrating security controls into IT operational, software development and project management processes. Gene is a certified IS auditor, and is part of the Institute of Internal Auditors GAIT task force that developed and published the four GAIT Principles in January 2007, designed to help management appropriately scope the IT portions of SOX-404. In 2007, *ComputerWorld* added Gene to the "40 Innovative IT People Under The Age Of 40" list, and was given the Outstanding Alumnus Award by the Department of Computer Sciences at Purdue University for achievement and leadership in the profession.

Paul Love, CISSP, CISA, CISM, Security+, has been in the IT field for over 15 years. Paul holds a masters of science degree in network security and a bachelor's in information systems. He has coauthored three security books, contributed to multiple Linux/Unix books, and has been the technical editor for over 10 best selling Linux and Unix books. Paul ran a successful Linux portal site during the dot com era and has been an avid Unix/Linux user and administrator both professionally and as a hobby for many years. Paul is currently the director of information security at The Standard.

Donn B. Parker is a retired SRI International information security consultant. He has specialized in information security and computer crime research for 40 of his 55 years in the computer field. He has lectured extensively and written numerous books, papers, articles, and reports in his specialty based on interviews of more than 200 computer criminals and reviews of the security of 250 large corporations. His sixth book, *Fighting Computer Crime, a New Framework for Protecting Information*, was published by John Wiley & Sons in 1998. Mr. Parker received many of the awards given in information security. He formed the International Information Integrity Institute (I-4) at SRI that has been serving 75 international corporate members for 22 years to keep them aware of the most advanced information security concepts and controls. Mr. Parker received a master of arts degree in mathematics from the University of California, Berkeley in 1954. He is a member of the Association for Computing Machinery (as well as a fellow and national officer) and the Information Systems Security Association.

Ben Rothke is the technical editor of this volume. He is a senior security consultant with BT Professional Services and has over 15 years of industry experience in information systems security and privacy. Prior to joining BT, Ben was with AXA, Baltimore Technologies, Ernst & Young, and Citicorp, and has provided security solutions to many Fortune 500 companies. Ben is the author of *Computer Security—20 Things Every Employee Should Know* (McGraw-Hill), and a contributing author to *Network Security: The Complete Reference* (Osborne) and *The Handbook of Information Security Management* (Auerbach) and writes security book review for *Security Management* and *Slashdot*. Ben is also a frequent speaker at industry conferences, such as CSI, RSA, MISTI, and NetSec and is a certified information systems security professional (CISSP), certified information security manager (CISM), and PCI QSA (qualified security assessor) and a member of ASIS, CSI, and InfraGard. He can be reached at ben.rothke@bt.com.

Dan Schutzer is currently the executive director of the Financial Services Technology Consortium (FSTC), responsible for its day-to-day operation. (FSTC) is the financial industry's original collaborative forum, providing a safe, effective, and reliable venue for financial institutions, technology companies, and academia to explore today's strategic business-technology issues. Its initiatives have resulted in many important new standards, concepts, and products. He is also a member of the BITS Advisory Council, an ASC X9 board member and a fellow of the New York Academy of Sciences. Dan was previously a director and senior vice president of Citigroup for over 23 years. During that time he worked in almost all the areas of Citigroup, ranging from trading to retail banking to security and corporate technology. He ran Citigroup's Advanced Technology for a number of years. Dan also worked as the technical director of naval intelligence, technical director of Navy Command, Control, and Communications, Sperry Rand, Bell Laboratories, IBM, and Syracuse University. Dan has a Ph.D. and a M.S.E.E. from Syracuse University, and a B.S.E.E. from City College of New York. He has authored over 65 publications and 7 books. Dan can be reached at dan.schutzer@fstc.org.

Thomas J. Smedinghoff is a partner in the privacy, data security, and information law practice at the law firm of Wildman Harrold, in Chicago. Mr. Smedinghoff is a member of the U.S. Delegation to the United Nations Commission on International Trade Law (UNCITRAL), where he participated in the negotiation of the United Nations Convention on the Use of Electronic Communications in International Contracts. He is also the chair of the International Policy Coordinating Committee of the American Bar Association Section of Science & Technology Law. He was also an American Bar Association representative to the Drafting Committee for the Uniform Electronic Transactions Act (UETA), and chair of the Illinois Commission on Electronic Commerce and Crime (1996–1998) that wrote the Illinois Electronic Commerce Security Act. He can be reached at smedinghoff@wildman.com.

George Spafford is a principal consultant with Pepperweed and an experienced practitioner in business and IT operations. He is a prolific author and speaker, and has consulted and conducted training on regulatory compliance, IT governance, and process improvement in the United States, Australia, New Zealand, and China. Publications include coauthorship of *The Visible Ops Handbook* and *Visible Ops Security*. George holds an M.B.A. from Notre Dame, a B.A. in materials and logistics management from Michigan State University, and an honorary degree from Konan Daigaku in Japan. He is a ITIL Service Manager, TOCICO Jonah, and a certified information systems auditor (CISA). George is a current member of the IIA, ISACA, ITPI, ITSMF, and the TOCICO.

Joel Weise has worked in the field of information security for almost 30 years. As the principal engineer and chief technologist for the Sun Client Services Security Program Office, he designs system and application security solutions for a range of different enterprises. Joel is also a leading expert on legal and regulatory issues as they relate to information security. Joel is the Sun Microsystems ANSI representative, a member of the *Information Systems Security Association Journal* Editorial Advisory Board, and author of various information security publications. His current research work is focused on the elaboration of adaptive security, complex adaptive systems, and security maturity modeling.

Index